OXFORD CLASSICAL MONOGRAPHS

*Published under the supervision of a Committee of the
Faculty of Literae Humaniores in the University of Oxford*

The aim of the Oxford Classical Monographs series (which replaces the Oxford Classical and Philosophical Monographs) is to publish books based on the best theses on Greek and Latin literature, ancient history, and ancient philosophy examined by the Faculty Board of Literae Humaniores.

Canons of Style in the Antonine Age

Idea-Theory in its Literary Context

IAN RUTHERFORD

CLARENDON PRESS · OXFORD
1998

Oxford University Press, Great Clarendon Street, Oxford OX2 6DP

Oxford New York

Athens Auckland Bangkok Bogotá Buenos Aires Calcutta
Cape Town Chennai Dar es Salaam Delhi Florence Hong Kong Istanbul
Karachi Kuala Lumpur Madrid Melbourne Mexico City Mumbai
Nairobi Paris São Paolo Singapore Taipei Tokyo Toronto Warsaw

and associated companies in
Berlin Ibadan

Oxford is a trade mark of Oxford University Press

Published in the United States
by Oxford University Press Inc., New York

British Library Cataloguing in Publication Data
Data available

Library of Congress Cataloguing in Publication Data
Canons of style in the Antonine age: idea-theory in its
literary context / Ian Rutherford.
(Oxford classical monographs)
Includes bibliographical references and index.
1. Greek prose literature—History and criticism—Theory, etc.
2. Hermogenes, 2nd cent. Peri ideōn. 3. Greece—History—146
B.C.–323 A.D. 4. Criticism—Greece—History. 5. Rhetoric, Ancient.
6. Style, Literary. I. Title. II. Series.
PA3557.R88 1997   808'.00938'09015–dc21   96–45145
ISBN 0–19–814729–5

1 3 5 7 9 10 8 6 4 2

Typeset by Joshua Associates Ltd., Oxford
Printed in Great Britain on acid-free paper by
Biddles Ltd., Guildford and King's Lynn

Preface

This book is the final product of my doctoral dissertation, 'Technique and Innovation on *Idea*-Theory: Six Studies in the *Idea*-Theory of Hermogenes and Ps.-Aristides' (Oxford, 1986), masterfully supervised by Professor D. A. Russell. There has been a change of emphasis, away from rhetorical technique (an area well covered by M. Patillon, in his study of Hermogenes which appeared in 1986), and toward the relationship between Hermogenes and contemporary literature. The reworking was largely carried out while I was a Junior Fellow at the Center of Hellenic Studies in the Fall of 1992, and I would like to thank the staff there for all forms of assistance. All along, I have been greatly assisted by the labours of Dr Doreen Innes, of St Hilda's College, Oxford. I would also like to acknowledge the help of Professors E. Asmis, E. Bakker, G. Kennedy, D. Obbink, D. Schenkeveld, E. Schütrumpf, R. Webb, and C. Wooten and Dr I. Sluiter. For those errors of fact and judgement that remain, the responsibility is mine alone.

I. R.

July 1994

Contents

Introduction: Literature and Rhetoric in the Second Century CE

The subject of this study is the relationship between a literature and a stylistic theory. The literature is the Greek literature of the so-called Second Sophistic, the renaissance of Greek culture which began in the first century CE and flourished through the second century CE, reaching a peak in the reigns of Hadrian (117–38 CE), Antoninus Pius (138–61 CE), and Marcus Aurelius (161–80 CE).[1] The literary masters of this era are the great epideictic orators, the 'sophists' who gave the movement its name, such as Dio of Prusa, Herodes Atticus, Aelius Aristides, Polemo of Laodicea, Dionysius of Miletus, Scopelion of Clazomenae, or Lollianus of Ephesus. Few of their rhetorical works survive, with the exception of the extant speeches of Aelius Aristides, and most of our evidence for their careers and their works comes from Flavius Philostratus whose *Lives of the Sophists* dates from the early third century CE.

Oratory was not the only genre that flourished in this period, and there is much prose literature which would not be described as primarily rhetorical (poetry is nowhere near so important). One of the main genres was the novel, brought to perfection in this period by novelists such as Achilles Tatius and Xenophon of Ephesus. Arrian of Nicomedia wrote philosophical recollections of Epictetus and also history, in both cases imitating Xenophon. Lucian of Samosata wrote comic dialogues, and satirical prose works of all sorts. Another important genre is the miscellany, illustrated by the major works of Aelian of Praeneste (*Varia Historia*, *De Natura Animalium*). Other genres were collections of descriptions of artworks or scenes (εἰκόνες, such as those of Philostratus of Lemnos) and fictional letters (examples survive by

---

[1] Surveys of literature of the period include Bowersock (1969), Reardon (1971), Easterling and Knox (1985), 665–713 (contributions by G. Bowersock, E. Bowie).

Aelian, Alciphron, and Flavius Philostratus). Even Aelius Aristides was best known for a non-rhetorical work, a desultory
narrative of his illnesses and incubation in the temple at Pergamum in several books, called *Hieroi Logoi*.

One of the most striking features of the prose literature of this
period is its strong allegiance to earlier literary models. The most
popular models were the great prose-writers of the fifth–fourth
century—Demosthenes, Plato, Xenophon, Thucydides, and
sometimes Critias. Some writers are strictly conservative ('Atti-
cists'), others adopt styles of composition and delivery believed to
have developed in the post-classical and modern period, and
associated with the rhetorical schools of the Eastern Greek world
('Asianism' is a term sometimes used for this aspect). Even among
the more conservative writers, there are variations in attitude:
some regard the classics as superior to anything the modern age
could produce, but others think of themselves as equal or superior
to any ancient model (for example, Aelius Aristides).

As we might expect, there was a good deal of interest in literary
theory during this period. This can be thought of as not so much
'poetics', since poetry is a comparatively insignificant genre, but
rather as 'prosaics'—the theory of prose.[2] Some contributions to
prosaics are cast in literary form: examples include Dio of Prusa's
Peri Logou Askeseos, Aristides' *Peri Tou Paraphthegmatos*, and
Lucian's *Quomodo Historia Conscribenda Sit*. But most theoretical
works on prose were in the subliterary form of rhetorical manuals;
in particular, we begin to find a new type of stylistic theory, the
so-called *idea*-theory, heavily dependent on earlier rhetorical
theories of style. It is set out in three surviving works. The first
is the *Peri Ideon* attributed to Hermogenes of Tarsus, himself a
brilliant orator who tasted fame while still an adolescent during
the reign of Marcus Aurelius.[3] The other two works were
formerly attributed to Aristides: the *Peri Politikou Logou*, and
the *Peri Aphelous Logou*. All three set out complex analyses of
major writers, principally Demosthenes (*Peri Ideon*, *Peri Politikou
Logou*) and Xenophon (*Peri Aphelous Logou*), who are presented as
ideal models for stylistic emulation.

---

[2] For the apparently recent term 'prosaics', see Morson and Emerson (1990),
15 n. 1; Kittay and Godzich (1987).

[3] Philostratus, *Bioi Sophiston* 577–8; for the life of Hermogenes, see Radermacher (1912).

I call such ideal models for the styles of writers, canons of style. The *idea*-theorists do not use the Greek word κανών in this sense (they use ἰδέα), but it is common in other stylistic writers, such as Dionysius of Halicarnassus.[4] Modern readers may be more used to the idea of a literary canon as a selection of highly valued works. It should be stressed at the outset that a κανών in the ancient sense and a literary canon in the modern sense are not the same. Still, there is some intersection, since a list of preferred authors will constitute a reading list of the sort that we find in Dionysius, *Peri Mimeseos*, Quintilian, *IO* 10. 1, and in Hermogenes, *Peri Ideon* 2. 10–12. An ancient rhetorician would never have called such a list a κανών, but he might have referred to it as a series of κανόνες, as Phrynichus Arabius in his *Sophistike Proparaskeue* described a collection of ideal models as εἰλικρινοῦς . . . καὶ καθαροῦ καὶ Ἀττικοῦ λόγου κανόνας καὶ σταθμάς (standards and measures of pure and uncorrupted Attic language). The major difference remains the function: literary canons in our sense have nothing to do with stylistic emulation, or emulation of any other sort.[5]

My aim in this study is to explore the attitudes to literature implied by the theory of *ideai*, and the relationships between the κανόνες which it presents and the literary environment in which it developed. This subject has been touched on before, mainly by

[4] But in ancient literary criticism κανών has its original sense of 'standard', and it is often paired with ὅρος or στάθμη (ὅρος at *Dem. Lex.* 23 (178. 11); στάθμη at Ps. Dionysius, *Rhet.* 11. 1 (374. 22); the Latin is *lex operis*, as in Quintilian, *IO* 10. 1). Its most common applications are to an author who is regarded as an ideal model for literary μίμησις, particularly with respect to a particular style (in Dionysius of Halicarnassus, of invention at *Lys.* 18 (29. 20); *Is.* 20 (123. 21); Thucydides at *Dem. Lex.* 1 (130. 3) (the grand style); Plato at *Dem. Lex.* 23 (178. 11), 26 (186. 7); Homer in respect to *harmonia* at *Dem. Lex.* 41 (220. 6)); also sometimes with respect to a particular dialect (again in Dionysius) (*Lys.* 2 (9. 12), *Pomp.* 3 (239. 9)), or a particular genre (as in Lucian, *How to Write History*, cc. 6–8; 23). (The same word also sometimes refers to a technical principle in general, as at Ps. Dionysius, *Rhet.* 11. 1 (374. 22); also Dionysius, *Lys.* 24 (34. 18).)

[5] Phrynichus: Photius, *Bibl.* 158 (101a); cf. Schmid (1887–97), i. 206. We have another literary application of the word 'canon' when we speak of the canon of Demosthenes' works, meaning the set of those works judged to be authentic (see Ch. VI). That again is a modern concept, though again there is an oblique connection to the ancient usage of the word κανών, in so far as a common way of judging the authenticity of a work was to decide on what counted as the essential stylistic characteristics of the author, and to use those as a standard (κανών) by which to judge the rest (thus, at *Lys.* 12 (20. 17) Dionysius says that a speech that other people take as a κανών for Lysias is in fact spurious).

scholars interested in the literature of the Second Sophistic in
general, and particularly in older works on Aelius Aristides (since
Peri Politikou Logou and *Peri Aphelous Logou* were at one time
falsely attributed to him). But it has never been dealt with in
depth, because scholars working on the theory of *ideai* have
tended to concentrate on different questions (such as its origins,
or its influence on later centuries), while those interested in the
Second Sophistic have tended to pass over it as an eccentric
development, irrelevant to the main literary trends of the time.[6]
This reluctance to make use of it is understandable, because the
methodologies it presents can seem both abstruse and pedantic,
and it may seem difficult to see how they could have any relevance
outside the rhetorician's class-room. The challenge is to show that
there are after all connections, and this requires looking beyond
the individual *ideai* and the techniques that instantiate them, and
paying more attention to the general literary categories which they
articulate.

My starting point is a survey of the major texts of *idea*-theory
and their background (Chapter I). After that, I turn to a study of
sophistic influences (Chapter II), exploring the contribution of
sophistic declamation. After that, I move on to an examination
of the reading list in *Peri Ideon*, and I unpack the significance of
the major literary categories included there, exploring their
history and context (Chapter III). I devote a separate chapter
to the relation between prose and poetry, which has interesting
parallels in the literature of the Second Sophistic (Chapter IV).
After that I consider the subject of Xenophon, tracing changing
views of Xenophon's style in the early empire (Chapter V), and
exploring aspects of the relationship between *Peri Ideon* and *Peri
Aphelous Logou*. (To make these sections more accessible, I have
included a translation of *Peri Aphelous Logou* as an appendix.)

After that I turn to Demosthenes himself, showing how his
image changes under the influence of sophistic declamation, and
how the need to find Demosthenic examples for even the rarest
and strangest stylistic techniques may have led rhetoricians to

---

[6] Scholars working on the theory of *ideai*: Hagedorn (1964) is concerned with
development, Kustas (1973) and Patterson (1970) with *Nachleben*. Patillon (1988)
has little to say about contemporary literature. Scholars of Second Sophistic: I note
the comparatively brief treatments in Reardon (1971), 99–102 and in Grube (1965),
338–9.

draw on works of unusual quality and in some cases dubious authenticity (Chapter VI). Finally, I move to the role of contemporary authors, and I focus on Aelius Aristides, mentioned twice in *Peri Ideon*, whose works contain several parallels to the theory of *ideai*, although his view of the proper relationship between writer and literary κανών is radically different, since whereas Hermogenes thinks of Demosthenes as the ideal orator, Aristides claims that position for himself, and in general seems to want to assert his ultimate independence from any classical model (Chapter VII).

I

Idea-Theory

1. THE MAJOR SOURCES

The practice of formulating judgements about texts in terms of
a system of qualities (usually called ἀρεται or ἰδέαι) of style is
very old in the Greek world. It had already reached a high level
of development by the time of Dionysius of Halicarnassus (first
century CE), but its golden period came later, in the second
century CE, when a modified terminology seems to have come
into use, including many new terms like περιβολή, ἀκμή, ἀφέλεια,
and βαρύτης. To this period can be dated the anonymous *Peri
Politikou Logou* (*On Political Language*) and *Peri Aphelous Logou*
(*On Plain language*), transmitted to us in the works of Aristides,
and hence sometimes known as Ps. Aristides A' and B', as well
as the much more elaborate *Peri Ideon* (*On Ideas*) of Hermogenes of Tarsus. All three of these works apply the system
of qualities to a single preferred author: Demosthenes in the
case of *Peri Ideon* and *Peri Politikou Logou*, Xenophon in the
case of *Peri Aphelous Logou*. For each quality they specify
appropriate techniques arranged in various levels, and they
illustrate these techniques with examples drawn mostly from
the preferred author.

The most complex of these theories is the one in *Peri Ideon*, and
its author probably wrote it in awareness of the other two. *Peri
Ideon* belongs to a group of five rhetorical works known as the
Corpus Hermogenicum. They are *Progumnasmata* (*Elementary
Exercises*), *Peri Staseon* (*On Stases* or *On Argumentative Stances*),
Peri Heureseos (*On Invention*), *Peri Ideon*, and *Peri Methodou
Deinotetos* (*On the Technique of Power*). Hermogenes claims in
Peri Ideon 378. 18 ff.) to have written works with titles corres-
ponding to the last four of these, so the first is presumably a later
addition. There is no reason to think that the second and fourth
are not correctly attributed, but the third and fifth are probably

spurious.[1] The sequence *Peri Staseon, Peri Heureseos, Peri Ideon, Peri Methodou Deinotetos* provided a complete course in public speaking in the manner of Demosthenes. It starts with *Peri Staseon*, which teaches you how to angle your argument, given the facts and the legal situation. The original *Peri Heureseos* must have covered composition and argumentation (the extant *Peri Heureseos* also dips into style). *Peri Ideon* itself provides an advanced course in style. The extant *Peri Methodou Deinotetos* presents a sequence of miscellaneous techniques covering both argumentation and style; the original Hermogenean work with this title may also have been a catalogue of techniques, with a stress on how Demosthenes manages to do everything with complete appropriateness.

The stylistic system of *Peri Ideon* consists of six general types in all, some of which are subdivided, making a total of seventeen forms. I present them in Table 1, accompanied by a brief summary of their content. The status of δεινότης is different from that of the other *ideai*. The others receive an exhaustive technique-by-technique analysis in the main part of the treatise (the part that I shall term the 'core'). But the section on δεινότης is one of several essays appended to the main section (this part I shall term the 'post-core'), which have a more discursive style.

The systems of *Peri Politikou Logou* and *Peri Aphelous Logou* are simpler. *Peri Politikou Logou* has σεμνότης, βαρύτης, περιβολή, ἀξιοπιστία (convincingness: cf. ἀλήθεια in *On Ideas*), σφοδρότης, ἔμφασις (force: this term usually means 'innuendo'),[2] ἐπιμέλεια (elegance: cf. κάλλος in *On Ideas*), γλυκύτης, σαφήνεια and καθαρότης, βραχύτης, and συντομία, and finally κόλασις (pruning, i.e. pruning back excessive amplification). *Peri Politikou Logou* lacks the two-tier architecture of *On Ideas*, and there is much less recognition of ἦθος and the lighter styles: thus, βαρύτης is not in *Peri Politikou Logou* associated with ἦθος, and *ideai* like γλυκύτης, σαφήνεια/καθαρότης and βραχύτης/συντομία are treated very briefly. It has been argued, I think rightly, that *Peri Politikou Logou* was a source for Hermogenes in *On Ideas*.[3] It can be seen that one

---

[1] In general see Radermacher (1912); Kennedy (1983). On *Peri Methodou Deinotetos* see Bürgi (1930). On *Peri Heureseos* see App. A.

[2] For the sense of ἔμφασις, see Rutherford (1988).

[3] See Schmid (1917) and (1926). There were other works on similar subjects by Basilikos and Zeno: see Syrianus, 13. 9.

TABLE I. *Stylistic System of* Peri Ideon

Name of idea	Description
1. σαφήνεια (clarity)	
καθαρότης (purity)	absence of amplification
εὐκρίνεια (distinctiveness)	clarity in presentation of material, e.g. listing points
2. μέγεθος (grandeur)	
σεμνότης (solemnity)	talking about sublime subjects, like gods
περιβολή (envelopment)	stylistic amplification and complexity
(μεστότης)	(an extreme form of περιβολή)
λαμπρότης (brilliance)	direct grandeur appropriate to encomium
τραχύτης (roughness)	milder aggression
σφοδρότης (vehemence)	fiercer aggression
ἀκμή (peak)	combination of λαμπρότης and τραχύτης/σφοδρότης
3. κάλλος (beauty)	syntactic symmetry
4. γοργότης (agility)	short clauses
5. ἦθος (character)	
ἀφέλεια (plainness)	naïve and simple sentiments
γλυκύτης (sweetness)	effect of lyric poetry, sensuality, personification
δριμύτης (pungency)	verbal wit
ἐπιείκεια (reasonableness)	impression of being a decent person
ἀλήθεια (veracity)	emotional language giving impression of spontaneity
βαρύτης (gravity)	sternness, especially manifested in self-reproach
6. δεινότης (power)	rhetorical skill in the appropriate use of speech

change he has made is to create a category of ἦθος with six subdivisions to correspond to the six parts of μέγεθος, filling it with a number of *ideai* from different sources, among them βαρύτης.

Peri Aphelous Logou presents quite a different picture. The main focus here is of course ἀφέλεια, but the author also discusses ὗθος, σεμνότης, περιβολή, γλυκύτης, κάλλος, ἀξιοπιστία. The stylistic

palette is shifted in the direction of the plain style. It has some-
times been suggested that *Peri Aphelous Logou* was influenced by
On Ideas, but I think it is more likely, in fact, that *Peri Aphelous
Logou* or something like it was known to Hermogenes (see
Chapter V).

The *Corpus Hermogenicum* was the subject of many commentaries, not all of them edited even now. The earliest, covering all of
Hermogenes and Ps. Hermogenes, is attributed to the Neoplaton-
ist Syrianus from the fifth century. But most of them come from a
later period: an anonymous commentary, on *Peri Staseon* and *Peri
Heureseos*, dates from the tenth century; a commentary on *On
Ideas*, attributed to John Siceliotes, dates from the eleventh
century; and a commentary attributed to Maximus Planudes on
all of Hermogenes and Ps. Hermogenes probably dates to the
thirteenth century. In addition, from the twelfth century comes a
lengthy commentary on *On the Technique of Power* by Gregory of
Corinth.[4]

These commentaries are only an aspect of the rich *Nachleben*
enjoyed by Hermogenes' system. We see this in Eustathius'
application of it to the style of Homer, and in Theodorus
Metochites' application of it to a comparison of Aristides and
Demosthenes. Many of the stylistic descriptions found in Photius
are also indebted to it. It also had some influence on the
Renaissance, after a Latin translation was published by Sturm
in 1571 CE.[5]

Why was it so influential? Not simply because the quasi-
philosophical terminology appealed to the tastes of the Byzan-
tines.[6] Above all, the reason was that it was a good system: the
stylistic observations were impressive, as far as they went, and
based on specific features of texts rather than on hazy aesthetic
judgements, and the system was consistent and easy to understand, and not any more complicated than it had to be. In all of

---

[4] Syrianus: ed. Rabe; Maximus Planudes: Walz, v; John Siceliotes: Walz, vi;
anonymous, on *Peri Staseon* and *Peri Heureseos*: Walz, vii; Gregory of Corinth:
Walz, vii. On these, see Kustas (1973), 21; Kennedy (1983), 115–16.

[5] On Byzantine influence, the major work remains Kustas (1973); on Eustathius,
see Lindberg (1977); on Theodorus, see Gigante (1969). Photius displays knowledge of *idea*-theory, e.g. at c. 141 (98b) on Basileios; c. 160 (102b) on Choricius of
Gaza; c. 165 (107b) on Himerius; c. 181 (126b) on Damascius of Damascus. For the
Western Renaissance, Patterson (1970).

[6] Kustas (1973).

these respects it was preferable to the system of Dionysius of Halicarnassus.

2. THE SYSTEM OF STYLISTIC QUALITIES AND ITS BACKGROUND

Greek stylistic theory is a *continuum*. The earliest theoretical account that survives is Aristotle's *Rhetoric* but Aristotle's theory is extremely simple compared with what follows, recommending a single virtue of style with four subdivisions:[7] ἑλληνισμός (i.e. grammatical correctness), σαφήνεια (clarity), ὄγκος (ornamentation), and τὸ πρέπον (appropriateness). These four qualities also formed the basis for Theophrastus' theory of style (it was perhaps Theophrastus who gave ornamentation the name κατασκευή) and for that of the Stoics who took over the Theophrastean list, but added συντομία.[8] These basic qualities come through in *idea*-theory, with the exception of ἑλληνισμός, which is rejected probably on the grounds that it is a grammatical rather than a rhetorical quality.

TABLE 2. *Peripatetic/Stoic Virtues and Hermogenes' System*

Peripatetic/Stoic virtues	Hermogenes, *On Ideas*
ἑλληνισμός	—
σαφήνεια	σαφήνεια
κατασκευή	μέγεθος, κάλλος
πρέπον	ἦθος, δεινότης
(συντομία)	γοργότης

Another important tenet of ancient stylistic theory that we have to take account of is the idea that the ideal style is a mean between grand and low (already in Aristotle), and, congruent to this, the thesis that there are three styles: grand, medium, and low. The three-style theory may go back to Theophrastus, who saw the style of Thrasymachus as an ideal medium (the συστροφή style).[9]

---

[7] The word ἀρετή, e.g. at *Rhet.* 3. 2. 1, 1404^b.

[8] Theophrastus: Cicero, *Orator*, 79; Stoics: Diogenes Laertius, 7. 59 (Zeno). A good survey of the development of stylistic theory in Russell (1981*b*), 129 ff.

[9] Aristotle, *Rhet.* 1404^{b}3–4; Theophrastus on Thrasymachus: Dionysius of

Other sources connect three styles with three rhetorical functions, linking a high style with emotion (πάθος *movere*), a lower style with explanation (πρᾶγμα, *docere*), and a middle style with pleasure (ἦθος, *delectare*).[10] This structure is very important in ancient stylistic theories, but it is so basic that it is sometimes invisible. In *On Ideas*, some of the qualities are higher, some lower, and some in between, and they can be represented as in Table 3.

TABLE 3. *The Three-Style Theory and Hermogenes' System*

Higher	Middle	Lower
πάθος, *movere*	ἦθος, *delectare*	πρᾶγμα, *docere*
		σαφήνεια
μέγεθος		
	κάλλος	
		γοργότης
ἦθος	ἦθος	ἦθος
(ἀλήθεια, βαρύτης)	(γλυκύτης, δριμύτης)	(ἀφέλεια, ἐπιείκεια)

Generally, in a good style (which for Hermogenes means the style of Demosthenes), elements of different types will be mixed, and in particular, elements from the various *ideai* associated with μέγεθος are interspersed with elements from γοργότης (agility), and from the various *ideai* associated with ἦθος.

A slightly different development is the system of Ps. Demetrius, *Peri Hermeneias*, probably to be dated to the first century BCE.[11] Demetrius distinguishes four χαρακτῆρες, which are not so much necessary virtues, as alternative stylistic colours: the grand (μεγαλοπρέπής), the elegant (γλαφυρός), the forceful (δεινός), and the slim (ἰσχνός). They correspond to qualities in *On Ideas* roughly as shown in Table 4. As in *idea*-theory, qualities can be mixed (*Peri Hermeneias* 36). Unlike *idea*-theory, the four χαρακτῆρες have neighbouring faults (ψυχρός, κακόζηλος, ξηρός, ἄχαρις), which are also described as χαρακτῆρες.

The third system of stylistic qualities seems to combine the

Halicarnassus, *Dem. Lex.* c. 3. On this difficult issue, see the sensible discussion by Innes (1985).

[10] Cicero, *Orator* 69–70; Fantham (1973).
[11] G. Morpurgo-Tagliabue (1979); Innes (1985). Cf. Ch. III n. 40.

TABLE 4. *The Stylistic Systems of Demetrius
and Hermogenes*

Demetrius	Hermogenes
μεγαλοπρεπής	μέγεθος, σεμνότης
γλαφυρός	ἦθος, γλυκύτης
ἰσχνός	σφοδρότης, ἀλήθεια
δεινός	καθαρότης

theory of Aristotelian ἀρεταί and Demetrian χαρακτῆρες, and to
elaborate it a little. This is the theory of stylistic ἀρεταί of
Dionysius of Halicarnassus. Dionysius is the only earlier rhetorician Hermogenes mentions (the reference comes in connection
with his analysis of the οὐ βεβηκυῖαι (unsteady) ἀναπαύσεις appropriate to the *idea* κάλλος).[12] Dionysian ἀρεταί correspond in some
degree to the qualities used by the *idea*-theorists, though his
vocabulary shows greater differences. Table 5, illustrating correspondences, is based on the work of Dieger Hagedorn, who has
done more than any other scholar to figure out the relationship (I
have added a column with the *ideai* in *Peri Politikou Logou*).[13]
None of these correspondences is an exact fit, and some are very
approximate. In general, it is important to emphasize that there
are aspects of *idea*-theory which are not found before the second
century; sophistic declamation may have been a factor here (see
Chapter II); the taste for Xenophon was perhaps another (see
Chapter V).

Idea-theory analyses style by dividing it into different levels or
strata: subject matter or thought (πράγματα, ἔννοια, γνώμη, ἐπινόημα), figure (σχῆμα), diction (λέξις, ἀπαγγελία), composition of
diction (σύνθεσις), rhythm and clausula (ῥυθμός, ἀνάπαυσις). This

---

[12] *À propos* of an anapaestic ἀνάπαυσις in the first sentence of *Against Leptines*
(311. 7 ff.), Hermogenes observes that Dionysius had somewhere suggested that an
anapaestic clausula was βεβηκυῖα (though we find no such suggestion in his extant
works). However, Dionysius uses terms like βεβηκώς and βάσις to characterize the
clausulae appropriate to the αὐστηρὰ ἁρμονία and Hermogenes may have borrowed
this from him. For the terms βεβηκώς/βάσις in Dionysius, see Geigenmüller (1908),
76. In *Peri Ideon* βεβηκυῖαι ἀναπαύσεις are appropriate to σεμνότης (see 293. 11 ff.).

[13] Hagedorn (1964), 77; for the system of Dionysius, see Geigenmüller (1908),
Bonner (1935).

TABLE 5. *The Stylistic Systems of Dionysius and Hermogenes (after Hagedorus)*

Dionysius	Peri Politikou Logou	Peri Ideon
σαφήνεια	σαφήνεια καὶ καθαρότης	καθαρότης
virtus narrationis σαφήνεια		εὐκρίνεια
μεγαλοπρέπεια	σεμνότης	σεμνότης
δεινότης	σφοδρότης, ἔμφασις	τραχύτης, σφοδρότης, ἀκμή
καλλιλογία	λαμπρότης	
περιττολογία	περιβολή	περιβολή
ἡδονή, χάρις	ἐπιμέλεια, γλυκύτης	κάλλος, γλυκύτης
συντομία, συστροφή	βραχύτης καὶ συντομία	γοργότης
ἠθοποιία		ἐπιείκεια
λεκτικὸς τόπος of ἠθοποιία } (virtus narrationis πιθανότης)		ἀφέλεια
δεινότης	ἀξιοπιστία	ἀλήθεια
πρέπον		δεινότης

feature is also inherited from the stylistic tradition: Demetrius and the author of *Peri Hupsous* both organize their analysis by strata (Dionysius, however, does not). Table 6 shows how the different strata are deployed in different rhetoricians. The distribution of strata in *On Plainness* and in *On Political Language* is comparatively simple, and (except for details of terminology) continues that of earlier stylistic theory. Hermogenes' system seems more complex; he has eight strata, though that number is produced by the artificial separation of rhythm and clausula.

The strangest stratum in Hermogenes is μέθοδος, and it is worth a closer look. Μέθοδος comes in two varieties. The first has to do with modifying the innate stylistic properties of ἔννοιαι (thoughts). Some μέθοδοι completely transform the quality of the ἔννοιαι that they are applied to;[14] others present the ἔννοιαι of an *idea* as they are, preserving their proper quality.[15] Most come somewhere in between, altering the quality of a ἔννοιαι but to a limited extent. Sometimes this is rhetorically desirable: for example, offensive τραχεῖαι ἔννοιαι have to be made to seem plainer by μέθοδοι (256. 21 ff.); in other cases it is stylistically desirable, for example (266. 1 ff.) a sustained λαμπρὰ ἔννοια is fragmented for the sake of variety. Other μέθοδοι disguise, for example περιβολή can be covered up (227. 2 ff.) by μέθοδοι and made to look like καθαρότης, the opposite quality.

Μέθοδος can also have to do with linking stylemes, for example the μέθοδος of ἀφήγησις discussed in the section on καθαρότης (228. 21 ff.). Only slightly different are those μέθοδοι which have to do with the order in which ἔννοιαι are placed: ἀναστροφή (reversing) of the order of ἔννοιαι (282. 15 ff.); and the μέθοδοι of εὐκρίνεια, which have to do with the order in which points will follow.[16] When the word μέθοδος is used with this application, there may be a suggestion of its earlier meaning of 'pursuit, approach'.

Hermogenes says in his introduction that μέθοδος continues the category figure (σχῆμα) of thought (222. 21–2). A figure of thought would usually have meant a stylistically significant pattern not

---

[14] Thus, a μέθοδος generates βαρύτης from ἐπιεικεῖς *thoughts* (364. 17 ff.); the μέθοδος—which turns out to consist of irony—does not merely adapt the ἐπιεικής *thought*, but transforms it, leaving no trace of the ἐπιείκεια behind.

[15] For example, the *thoughts* of τραχύτης (255. 25 ff.) are defined as ones that involve reproach, while the μέθοδος of τραχύτης is (258. 1 ff.) to introduce such *thoughts* without concealment.

[16] See App. A. 2, p. 106.

Table 6. Stylistic Strata in Different Ancient Stylistics

	Demetrius	Peri Hupsous	Peri Politikou Logou	Peri Aphelous Logou	Peri Ideon
Thought	πράγματα διάνοια	ἔννοια (πάθος)	γνώμη	ἐπινόημα (μεταχείρισις)	ἔννοια μέθοδος
Figure		σχῆμα διάνοιας	σχῆμα	σχῆμα	σχῆμα
Diction	λέξις σύνθεσις	λέξις σύνθεσις	ἀπαγγελία	λέξις	λέξις σύνθεσις
Rhythm			ῥυθμός	ῥυθμός	ῥυθμός ἀνάπαυσις

reducible to a superficial lexical pattern but inhering in a syntactic formula,[17] but few traditional figures of thought are found among the μέθοδοι (there are in fact rather more of them among the σχήματα). The common factor in fact seems to be the idea that figure of thought implies oblique and indirect expression, which is sometimes found in earlier rhetorical writings (see Appendix B).

Hermogenes uses a philosophical veneer, and it seems to recall Plato. This is explicitly at 297. 10, where he cites the *Phaidros* (264c) for the view that every λόγος should have a beginning, a middle, and an end, except that Hermogenes is talking about the distribution of stylemes, whereas Plato had in mind the thematic organization of the speech. The term μέθοδος could also be borrowed from the *Phaidros* (270c–d). Furthermore, the term *idea* itself has an obvious philosophical background,[18] and Hermogenes' way of talking about *ideai* as abstract entities seems to echo Plato. *Ideai* can be mixed (231. 18 ff.):

σχεδὸν γὰρ ἅπασαι αἱ ἰδέαι τῶν λόγων δι᾽ ἀλλήλων εὑρίσκονταί τε καὶ γίνονται καταφανεῖς ἤτοι κατὰ ἀφαίρεσιν καὶ χωρισμόν, ὥσπερ ἐνταῦθα πεποιήκαμεν, οἷον ὅτε ἐλέγομεν, ὅτι σχήματά ἐστι καθαρὰ ὅσα τῶν τῆς περιβολῆς ἐστιν ἀπηλ-λαγμένα, ἢ κατὰ πρόσθεσιν, ὥσπερ ὅτε ἔφαμεν σαφήνειαν ὑπ᾽ εὐκρινείας γίνεσθαι καὶ καθαρότητος

(For almost all the stylistic *ideai* are found interwoven with each other, and become manifest either by subtraction and separation, as we did here, for example when we said that the pure figures are those that are removed from *peribole*, or by addition, as when we said that clarity results from distinctiveness and purity.)

This recalls Plato's *Sophist* (235b, δι᾽ ἀλλήλων at 259a6). Elsewhere, Hermogenes argues that opposite *ideai* can coexist (279. 17), and this recalls the quasi-mystical doctrine of 'unity of opposites' associated with the Presocratic philosopher Heraclitus of Miletus.[19] The link between rhetoric and a complex system of classes and species recalls also Socrates' account of the division and combination of natural kinds at *Phaidros* 265e, except that these kinds have to do with the subject matter of rhetoric, not its medium.[20]

There are two other suggestions of philosophy. One is the

---

[17] Alexander Numeniou, 10. 14 ff.; Quintilian, *IO* 9. 1. 17.
[18] For the term *idea*, see Panofsky (1968), c. 1.
[19] Diels and Kranz (1954) Heraclitus B60, 62, 67.
[20] On Hermogenes' attitude to Plato, see III. 4.

discussion of ἀκμή, where Hermogenes debates the issue whether this quality, which he sees as a combination of the *ideai* λαμπρότης and σφοδρότης/τραχύτης, can be said to have any independent existence of its own, and he uses the term γενέσεως ὑπόστασις, which must mean 'foundation for becoming', or 'capacity for self-generation'. Ὑπόστασις means 'essence' in late philosophical texts, though the combination γενέσεως ὑπόστασις has no philosophical parallel.[21]

The other case is the term ἐνδιάθετος in his discussion of ἀλήθεια. We have an excellent discussion of it development in philosophy by Pohlenz, mainly concerned with the origins of the term, and by Mühl, tracing its use in early Christian theology. Ἐνδιάθετος λόγος—internal reflective language, the language of thought—was the theoretical complement of προφορικὸς λόγος—expressive language. Animals can have the latter, the former is peculiar to man. Perhaps the philosophical term entered everyday life to denote sincere feelings. But Hermogenes' use of the word seems to latch on to the philosophical sense. This is shown by the fact that for him as for the philosophers, what is ἐνδιάθετος is the λόγος, and also by the fact that the conjunction of ἀληθής and ἐνδιάθετος occurs also in Philo, where, as Pohlenz notes, it seems to be borrowed from a Stoic source. The result is a paradox: ἐνδιάθετος λόγος is reducible to a species of προφορικὸς λόγος, from which the philosophers rigidly distinguished it. Outward utterance can embody the language of internal thought.[22]

What are we to make of this veneer of philosophy? Was Hermogenes a frustrated philosopher? Was he responding to the revival of Platonism? The latter seems unlikely, since if you compare him with Ps. Longinus, what stands out is neglect of typically Platonic concepts such as inspiration and genius (see II. 3). A more likely explanation is that rhetoricians were sensitive, as they always had been, to charges from the philosophers that rhetoric lacked a true methodology (a contemporary version of this attack was the one made by Sextus Empiricus in *Against the*

---

[21] For the general sense of ὑπόστασις, see Dörrie (1955), 65. Hermogenes also uses ὑπόστασις to denote the 'so . . . that . . .' construction (290. 17 ff., also *Peri Politikou Logou* cc. 67 ff. (27. 24 ff.), Anonymous *Peri Skhematon* 24 in Spengel (3. 128. 12 ff.), and in this case also ὑπόστασις seems to mean 'substantiation', i.e. the '. . . that . . .' clause substantiates and expands the antecedent: see Syrianus, *Commentary on Hermogenes* 60. 24 ff.; LSJ s.v.; Kustas (1973), 137.

[22] See Mühl (1962) and Pohlenz (1939), appendix.

Rhetoricians (= *AM* 2)). Following the hint of Socrates in the *Phaidros*, Hermogenes wanted to produce a rhetorical theory which had at least the appearance of being intellectually respectable.

3. HERMOGENES ON DEMOSTHENES

One could be forgiven for thinking that the real subject of *Peri Ideon* is to praise Demosthenes, and that its ostensible function of providing a general course in stylistics is a masquerade. Hermogenes has three connected theses about Demosthenes. The first is that he uses all the *ideai*, even ones you would not expect (like ἀφέλεια). This is an old idea in Greek rhetoric. Dionysius (*Dem. Lex.* 8) had described the Protean versatility of Demosthenes:

ἐξ ἁπάντων δ' αὐτῶν ὅσα κράτιστα καὶ χρησιμώτατα ἦν ἐκλεγόμενος συνύφαινε καὶ μίαν ἐκ πολλῶν διάλεκτον ἀπετέλει, μεγαλοπρεπῆ λιτήν, περιττὴν ἀπέριττον, ἐξαλλαγμένην συνήθη, πανηγυρικὴν ἀληθινήν, αὐστηρὰν ἱλαράν, σύντονον ἀνειμένην, ἡδεῖαν πικράν, ἠθικὴν παθητικήν, οὐθὲν διαλλάττουσαν τοῦ μεμυθευμένου παρὰ τοῖς ἀρχαίοις ποιηταῖς Πρωτέως

(Selecting the most powerful and most useful elements from all of them, he wove together and effected a single style, grand and plain, excessive and non-excessive, unusual and usual, panegyrical and veracious, austere and delightful, tense and relaxed, sweet and bitter, full of character and full of emotion, different in no way from the Proteus described in myth by ancient poets)

Hermogenes' second thesis is that in using all the *ideai* Demosthenes uses them all perfectly. His ability in this direction is identified with δεινότης.[23] There is also a third thesis which is that his perfect use of *ideai* takes the form of combining them. Hermogenes has a rich conceptual apparatus to describe how Demosthenes mixes styles. Most commonly they are said to reinforce each other, as in the case of σφοδρότης and λαμπρότης combining to produce ἀκμή. But he is more interested in cases of conflict between qualities, in which a speaker uses one quality to disguise another, so that one is real and the other only an appearance (for example, the account of the use of καθαρός strata to disguise περιβολή at 228. 19 ff.); or in which he pretends to be fair or clear, but actually aims to confuse (an informed listener or

[23] On δεινότης, see Rutherford (1994*b*).

reader will notice a conflict between the appearance and the δεινότης underlying it) or puts complex things simply (ἐπιπολαῖος βαθύτης, 'superficial depth' is the name for this) or says many things while appearing to say the same thing, or *vice versa*; or uses one quality as a correction (διόρθωσις) or relief (παραμυθία) for an undesirable stylistic effect.

To see how this works out, consider *De Corona* 18, discussed several times in *On Ideas*, a passage in which Demosthenes begins the narrative of his political career:

τοῦ γὰρ Φωκικοῦ συστάντος πολέμου, οὐ δι' ἐμέ (οὐ γὰρ ἔγωγ' ἐπολιτευόμην πω τότε) πρότων μὲν ὑμεῖς διέκεισθε ὥστε Φωκέας μὲν βούλεσθαι σωθῆναι, καίπερ οὐ δίκαια ποιοῦντας ὁρῶντες, Θηβαίοις δ' ὁτιοῦν ἂν ἐφησθῆναι παθοῦσιν, οὐκ ἀλόγως οὐδ' ἀδίκως αὐτοῖς ὀργιζόμενοι . . .

(When the Phocian war started, not through me (for I was not yet in politics), first you were disposed to want the Phocians on the one hand to escape ruin, although you saw that they were doing wrong and to be delighted at the Thebans on the other hand suffering any misfortune, out of an anger towards them that was neither irrational nor unjust . . .)

The overall effect comes from a combination of elements that provide a broad envelope or framework—initial subordination from the genitive absolute, the μέν . . . δέ . . ., and elements that break up this framework—in this case the parenthesis which starts with 'not through me . . .'. The aesthetic quality associated with the former is περιβολή, a quality which inheres in a wide range of forms of syntactical complexity present in sentences, particularly characteristic of the complex periods of Demosthenes; on the other hand, the quality associated with the disruptive parenthesis is γοργότης. Γοργά parentheses are common catalysts for grand qualities. One sees the same pattern in *Against Aristogeiton* 1. 15, where a sentence that would otherwise have been excessively σεμνός is broken up by a *parenthetic* clause which is described as a ὑποστροφή or a 'twist' in the narrative:

ἅπας ὁ τῶν ἀνθρώπων βίος, ὦ ἄνδρες Ἀθηναῖοι, <u>κἂν μεγάλην πόλιν οἰκῶσι κἂν μικράν</u>, φύσει καὶ νόμοις διοικεῖται.

(The whole life of human beings, men of Athens <u>whether they dwell in a large state or a small one</u>, is governed by nature and by the laws.)

The message is: a good Demosthenic sentence contains features that instantiate contrasting stylistic qualities. In some senses this

is a continuation of a very old idea in Greek stylistics that good
style is a mean, but the dynamic application we find here—
Demosthenic language is a continuous tension between elements
with conflicting stylistic properties—is probably new with *idea*-
theory.

Hermogenes' approach to Greek stylistics is both sensitive and
pedantic. He postulates rules ('feature *x* produces quality *y*'),
which then turn out to have many exceptions. Every linguistic
feature in Demosthenic text can be of stylistic significance; it is
not a question of specially marked features; nothing goes unnoticed. The educated listener or reader does not just experience
all of these qualities simultaneously. Rather he experiences them
one after another in quick succession. The effect is linear, as one
after another of a series of textual features elicit different
responses. Demosthenic language contains so much stylistic
information that an audience could easily miss much of it—as
Aelius Aristides complains that his audiences miss much of his
art.[24] How successful this form of analysis is, and how faithfully it
captures the spirit of Demosthenes' style, are not questions I want
to address in this monograph. But the general view among experts
seems to be that the system is very successful, and certainly more
successful than that of Dionysius.[25]

If we look at the bigger picture, one thing that emerges about
Hermogenes' approach to Demosthenes is that he tends to unify
stylistic virtues which other rhetoricians regarded as discrete.
Thus, δεινότης, which had been associated with Demosthenes
since the time of Demetrius at least, but redefined by succeeding
generations of rhetoricians, now turns out to be essentially the
ability to use all *ideai* well.[26] Furthermore, in *Peri Ideon* the
mixing of qualities very often comes about *via* μέθοδος. Hermogenes claims that the concept of μέθοδος continues the earlier
concept of figure of thought (σχῆμα διανοίας), and sense can be
made of this claim, as long as we look to the concepts behind
ancient figure-theory rather than to individual figures (App. B).
Figures of thought were an area in which Demosthenes was
supposed to show unparalleled skill, but they were not always
considered to be central to his style (Dionysius, for example,

[24] *Peri Tou Paraphthegmatos*, cited in Ch. VII.
[25] See most recently Wooten (1989); also Russell (1981*b*).
[26] On δεινότης, see pp. 28 ff.

manages never to mention them). Hermogenes takes a different route: he transforms the concept of 'figure of thought, giving it a new name (μέθοδος), and broadening its application from individual *formulae* to the more general idea of indirect expression of thought, which is linked to the process of mixing *ideai* together, since a typical μέθοδος involves taking a thought that would naturally be expressed in *idea x*, and factoring into it elements that belong to *idea y*, so as to produce a well-blended combination. In this way, Hermogenes reinterprets Demosthenes' traditional expertise in the use of figures of thought so as to make it an instrument of his Protean versatility. Thus, though to a reader approaching *Peri Ideon* for the first time it may present a somewhat desultory appearance, in fact the theory behind it turns out to be a peculiarly neat synthesis of earlier rhetorical ideas about Demosthenes.

II

Sophistic Influences

I. THE SOPHISTIC STYLE IN *PERI IDEON*

The immediate intellectual environment of *idea*-theory was without doubt the living tradition of declamation practised throughout the Roman empire, dominated by superstar-sophists, among them Hermogenes himself, whose careers Philostratus charts in *Lives of the Sophists*. To judge from this account, which is our main source, they wrote in many styles, ranging from the comparatively restrained to the grand and eccentric. It seems likely that some at least of their styles were close to the classical ones recommended by *idea*-theorists. Those of Nicostratus and Aristides probably belong here. Also that of Herodes Atticus, with its strong Critian flavour,[1] and that of Polemo, which was Demosthenic.[2] But others

---

[1] Herodes Atticus (*Vit. Soph.* 564): ἡ δὲ ἁρμονία τοῦ λόγου ἱκανῶς κεκολασμένη καὶ ἡ δεινότης ὑφέρπουσα μᾶλλον ἢ ἐγκειμένη, κρότος τε σὺν ἀφελείᾳ καὶ κριτιάζουσα ἠχὼ καὶ ἔννοιαι οἷσι μὴ ἑτέρῳ ἐνθυμηθῆναι κωμική τε εὐγλωττία οὐκ ἐπείσακτος, ἀλλ' ἐκ τῶν πραγμάτων, καὶ ἡδὺς ὁ λόγος καὶ πολυσχήματος καὶ εὐσχήμων καὶ σοφῶς ἐξαλλάττων, τὸ πνεῦμα τε οὐ σφοδρόν, ἀλλὰ λεῖον καὶ καθεστηκὸς καὶ ἡ ἐπίπαν ἰδέα τοῦ λόγου χρυσοῦ ψῆγμα ποταμῷ ἀργυροδίνῃ ὑπαύγαζον. προσέκειτο μὲν γὰρ πᾶσι τοῖς παλαιοῖς, τῷ δὲ Κριτίᾳ καὶ προσετετήκει καὶ παρήγαγεν αὐτὸν ἐς ἤθη Ἑλλήνων τέως ἀμελούμενον καὶ περιορώμενον. (The constituency of his style was sufficiently restrained, and it had a power which crept up on you rather than launching an assault. It combined impact with plainness, with a sonorousness that recalled Critias; his ideas were the sort that would not occur to anyone else; he had a humorous eloquence which was not extraneous, but derived from the subjects themselves; his diction was pleasing and abounded in figures and had grace and skilful variety; his breath was not vehement but smooth and steady. In general, his type of eloquence was like gold dust shining beneath a silvery eddying river. For while he devoted himself to all the older writers, from Critias he was actually inseparable, and brought him into familiarity among the Greeks, since he had been neglected and overlooked up to that point.) On Herodes Atticus and Critias, see Schmid (1887–97), i. 193.

[2] Polemo of Laodicea (*Vit. Soph.* 542): ἡ δὲ ἰδέα τῶν Πολέμωνος λόγων θερμὴ καὶ ἐναγώνιος καὶ τορὸν ἠχοῦσα, ὥσπερ ἡ Ὀλυμπιονικὴ σάλπιγξ, ἐπιπρέπει δὲ αὐτῇ καὶ τὸ Δημοσθενικὸν τῆς γνώμης, καὶ ἡ σεμνολογία οὐχ ὑπτία, λαμπρὰ δὲ καὶ ἔμπνους, ὥσπερ ἐκ τρίποδος. (Polemo's style of eloquence is heated, combative, and ringing, like the trumpet at the Olympic games. A conspicuous element in it is a Demosthenic quality of thought. It has a solemnity which is not sluggish, but brilliant and inspired as though delivered from a tripod.) Polemo's style is high, but described in

were probably more modern and more outlandish in their effects than anything the *idea*-theorists would have condoned. For example, it is difficult to believe that the technique of finishing one's speech with an ᾠδή, which Philostratus describes more than once, is something the *idea*-theorists would have approved of.[3] Whether we should think of a special Asianist style distinguished from the classical style remains difficult to tell, but there were flamboyant styles of declamation-performance that classicists like Hermogenes would have regarded as decadent.[4] So that, whereas there might be a tendency to think of the major stylistic isobar in this period as lying between the Demosthenic and the Xenophontic, we get a glimpse that there was another one just as important between a flamboyant style of declamation-performance, perhaps perceived as modern and of foreign origin, and a more restrained one, which tended to be associated with ancient simplicity and the Greek past.

Since many such declaimers of the period seem to have applied to themselves the title σοφιστής, and traced their profession back to the sophists of the classical period, and in particular the 'Second Sophistic' founded by Aeschines, we might begin by looking at the few explicit references to sophists or sophistic style in *Peri Ideon*.

Contemporary sophists are not much in evidence in *idea*-theory. Only two are mentioned by the theorists, both in *On Ideas*. One is Aelius Aristides, the famous orator and valetudinarian, who is mentioned as a model for σεμνότης and for ἀλήθεια; I discuss the portrayal of Aristides in *On Ideas* more fully in Chapter VII. The other is Titus Aurelius Nicostratus, from Macedonia, who is mentioned as a model of ἀφέλεια. Suda informs us that he wrote a Δεκαμυθία and a Πολυμυθία (apparently collections of fables), Εἰκόνες (*ekphrases* to be compared with those of Philostratus), Θαλάττουργοι (imitations of letters by workmen along the lines of those by Aelian?), and Ἐγκώμια. Hermogenes, *Peri Ideon* 407. 15–16, also mentions μῦθοι δραματικοί, which are probably novels.[5]

more classical terms, without mention of, for example, περιβολή. The description in two phenomena associated with major religious centres: the games (Olympia) and the oracle (Delphi).

[3] Of Favorinus of Arelate: *Vit. Soph.* 491; of Dionysius of Miletus at *Vit. Soph.* 513; of Hadrian of Tyre at *Vit. Soph.* 171; also the *canticum* at Cicero, *Orator* 57.

[4] Asianism and Atticism, Wilamowitz-Moellendorf (1900), Bowersock (1969).

[5] See Stegemann (1936); Rohde (1900), 378–9.

If *idea*-theory has little to say about contemporary sophists, it is a little more informative about the ancient sophists. In the chapter on δεινότης (2. 9) the abstract category of language which 'seems to be δεινός but is really not' turns out to be the sophistic style, associated with Gorgias (cf. also 248. 21), Meno, and Polus, particularly as portrayed by Plato. This style is superficially impressive, but actually empty (397–8), because grand and beautiful ἔννοιαι and σχήματα are not used with the appropriateness that is the mark of true δεινότης.[6] The same style is also attributed to the orator Aristogeiton because he uses abusive language and invective before the ἀπόδειξις section of his speeches.[7]

Three other ancient sophists deserve to be mentioned also. First, there is Antiphon the sophist, author of *Peri Aletheias*, whose style Hermogenes discusses in 2. 11, hedging on the question of whether he is the same as Antiphon of Rhamnous, the oligarch mentioned by Thucydides.[8] His style exemplifies the same φαινομένη δεινότης that Hermogenes attributes to the sophists in 2. 9. It is interesting that Hermogenes stresses that it was Antiphon the author of *Peri Aletheias* who was an influence on Thucydides. I suspect that Hermogenes makes this point in order to suggest that Thucydides' style has a sophistical element. There seems to have been a tradition that Rhamnousian Antiphon influenced Thucydides (based perhaps on Thuc. *Hist*. 8. 68. 1; cf. Marcellinus *Vit. Thuc.* 22). But the author of *Peri Aletheias* was not a good stylistic κανών (nothing but grandeur used inappropriately, resulting in obscurity), and it was in following him, I take the argument to be, that Thucydides himself fell into error.[9]

[6] See Voit's (1934) analysis. Hermogenes uses the word σοφιστικός once independently in the section on political language (381. 27) as one of a pair of terms with λαμπρός to describe the effect of long clauses if they are not broken up in a Demosthenic manner.

[7] Compare also 257. 22, where Aristogeiton is described as using unmitigated τραχύτης.

[8] At 399. 21 Hermogenes seems to suggest that both Antiphons were οἱ σοφιστεύσαντες. Modern opinion seems to be that the sophist and the orator were distinct, and the situation may even be more complex than that, since the author of the extant *Tetralogies* could be yet another Antiphon. There seems to be a sense that the stylistic argument is not sufficient to distinguish them. See Kerferd (1981), 49–51; Morrison (1961).

[9] This represents a change of emphasis from Dionysius, who admires Demosthenes and also Thucydides, but thinks rather less of Plato. Hermogenes' view of Thucydides is not high. He rarely cites him in the core (one of the rare exceptions

Second, there is Critias, mentioned as one of the political orators in *On Ideas* 2. 10. He is not associated with sophistry in *Peri Ideon* (though Hermogenes compares him to Antiphon), but classed with the ancient sophists in *Peri Aphelous Logou* 93. 20 (also at 77. 13). It may be that the position of Critias in both these authors reflects the influence of Herodes Atticus, who, according to Philostratus, did much to popularize Critias in Athens.[10]

Finally, there is Aeschines, whom Hermogenes characterizes as σοφιστοκὸς καὶ γαῦρος (sophistical and arrogant) (399. 4; cf. 401. 9). There seems to be a reference to the tradition that Aeschines became the founder of the Second Sophistic, having fled from Athens to Rhodes (*Vit. Soph.* 507). At any rate, this passage shows that the term σοφιστικός has a negative value for Hermogenes.

2. THE CONTRIBUTION OF SOPHISTIC DECLAMATION TO THE THEORY OF *IDEAI*

For more insight into the relationship between *idea*-theory and the Second Sophistic, we must examine its relation to the stylistic theory implied in Philostratus' *Lives of the Sophists*. Philostratus' model of style is bipolar, with a heavier end, associated with περιβολή, the sophistic style, the qualities ἀγών, πνεῦμα, ἐπιφορά, χολή, σεμνολογία, ῥοῖζος, and κρότος, and a lighter end, associated with ἀφέλεια, the political style, the forensic, dialectic, the archaic, ἀττικισμός and κόλασις (restraint).[11] I list some of the key terms in Table 7.[12] There are terminological similarities to *Peri Ideon, Peri*

---

is for his use of nouns rather than verbs in the section on σεμνότης—249 bottom). In the sketch of Thucydides' style in 2. 11 (409–10) it is presented as a failure: he aims at σεμνότης and κάλλος, but goes too far and ends up by becoming σκληρός, ἀσαφής, and ἀγλευκής (harsh, unclear, and lacking in sweetness). Thucydides is a κανών of nothing in particular.

[10] *Vit. Soph.* 564 (cited in n. 1 above). It may well be that the surviving speech περὶ πολιτείας which purports to be by Herodes was actually by Critias: see Wade-Gery (1945). The speech was edited by Albini (1968).

[11] On Philostratus' attitude to style, see Anderson (1986), 37.

[12] Some passages, besides those already cited, and those cited in other notes, are: (*a*) Aspasius of Ravenna (627): ἐπιμεληθεὶς δὲ τοῦ δοκίμως τε καὶ σὺν ἀφελείᾳ ἑρμηνεύειν πνεύματος τε καὶ περιβολῆς ἠμέλησε (He took care that his style was acceptable and plain, but he neglected breath and elaboration). Here then, ἀφέλεια is contrasted to πνεῦμα and περιβολή. (*b*) Athenodorus (*Vit. Soph.* 594): Ἀριστοκλέους μὲν γὰρ ἤκουσε παῖς ἔτι, Χρήστου δὲ ἤδη ξυνιείς, ὅθεν ἀπ' ἀμφοῖν ἐκράθη τὴν γλῶτταν ἀττικίζω τε κἀκ περιβολῆς ἑρμηνεύων (He attended lectures by Aristocles while still a boy, and by Chrestus when his understanding was more advanced; and from these two he

TABLE 7. *The Two Styles in Philostratus,*
Lives of the Sophists

σοφιστικός	πολιτικός
	δικανικός
περιβολή	ἀφέλεια
πνεῦμα	ἀττικίζω
	ἀρχαῖος

Politikou Logou, and *Peri Aphelous Logou,* but conceptual differences. Because the grand-sophistical style monopolizes one of the two stylistic poles, the contrasting pole attracts an unlikely alliance of qualities that have in common their opposition to the grand-sophistic style. The superimposition of the terms ἀφελής and πολιτικός here is surprising, in view of the situation in *Peri Aphelous Logou,* where they are antithetical. But a common hostility to the grand-sophistical style takes precedence.

One hypothesis that suggests itself is that Philostratus adapted his stylistic vocabulary from *Peri Ideon* and *Peri Politikou Logou,* or manuals like them, appropriating the vocabulary of classicizing literary stylistics for the more vigorous environment of sophistical declamation. But there is also an alternative hypothesis available: perhaps his deployment of the terms is in some respects faithful to usage established in the second century CE. For such a relationship to exist, he would have had to have drawn on contemporary accounts, perhaps works of criticism concerned with contemporary declaimers.

derived his well-tempered style, for he both Atticized and expressed himself by way of *peribole*). (*c*) Apollonius of Naucratis (*Vit. Soph.* 599): λόγου δὲ ἐπεμελήθη πολιτικοῦ καὶ εὖ κεκολασμένου, ἧττον δὲ ἀγωνιζομένου, περιβολὴ γὰρ ἄπεστιν αὐτοῦ καὶ πνεῦμα (the style he cultivated was political and well restrained, but less suited to controversy; for it lacked elaboration and breath); (*d*) Aristocles of Pergamum (*Vit. Soph.* 568): ἡ δὲ ἰδέα τοῦ λόγου διαυγὴς μὲν καὶ ἀττικίζουσα, διαλέγεσθαι δὲ ἐπιτηδεία μᾶλλον ἢ ἀγωνίζεσθαι, χολή τε γὰρ ἄπεστι τοῦ λόγου καὶ ὁρμαὶ πρὸς βραχύ, αὐτὴ τε ἡ ἀττίκισις, εἰ παρὰ τὴν τοῦ Ἡρώδου γλῶτταν βασανίζοιτο, λεπτολογεῖσθαι δόξει μᾶλλον ἢ κρότου τε καὶ ἠχοῦς ξυγκεῖσθαι (The quality of his style was bright and Attic, but it was more suited to dialogue than to contest, for it lacks indignation and spontaneous outbursts. And even his Atticism, compared with the language of Herodes, will seem delicately wrought, rather than forged from impact and sonorousness); (*e*) Philiscus the Thessalian (*Vit. Soph.* 623): his style was λάλος rather than ἐναγώνιος (colloquial rather than contentious).

Furthermore, not only could such critical terms have already been used of sophistical declamation in the second century, but it is even possible that some of them originated in this context. This hypothesis cannot be proved decisively for any term. But in some cases such an origin seems quite likely. One thinks, for example, of the term περιβολή, which is used by the *idea*-theorists in the sense of 'amplification', particularly with reference to a well-rounded and filled-out sentence, but which is specially associated with sophists in *Lives of the Sophists*,[13] and which surely starts off meaning 'costume', 'get-up', the sort of outfit that would have been most appropriate on a flamboyant sophist.[14]

Another term which may have started off in sophistic declamation is ἀκμή (λόγου), which means 'climax' or 'culminating effect', and is used both in *Peri Heureseos* and by Hermogenes in *Peri Ideon*. The author of *Peri Heureseos* uses it to refer to the effect of a sequence of clauses or sentences, where the same structure is repeated several times, or the intensity increases toward the end. Hermogenes, on the other hand, defines it as the effect of combining the effects of panegyric brilliance (λαμπρότης) with that of vehemence (σφοδρότης) to give the effect of a confident and controlled attack.[15] But it is interesting that the same technique of performance-climax is mentioned several times in *Lives of the Sophists* in connection with the sophists Scopelion, Aristides, Polemo, and Lollianus as a distinctive and virtuoso feature of their technique. For example, of Polemo (*Lives of the Sophists* 537):[16]

[13] Nicetes of Smyrna (*Vit. Soph.* 511): ὁ δὲ ἀνὴρ οὗτος τοῖς μὲν δικανικοῖς ἀμείνων ἐδόκει τὰ δικανικά, τοῖς δὲ σοφιστικοῖς τὰ σοφιστικὰ ὑπὸ τοῦ περιδεξίως τε καὶ πρὸς ἄμιλλαν ἐς ἄμφω ἡρμόσθαι. τὸ μὲν γὰρ δικανικὸν σοφιστικῇ περιβολῇ ἐκόσμησεν, τὸ δὲ σοφιστικὸν κέντρῳ δικανικῷ ἐπέρρωσεν (He was a man who to men with forensic interests seemed to be better at forensic subjects, and again to men with sophistic inclinations seemed to do better on sophistic themes, because of the intelligence and competitiveness with which he adapted himself to both styles. For he adorned the forensic style with sophistic *peribole*, while he strengthened the sophistic style with a forensic sting); Theomnestus of Naucratis (*Vit. Soph.* 486): καὶ Θεόμνηστον δὲ τὸν Ναυκρατίτην ἐπιδήλως φιλοσοφήσαντα ἡ περιβολὴ τῶν λόγων ἐς τοὺς σοφιστὰς ἀπήνεγκεν (Again, Theomnestus of Naucratis was conspicuously a philosopher, but the *peribole* of his speeches caused him to be classed with the sophists).

[14] The term ἐφελκόμενα σχήματα ('figures that draw a train'), used in connection with περιβολή by Hermogenes, seems to preserve the metaphor.

[15] Here *Peri Ideon* may presuppose *Peri Heureseos*: see App. A.

[16] Other cases: of Scopelion of Clazomenae (*Vit. Soph.* 519): θαυμασιώτερος . . . περὶ τὰς ἀκμαιοτέρας τῶν ὑποθέσεων καὶ πολλῷ πλέον περὶ τὰς Μηδικὰς, ἐν αἷς οἱ Δαρεῖοί

φησὶ δὲ αὐτὸν ὁ Ἡρώδης καὶ ἀναπηδᾶν τοῦ θρόνου περὶ τὰς ἀκμὰς τῶν ὑποθέσεων, τοσοῦτον αὐτῷ περιεῖναι ὁρμῆς, καὶ ὅτε ἀποτορνεύοι περίοδον, τὸ ἐπὶ πᾶσιν αὐτῆς κῶλον σὺν μειδιάσματι φέρειν, ἐνδεικνύμενον πολὺ τὸ ἀλύπως φράζειν, καὶ κροαίνειν ἐν τοῖς τῶν ὑποθέσεων χωρίοις οὐδὲν μεῖον τοῦ Ὁμηρικοῦ ἵππου.

(Herodes says also that he would jump up from his chair at moments of peak in his theme, such was his excess of excitement, and when he rounded off a period, he would deliver the final clause with a smile, as if to show that he could do so without effort, and at certain points in his argument he would stamp the ground, no less than the horse in Homer. [*Iliad* 6. 507]) (after Wright)

Again, I could see the concept of ἀκμή (λόγου) as having originated in the performance of sophistic declamation, and as having been transferred from there to classical stylistic theory.

Another *idea* which may have originated in sophistic declamation is βαρύτης. This is one of the hardest *ideai* to understand. According to *Peri Politikou Logou* and *Peri Ideon* you produce it when you impersonate a certain tone of indignation and injured pride, sometimes reproaching the jury, protesting that you deserve the opposite treatment to what you have received, sometimes accusing yourself in irony (or 'figured language'), which is a calculated ploy to make the audience react in the opposite direction. As Hermogenes saw, this is in some sense the opposite of ἐπιείκεια, where the speaker tries his best to conciliate the audience, and represents himself as a nice guy; but in the role of βαρύτης, you start from the premiss that you are an important person who deserves respect, and has been treated badly.

τέ εἰσι καὶ οἱ Ξέρξαι (. . . he was more wonderful in his treatment of higher-pitched themes, especially those relating to the Persians, in which occur passages about Darius and Xerxes); of Aelius Aristides (*Vit. Soph.* 583–4): ἐπιλαμβάνονται δέ τινες καὶ ἀκμῆς τοῦ ἀνδρὸς ἐπὶ τοῦ παραιτουμένου τὸν τειχισμὸν τῆς Λακεδαίμονος. εἴρηται δὲ ὧδε· "μὴ γὰρ δὴ ἐν τείχει ἐπιπτήξαιμεν ὀρτύγων ἐναψάμενοι φύσιν." (And some criticize his [Aristides'] peak when he spoke in his role of the Spartan who argued against the fortifying of Sparta. It went like this: 'May we not cower within the walls, taking on the nature of quails'); of Lollianus of Ephesus (*Vit. Soph.* 527)— Lollianus takes it as his theme to denounce Leptines on account of his law, because the supply of corn has not reached Athens from Pontus: ὧδε ἤκμασεν· κέκλεισται τὸ στόμα τοῦ Πόντου νόμῳ καὶ τὰς Ἀθηναίων τροφὰς ὀλίγαι κωλύουσι συλλαβαί, καὶ ταὐτὸν δύνανται Λύσανδρος ναυμαχῶν καὶ Λεπτίνης νομομαχῶν (His climax was as follows: the mouth of the Pontus has been locked up by a law, and a few syllables keep back the food supply of Athens; so that Lysander fighting with his ships and Leptines fighting with his law have the same power') (trans. Wright). To sum up, then: the words ἀκμή/ἀκμαῖος/ἀκμάζω seem to refer to a climax in a declamatory performance, or, of a declamatory theme, the quality of accommodating such a performance.

I suggest that βαρύτης represents the stylistic counterpart of a type of declamation that we hear about in *Lives of the Sophists* and in other sources. The speaker had to pretend he was Demosthenes, in the closing years of his life, engaging in a sort of macabre brinkmanship with the Athenian *demos*, juxtaposing rebukes directed against them with ironic attacks on his own record, using 'figured language' to this end.[17] A particularly popular technique in all speeches of this type was to demand the death penalty for oneself—the reverse of Socrates' mistake in the *Apology*, but still a risky business, if used in real life. Philostratus attributes such speeches to Polemo of Laodicea (*Lives of the Sophists* 542; Kohl (1915), 293; 323; 311):

καὶ οἱ Δημοσθένεις τρεῖς, ὁ μετὰ Χαιρώνειαν προσαγγέλλων ἑαυτόν, καὶ ὁ δοκῶν θανάτου ἑαυτῷ τιμᾶσθαι ἐπὶ τοῖς Ἀρπαλείοις καὶ ὁ ξυμβουλεύων ἐπὶ τῶν τριήρων φεύγειν ἐπιόντος μὲν Φιλίππου, νόμον δὲ Αἰσχίνου κεκυρωκότος ἀποθνήσκειν τὸν πόλεμον μνημονεύσαντα.

(and the three on Demosthenes, one in which he denounced himself after Chaeronea, one in which he pretends that he deserves the death penalty for the affair of Harpalus, and on in which he advises the Athenians to take to their triremes and escape at the approach of Philip, and in which Aeschines had carried a law that anyone who mentioned the war should be executed.)

Similar in technique was a declamation by Dionysius of Miletus mentioned by Philostratus known as the *Epi Khaironeiai Threnos* (*Vit. Soph.* 522; Kohl (1915), 293),[18] and there were many others.[19]

---

[17] It is sometimes explicitly described as such in *Vit. Soph.* This point is made by Kohl (1915), 66 and by Drerup (1923), 150. In Philostratus we find it of Rufus of Perinthos at 597, where the technique is described as difficult; similarly of Polemo, 540 (Polemo was not good at them); Hermocrates of Phocis at 608; Antiochus of Aigai at 569.

[18] διεξιὼν γὰρ τὸν Δημοσθένην τὸν μετὰ Χαιρώνειαν προσαγγέλλοντα τῇ βουλῇ ἑαυτὸν ἐς τήνδε τὴν μονῳδίαν τοῦ λόγου ἐτελεύτησεν· "ὦ Χαιρώνεια πονηρὸν χωρίον." καὶ πάλιν "ὦ αὐτομολήσασα πρὸς τοὺς βαρβάρους Βοιωτία. στενάξατε οἱ κατὰ γῆς ἥρωες, ἐγγὺς Πλαταιῶν νενικήμεθα." καὶ πάλιν ἐν τοῖς κρινομένοις ἐπὶ τῷ μισθοφορεῖν Ἀρκάσιν "ἀγορὰ ππολέμου πρόκειται καὶ τὰ τῶν Ἑλλήνων κακὰ τὴν Ἀρκαδίαν τρέφει," καὶ "ἐπέρχεται πόλεμος αἰτίαν οὐκ ἔχων." (For when reciting an account of Demosthenes as he denounced himself before the *boule* after Chaeronea, he finished his speech with this monody: 'O Chaeronea, wicked place!' and again: 'O Boiotia, you who have deserted to the barbarians! Lament, heroes beneath the earth! It is close to Plataea that we have been defeated!' And again, in the description of the Arcadians on trial for being mercenaries, he said: 'A market-place of war has been set up, and the woes of the Greeks nourish Arcadia,' and 'There comes upon us a war for which there is no cause.') This passage is discussed in Norden (1898), 413.

[See p. 30 for n. 19]

These reflections on how sophistic declamation may have contributed to the development of the theory of *ideai* suggest that a modification should be made to the orthodox view of its development. The orthodox view, masterfully formulated by Hagedorn, is that the system of *ideai* as we see it in *Peri Ideon* represents a linear development from the ἀρεταὶ λέξεως of earlier rhetoric, best exemplified in the stylistic works of Dionysius of Halicarnassus. That this represents a large part of the truth is not something I want to contest. But at the same time I have come to believe that the system of ἀρεταὶ λέξεως may have been enriched by new qualities such as βαρύτης, ἀκμή, and περιβολή which developed in response to sophistical declamation.

What makes this especially plausible is that some of the qualities that I have found parallels for in *Lives of the Sophists* are exactly the ones that have no precedent in the works of Dionysius. That is particularly true of βαρύτης and ἀκμή, for example.[20] For Hagedorn, περιβολή has an antecedent in the quality περιττολογία in Dionysius. However, whereas περιβολή is a desirable quality of style, inhering in various complex forms of sentence structure,[21] περιττολογία in the system of Dionysius is a fault.[22] Now, although

---

[19] Kohl (1915) 293, 296, 298 (Philip demands Demosthenes after Chaeronea, and Demosthenes proposes that he be given up), 299, 300, 302, 304 (Philip asks for the triremes; Demosthenes proposes that the crews be sent also), 314–15 (Demades proposes that Philip be worshipped; Demosthenes objects and is defeated, so he proposes that a temple be founded to him), 324–5 (Demosthenes proposes a death sentence for himself after the Harpalus affair).

[20] In each case the closest precedent would seem to be among the techniques listed in the section on δεινότης in Demetrius, *Peri Hermeneias*.

[21] Περιβολή inheres mainly in long, complex sentences which feature (1) progression from a general point to a particular one (*Peri Politikou Logou* 20. 2 ff., *Peri Ideon* 278. 13 ff.); (2) hyperbaton and reversal of points (*Peri Politikou Logou* 22.10 ff., *Peri Ideon* 282. 15 ff., 294. 11 ff.); and (3) σχήματα such as ὑπόστασις ('so . . . that . . .') (*Peri Politikou Logou* 27. 22 ff., *Peri Ideon* 290. 16 ff.), μερισμός (. . . μὲν . . . δὲ . . .) (*Peri Politikou Logou* 30. 23 ff., *Peri Ideon* 290. 21 ff.); and πλαγιασμός (the genitive absolute construction) (*Peri Politikou Logou* 34. 3 ff., *Peri Ideon* 288. 13 ff.).

[22] At *Dem. Lex.* c. 5, 137. 7 ff. in a description of the styles of Plato: ὅταν δὲ εἰς τὴν περιττολογίαν καὶ τὸ καλλιεπεῖν . . . ἄμετρον ὁρμὴν λάβῃ, πολλῷ χείρων ἑαυτῆς γίνεται . . . ἐκχεῖται δ᾽ εἰς ἀπειροκάλους περιφράσεις πλοῦτον ὀνομάτων ἐπιδεικνυμένη κενόν, ὑπερ-ιδοῦσά τε τῶν κυρίων καὶ ἐν τῇ κοινῇ χρήσει κειμένων τὰ πεποιημένα ζητεῖ καὶ ξένα καὶ ἀρχαιοπρεπῆ. (But when he launches himself unrestrainedly into impressive and decorated language, he does himself far less than full justice . . . [his style] abandons itself to tasteless circumlocutions and an empty show of verbal exuberance and, in defiance of correct usage and standard vocabulary, seeks artificial, exotic, and archaic forms of expression.) (Trans. Usher, 1974.)

Hermogenes seems to think that ideally you mix περιβολή with other qualities, like γοργότης, to produce an ideal blend of long/slow and short/rapid elements, περιβολή by itself is not a faulty quality. So I would suggest that περιβολή is without a precise correlate in Dionysius, and that it may have been a contribution of sophistic declamation.

3. TECHNIQUE AND ITS APPEARANCE

The concept of technique and its appearance is very important in *Peri Ideon*. We find this, for example, in connection with the stratum μέθοδος on *On Ideas*. Μέθεδος means 'way of adapting a thought'. But you see it even more in the quality δεινότης, which Hermogenes defines as basically 'skill in the correct use of elements of language'. The main account comes in *Peri Ideon* 2. 9, where Hermogenes distinguishes three types of δεινότης.

(i) Language that both is and appears to be δεινός, which is common in the grand deliberative speeches of Demosthenes and is mainly a matter of ἔννοιαι that are paradoxical or complex and of *strata* drawn from the sub-species of μέγεθος.[23]

(ii) Language that does not appear to be δεινός but actually is, which is characteristic of Demosthenes' private speeches and of Lysias and consists in concealing your rhetorical strategy beneath a plain stylistic appearance (376. 5 ff.). This type of δεινότης appropriates the alternative sense of δεινότης in earlier stylistic theory: that of 'force'.

(iii) Language that appears to be δεινός but is not really so, which is characteristic of Gorgias and of the sophists and comes about when grand λέξις, σχήματα, and κῶλα are used inappropriately to express ἔννοιαι that are superficial and common (377. 10 ff.).

If you consider the tripartition as a whole, what emerges is that the appearance of δεινότης plays two roles: on the one hand, by itself, without an underlying sense of καιρός, it is sophistical. But on the other hand, when combined with a sense of appropriate use, it is an essential component of Demosthenic style.

[23] 373. 8 ff. See Voit (1934), 57–8, who seems to me to overestimate the degree to which this type reduces to μέγεθος.

The concept of technique is thus of great value in *Peri Ideon*. Hermogenes is very much aware that the audience of a speech is on the lookout for clever techniques. In the section on κάλλος he mentions the proem of Isocrates' *Panathenaikos*, which describes the audience reaction to techniques like *parisosis* (298. 3, referring to *Panath.* 2). In some passages he suggests that Demosthenes and other classical authors deliberately call attention to their technique, as in a passage from *Against Aristocrates* (20) cited in the section on ἐπιείκεια, where Demosthenes is supposed to state that he is going easy on his opponent (i.e. he shows off his ἐπιείκεια):[24]
καὶ θεάσασθε, ὦ Ἀθηναῖοι, ὡς ἐπιεικῶς καὶ ἁπλῶς χρήσομαι τῷ λόγῳ, ὃς εἰς μὲν ταύτην τίθεμαι τὴν τάξιν αὐτόν, ἐν ᾗ πλείστης ἂν τυγχάνοι τιμῆς (And observe, Athenians, how fairly and simply I use language, in that I place him in the category in which he would be most honoured). Demosthenes is also supposed to describe some of Aeschines' words as σεμνός, referring to the *idea* (250. 5; *Or.* 18. 35). And Xenophon too goes in for this form of self-advertisement, himself applying 'sweet' to a term, a technique which Hermogenes thinks belongs to γλυκύτης (335. 20; *Kyn.* 5. 33).

The idea that the display and appreciation of technique is a large part of the transaction between orator and audience that takes place during a rhetorical performance is an old one. But one would expect to find it emphasized in the context of epideictic oratory, and declamation. This tendency becomes acute during the Second Sophistic. A particularly uninhibited statement of the view that the point of sophistical declamation is to display technique is found in Aelius Aristides' work, *Peri Tou Paraphthegmatos*. The premiss of this is that Aristides had been criticized for praising himself by making a remark in passing (παράφθεγμα) in

[24] *Against Aristocrates* is a speech frequently associated with δεινότης in *Peri Ideon*. It is cited a couple of times in the section on εὐκρίνεια for passages in which Demosthenes lists a number of points he is going to make, usually with the purpose of misleading the audience. These passages seem to come from *Peri Heureseos*; see App. A. And he also cites it in the section on γλυκύτης for the passage about the origin of the Areopagus at Athens—a passage expressed in unusually sweet and simple language. Hermogenes remarks on the anomalous style, and promises to discuss the passage more in *Peri Methodou Deinotetos*. These are not the only occasions on which δεινότης is mentioned in the core of *Peri Ideon*, nor the only occasions when Hermogenes cites from *Against Aristocrates*. Nevertheless, the correlation between references to δεινότης and citations from *Against Aristocrates* is high enough to make me think that Hermogenes had a special interest in δεινότης in this speech.

the course of a prose hymn in honour of Athena. The speech is a defence of that παράφθεγμα, and most of it is given over to a catalogue of illustrations of self-praise on the part of Greek authors, but it also includes passages describing the abilities and functions of the ideal orator. Aristides begins from the premiss that παραφθέγματα are necessary because otherwise the orator's technique would go unnoticed, and he goes on to describe the orator's skill in mixing different qualities of language and combining various techniques.[25] After this Aristides goes on to describe the orator's reactions upon not being appreciated correctly:

ὁ δέ ῥήτωρ ὑπὲρ αὐτῶν ῥήγνυται. τί φῄς; οὐχ ὁρᾷς τὸ ἀγώνισμα οὐδὲ ἀπό πολλοῦ, ἀλλ᾽ εἰς ἑκάτερον, φησί, τῶν αὐλῶν ἐμοῦ χωρὶς αὐλοῦντος καὶ πάσαις ἅμα ταῖς ἁρμονίαις χρωμένου κάθησαι πρὸς ἑνός τινος τῶν δακτύλων κίνησιν βλέπων, ὥσπερ ἂν εἰ καὶ ἐν λύρᾳ ἢ κιθάρᾳ πάντων ὁμοῦ δεικνυμένων μιᾶς χορδῆς ἤχου δοκοίης ἀκούειν.

(But the orator bursts with anger for this reason. What do you say? You do not see the contest, not even in the smallest degree. But, he says, although I play each flute separately, and at the same time use all the harmonies, you sit gazing at the movement of one of my fingers, as if when every technique was being displayed at the same time on a lyre or a harp, you would seem to hear the sound of a single chord.) (Trans. Behr, 1981)

In traditional oratory, the aim is to influence the audience by getting them on your side. Here, the orator aims to show off his skill, and if the audience are not up to appreciating it, the problem is theirs. The ostensible aim of *Peri Tou Paraphthegmatos* is to show that this attitude is well established in Greek literature, but even if that is so, it had never been given the attention it received from Aristides (see Chapter VII).

Such a concentration on technique and its appearance is unusual in Greek stylistic theory. It is probably more common for the appearance of technique to be criticized, on the grounds that in a democracy, where everyone is supposed to have an equal right to speak, a sense that a speaker is trained can obstruct the process of persuasion. Of course, that's an idealized position. In practice, a sense that a speaker is trained can just as easily contribute to his persuasiveness.

Thus, in Dionysius of Halicarnassus we find no great stress on

[25] I cite this passage in Ch. VII.

the appearance of technique in Demosthenes.[26] The effect that the orator tries to have on his audience is rather one of emotional force. Dionysius also believes that there is much to be said for a style that seems to be natural, like that of Lysias.

Dionysius' friend Caecilius held the slightly different view that there was something showy and technical about the style of Demosthenes, particularly its deliberate and frequent use of σχήματα διανοίας, and probably though of this as a quasi-fault. He contrasts this with the earlier style of Antiphon, which is free of deliberate σχήματα διανοίας, and comparatively simple and natural (fr. 103).

Caecilius' views on τὸ ὕψος were challenged by Ps. Longinus. And it may well be Caecilius' view that he is taking on when in c. 2 he argues that τὸ ὕψος is not just a matter of nature, but needs technique also. However, he shies away from admitting that a technical appearance is a desirable thing. This comes out particularly à propos of the study of De Corona 188 (the 'Marathon Oath') in c. 16–17. This σχῆμα διανοίας is a product of technique (what would naturally be an example is artificially cast in the form of an oath). But Ps. Longinus thinks that Demosthenes achieves τὸ ὕψος precisely by concealing the technique under a show of brilliance. Technique is manifestly not something which you flaunt.

Ps. Longinus does not share Hermogenes' view that technical skill is the essential quality of a supreme stylist and that its appearance is the supreme stylistic quality. Consider the comparison of Hyperides and Demosthenes in Peri Hupsous c. 34. Caecilius, Ps. Longinus objects, had preferred Lysias to Plato on the grounds that Lysias has more virtues, while Plato has faults. To show the absurdity of such an approach, Ps. Longinus compares Hyperides and Demosthenes. Hyperides, he argues,

---

[26] Though cf. Dem. Lex. 10; 148. 14 ff., according to which Thucydides has no regard for καιρός, while Demosthenes avoids this fault, but still gives the impression of δεινότης. The difference between the contrast drawn here and δεινότης types (i) and (iii) in Peri Ideon—the fact that Dionysius does not seem to think in terms of a 'real' form of δεινότης and the fact that it is not Thucydides whom Hermogenes regards as characteristic of type (iii)—are not as striking as the similarities. Furthermore, if Hermogenes was familiar with Dem. Lex. 10, it could be this that suggested to him the idea of associating δεινότης with τὸ πρέπον, for Dionysius' point about the appearance of δεινότης and τὸ πρέπον being at variance could easily have been extended into a general theorem that real δεινότης and τὸ πρέπον are identical.

has a much more varied and versatile style. Demosthenes, by contrast, is monotonous and incompetent at a variety of virtues (34. 3):

ὁ δὲ Δημοσθένης ἀνηθοποίητος, ἀδιάχυτος, ἥκιστα ὑγρὸς ἢ ἐπιδεικτικός, ἁπάντων ἑξῆς τῶν προειρημένων κατὰ τὸ πλέον ἄμοιρος· ἔνθα μέντοι γελοῖος ἔναι βιάζεται καὶ ἀστεῖος οὐ γέλωτα κινεῖ μᾶλλον ἢ καταγελᾶται, ὅταν δὲ ἐγγίζειν θέλῃ τῷ ἐπίχαρις εἶναι, τότε πλέον ἀφίσταται.

(Demosthenes, by contrast, has no sense of character. He lacks fluency, plainness and capacity for the epideictic manner; in fact he is practically without all the qualities I have been describing. When he forces himself to be funny or witty, he makes people laugh at him rather than with him. But when he wants to be close to being witty, it is then that he is most distant from it.) (Trans. Russell and Winterbottom, 1972)

In the end Demosthenes is superior because of his great emotional intensity (δεινότης). On the one hand, he is presented as monotonous, and incompetent in the use of a range of styles; on the other hand, Ps. Longinus rejects the principle that stylistic virtuosity is a good thing in itself at all. Technical virtuosity manifested in versatility is not the highest good, just as a certain number of technical flaws are pardonable. More generally, Ps. Longinus recognizes the highest qualities in literature as being something beyond art: the possession of great thoughts, the acquisition of which comes about in various ways, for example by studying great writers of the past or by contemplating nature, but which is particularly difficult in the modern era, where men are slaves to their vices (c. 44).[27] Hermogenes would have agreed

---

[27] The question of the relationship between the *Peri Ideon* and *Peri Hupsous* arises. It is not possible to determine the chronological relationship between them, because the date of *Peri Hupsous* remains uncertain. The best approach, perhaps, is to speculate on what Ps. Longinus and Hermogenes would have thought of each others' work. Ps. Longinus, I suggest, would have thought of Hermogenes as blind to the importance of great thoughts in literature, and hence insensitive to the greatness of Plato, fixated on the concept of technical ability, and false in his beliefs that the greatest rhetorical virtue is versatility and that Demosthenes instantiates this (Plato might be a better example). Hermogenes would obviously disagree with Ps. Longinus about versatility and Demosthenes. On the subject of τὸ ὕψος there are two things that he might say: either that it can be reduced to some of the *ideai* in his own system (σεμνότης, λαμπρότης, ἀκμή are the obvious candidates); or that the quality that Ps. Longinus is describing is not rhetoric at all but something more like intellectual greatness. Rhetoric, he would maintain, is purely a matter of technical rules, and to pretend anything else is

with the positive evaluation accorded Demosthenes, but for him it is precisely due to his supreme virtuosity.

self-deception or intellectual snobbery. Speaking as well as Demosthenes requires only a perfect mastery of the rules of rhetoric, so that a supposed decline in political or moral conditions is no impediment; but equally, because Demosthenes is a perfect master, no one will ever speak better.

III

Politikos and Panegurikos: The Reading List in Peri Ideon

1. HERMOGENES' SURVEY OF LITERATURE

In the survey of literature presented in the closing chapters of *Peri Ideon* (2. 10–12),[1] the major categories are ὁ πολιτικὸς λόγος and ὁ πανηγυρικὸς λόγος.[2] By ὁ πολιτικὸς λόγος Hermogenes means oratory, not just the deliberative branch, but the forensic and epideictic branches also. Ὁ πανηγυρικὸς λόγος, on the other hand, is a blanket term covering the rest of literature, which in effect means that it comprises both prose other than political oratory and poetry. The ideal form of ὁ πολιτικὸς λόγος is identical to Demosthenes' style, and is produced by a perfect blend of the eighteen *ideai* (221. 20 ff.; 305. 7 ff.; 380. 20 ff.). it has three main types, corresponding to the traditional three oratorical genres: συμβουλευτικός (deliberative), δικανικός (forensic), and πανηγυρικός (epideictic, the last to be distinguished from ὁ πανηγυρικὸς λόγος (384. 14 ff.; 388. 17–18).[3] In 2. 11 (περὶ τοῦ ἁπλῶς πολιτικοῦ) Hermogenes presents brief summaries of the style of the major Attic orators besides Demosthenes: Lysias, Isaeus, Hyperides, Isocrates, Dinarchus, Aeschines, Antiphon (both Antiphon of Rhamnous and Antiphon the Sophist), Critias, Lycurgus, and Andocides.

---

[1] The question of the relation between Hermogenes' survey of literature and the earlier surveys has (surprisingly) not been attempted before, either by scholars interested in Hermogenes (who, I suspect, have tended to look on the last chapters as peripheral to the rhetorical doctrine contained in the work), or by scholars interested in the history of reading lists, for example by L. Radermacher, *RE* 20 s.v. *Kanon*, 1873–8, O. Regenbogen, *RE* 40 s.v. *Pinax*, 1458–62 (this omission strikes me as the more difficult to explain).

[2] 2. 10 is somewhat misleadingly entitled περὶ τοῦ πολιτικοῦ in the manuscripts, since it deals with both categories. The contrast between these two categories is hardly met with in the earlier chapters of the work, though compare 216. 5 ff.

[3] Hermogenes illustrates the panegyric form of πολιτικὸς λόγος with the example of the Athenians and Spartans after the Persian War arguing about a procession, which should be identified with the one at Plataea: see Robertson (1986), 96.

The order seems to be one of degree of stylistic excellence, particularly as regards the quality δεινότης. Thus Lysias, Isaeus, and Hyperides are praised for their use of the quality δεινότης κατὰ μέθοδον, while Lycurgus and Andocides, who have only the epideictic and sophistical δεινότης κατὰ λέξιν, are on the whole criticized. Isocrates, Dinarchus, Aeschines, Antiphon and Critias come somewhere in between these two groups.

A statement at the end of the section indicates that Hermogenes sees Demosthenes and all the orators mentioned in 2. 11 except for Critias as belonging to a traditional group of ten (Antiphon of Rhamnous and Antiphon the Sophist apparently count as one for this purpose) (403. 13 ff.).

τῷ μὲν οὖν Δημοσθένει οἱ λοιποὶ τῶν δέκα, μεθ᾽ ὧν καὶ ὁ Κριτίας, ὑποτεταγμένοι οὑτωσί πως τὰ δεύτερα καὶ τρίτα τοῦ δικανικοῦ τε καὶ συμβουλευτικοῦ τῶν λόγων εἴδους ἀποφέρονται.

(The remainder of the ten, including Critias, are subordinate to Demosthenes and in this way carry off the second and third prizes for forensic and deliberative oratory.)

This is one of the first clear statements of the existence of a canon of ten orators. This testimony can be set alongside a passage from *Lives of the Sophists*, according to which the associates of Herodes Atticus flattered him with the observation that he belonged in the canon of the ten, and Herodes modestly replied that he was at any rate better than Andocides (suggesting that Andocides is tenth in the canon of ten, as he is in Hermogenes' list).[4] The notion of a canon of ten may well not go back much before the period of these authors.[5]

The ideal form of ὁ πανηγυρικὸς λόγος is the style of Plato, which is described at some length in 2. 10 (387. 5 ff.). In 2. 12 (περὶ τοῦ ἁπλῶς πανηγυρικοῦ) Hermogenes lists other authors in this class. The first group comprises Xenophon, Aeschines the Socratic, and Titus Aurelianus Nicostratus, the only near-contemporary writer

---

[4] *Vit. Soph.* 564–5 (72. 11 Kayser). See Ch. VII.

[5] Quintilian, *IO* 10. 1. 76, seems to imply that there were ten Attic orators, but ten is not the same as a canon of ten. In favour of knowledge of the canon of ten in Quintilian, see Cousin (1936), 559; against the same hypothesis, see Douglas (1956). Caecilius of Caleacte wrote a περὶ τοῦ χαρακτῆρος τῶν δέκα ῥητόρων according to Suidas (see Ofenloch (1888), 89 ff.), but we cannot infer very much from a mere title. There is certainly no sign of a group of ten in the works of Dionysius of Halicarnassus or in Cicero. For a good general discussion, see Anastassiou (1966), 103 ff.

whom Hermogenes includes in the survey.[6] The styles of these authors are said to be characterized by ἀφέλεια, and the two associated qualities γλυκύτης and δριμύτης,[7] and the predominance of this quality in these authors seems to be analogous to the predominance of δεινότης in ὁ πολιτικὸς λόγος. In this respect the style of these three authors seems to differ from that of Plato, which contained ἀφέλεια but was not dominated by it.[8] A second group of authors who fall within ὁ πανηγυρικὸς λόγος are the historians.[9] Detailed discussions are given of the styles of Herodotus, Thucydides, and Hecataeus; Theopompus, Ephorus, Hellanicus, and Philistus are mentioned, but not discussed at any length. Finally, ὁ πανηγυρικὸς λόγος also includes poetry;[10] in 2. 10–12 Hermogenes is interested principally in Homer, although in the main part of *Peri Ideon* he draws illustrations from other poets as well (see Chapter IV).

2. EARLIER READING LISTS

There exist earlier correlates to the panorama of Greek literature set out in *Peri Ideon* 2. 10–12. The most prominent, perhaps, is the reading list of Greek authors in the second book of Dionysius' *Peri Mimeseos* (*On Imitation*). This is particularly important from the view of view of this argument because we have reason to believe that Hermogenes knew the works of Dionysius and adapted them extensively in *Peri Ideon* (see Chapter I).

Dionysius planned three books on μίμησις, though he may never have completed the third. The survey of literature came in the second book of *Peri Mimeseos*, which survives in an epitome. The first book and the third (if it was written) seem to have been the more theoretical, dealing with the general question of μίμησις (Bk. 1) and the question of how one ought to imitate (Bk. 3), but the second was devoted to which authors were to be imitated and the larger part of it consists of a survey of authors from the

---

[6] For Nicostratus, see p. 23.

[7] For the close association between ἀφέλεια, γλυκύτης, and δριμύτης, see 339. 16 ff., 345. 3 ff.; for ἀφέλεια and γλυκύτης in Xenophon: 404. 20 ff.; in Aeschines the Socratic, 406. 22 ff.; in Nicostratus, 407. 10 ff. The same authors are presented as examples of ἀφέλεια in the core at 329. 8 ff.; Xenophon only at 328. 19 ff.

[8] For ἀφέλεια in Plato, see *Peri Ideon* 388. 12.

[9] 408. 9 ff. On historians in the list, see now Nicolai (1992), 324 ff.

[10] 389. 7 ff.; 391. 5 ff.; 412. 11 ff.

fourth century or earlier whose style he considers worth imit-ating.[11]

Dionysius deals with poetry first, beginning with Homer and the rest of epic, then lyric, and finally comedy, the only comedian mentioned being Menander (19. 5–22. 11; refs. to Usener's edn.). Then he motes on to prose. The first subdivision of prose he deals with is history (22. 12–26. 8), exemplified by Herodotus, Thucyd-ides, Philistus, Xenophon, and Theopompus. For the section on history we have a second source also, since Dionysius claims to reproduce the account of the historians from *Peri Mimeseos* B′ in his *Letter to Pompeius*. There are some differences between this and the epitome, and they are probably to be explained by the hypothesis that the *Letter to Pompeius* represents an earlier draft, though it has also been suggested that it might be an augmented version.[12] After history Dionysius moves to philosophy (26. 9–27. 7), mentioning Xenophon who therefore occurs twice in the list), Plato, and Aristotle; and here the last category is oratory (27. 12–29. 5), and he mentions the styles of Lysias, Isocrates, Lycurgus, Demosthenes, Aeschines, Hyperides.

Similar to Dionysius' list in many respects is the Greek side of the reading list that Quintilian provides for the young orator (*IO* 10. 1). Opinions vary on whether *Peri Mimeseos* was a direct influence on Quintilian, but the similarities are such that if there is no direct influence, we would have to postulate a common source.[13] Like Dionysius Quintilian divides literature up into

---

[11] *Epistula ad Pompeium* 766, 51. 1 ff.: πεποίηκα [καὶ] τοῦτο οἷς ⟨πρὸς⟩ Δημήτριον ὑπεμνημάτισμαι περὶ μιμήσεως. τούτων ὁ μὲν πρῶτος αὐτὴν περιείληφε τὴν περὶ τῆς μιμήσεως ζήτησιν, ὁ δὲ δεύτερος περὶ τοῦ τίνας ἄνδρας μιμεῖσθαι δεῖ ποιητάς τε καὶ φιλοσόφους, ἱστοριογράφους ⟨τε⟩ καὶ ῥήτορας, ὁ δὲ τρίτος περὶ τοῦ πῶς δεῖ μιμεῖσθαι μέχρι τοῦδε ἀτελής. ἐν δὴ τῷ δευτέρῳ περὶ Ἡροδότου τε καὶ Θουκυδίδου καὶ Ξενοφῶντος καὶ Φιλίστου καὶ Θεοπόμπου (τούτους γὰρ ἐγκρίνω τοὺς ἄνδρας ⟨ὡς⟩ εἰς μίμησιν ἐπιτηδειοτά-τους) τάδε γράφω. (I have done this in the manual I compiled on imitation in response to Demetrius. Of this work, the first book comprised the inquiry into imitation, the second was about which poets, philosophers, historians and orators should be imitated; the third is about how one should imitate, but it is still incomplete. In the second I wrote the following about Herodotus, Thucydides, Xenophon, and Philistus (these being the authors I judge are best suited to imitation).) See Usener (1889), 3 ff.

[12] For the theory that it is an earlier draft, see Usener; for the theory that it is an augmented version, Sacks (1983); more recently Heath (1989) has argued against Sacks and in favour of Usener.

[13] The case is most strongly put by Claussen (1873), 317 ff.; somewhat more sceptical and believing more in Ciceronian influence, Peterson (1891), xxii–xxxix; Cousin (1936), 563 ff. There is a good general study of the sources of Quintilian, *IO*

four main blocks, though the order is slightly different. He begins with poetry (10. 1. 51–72: a much fuller account than Dionysius'), then goes on to history (73–5), then oratory (76–80) and finally philosophy (81–4), whereas Dionysius had philosophy third and ended with oratory.[14]

Another point of contact between the two lists is that for the most part Quintilian includes only pre-Hellenistic authors. There are few exceptions: he includes some Hellenistic poets, commenting at this point that he is breaking with the practice of Aristarchus and Aristophanes of Byzantium who omitted Apollonius of Rhodes and all contemporary authors from their list.[15] (This statement is of great significance because it implies that in other respects he believed that his reading list followed the practice of the Alexandrian editors.)[16] Also, in his catalogue of Greek historians, he mentions Timagenes of Alexandria, who was active in the age of Augustus (10. 1. 75).[17] Quintilian's general rejection of post-Hellenistic Greek literature is in extreme contrast with the Roman part of his list where he includes contemporary authors and shows a certain disdain for earlier periods of Roman literature.

Exclusion of post-classical authors is one respect in which these reading lists show a degree of selectivity. But among classical authors selection has also taken place. Quintilian makes a revealing remark *à propos* of a group of three iambic writers mentioned at *IO* 10. 1. 60 when he says that this group represents a selection by Aristarchus.[18] A similar process must have taken place in other genres—one need only think of the tragedians.[19] That is not to say

10 by Tavernini (1953) who reaches the conclusion that although Quintilian certainly knew Dionysius, he was influenced by a wide variety of works on literary criticism. Bolaffi (1958) does not seem to mention Dionysius.

[14] I do not know how to explain the difference in the order of these two sections. Could it perhaps be that in the Latin half of the list Quintilian wants to end with the philosopher Seneca, or that he thought of philosophy as a more advanced stage in the curriculum?

[15] *IO* 10. 1. 54.

[16] Steinmetz (1964) argues strongly in favour of at least the poetry section of the list going back to the Hellenistic period. Since we know that Aristarchus thought that Menander was the second greatest poet after Homer, it may be significant that the lists of Dionysius and Quintilian begin and end with these two poets. So Steinmetz (1964), 462; also Körte (1936); Nicolai (1992), 287.

[17] The fragments of Timagenes are edited by Jacoby, *FGrHist* 88.

[18] 10. 1. 60: *tribus receptis Aristarchi iudicio scriptoribus iamborum.*

[19] Quintilian 10. 1. 66–8; Dionysius of Halicarnassus, *Peri Mimeseos.*

that the only authors included are ones that were approved of in every respect. Indeed, it is characteristic of the comments made about authors in these lists that they mix praise and criticism. It would be a mistake to think that the function of the lists was to provide canonical models; rather they provide examples which the modern student is supposed to engage and improve on, using his judgement (κρίσις, *iudicium*) to identify which elements are worth imitating and which are not.[20]

There is one point in which Quintilian, *IO* 10. 1 is a better parallel for Hermogenes' reading list than *Peri Mimeseos*. Quintilian and Hermogenes place their lists in a similar context: in both cases the reading lists follow a more abstract and general treatment of style, in Quintilian the whole of Books 8–9, in Hermogenes the main section of *Peri Ideon*. Quintilian's reading list is followed by a discussion of appropriateness (*IO* 11. 1), but Hermogenes also seems to have intended that the reading list, which comes at the end of *Peri Ideon*, should be immediately followed by *Peri Methodou Deinotetos*, which he seems to have intended should consist primarily of a discussion of appropriateness. It is unlikely that Hermogenes drew this principle of composition from Quintilian, but there is a distinct possibility, I think, that both might be drawing on a common principle of organization adopted in some Greek rhetorical treatise of the first century BCE or earlier.[21]

Another reading list that shows a similar pattern is the one that Dio of Prusa included in his *Peri Logou Askeseos* (*Or.* 18).[22] This list comprises authors whom Dio believes will be useful in the education of the man in political life (ὁ πολιτικός). It follows the same order as Quintilian: first poets (6 ff.); then historians (9–10); orators (11) (including a sub-group of four post-fourth-century Greek orators); and fourth οἱ Σωκρατικοί (13–19). This fourth category does not quite correspond to the philosophers of the earlier lists. The only example that Dio cites for this is Xenophon,

---

[20] This general exclusion of contemporary and recent authors is a point of contact between the ancient literary survey and the modern idea of the literary canons.

[21] This possibility has never been considered, as far as I know, although some people have been puzzled by the sequence of topics in Quintilian, *IO* 10. 1–11. 1, for example Schneider (1983).

[22] On Dio of Prusa's literary criticism, see Valgimigli (1912); Desideri (1978), 139–40; Jones (1978), 7–8.

and the exposition of his virtues takes up almost as much as the whole preceding part of the reading list.[23] This is a reflection of one of the principal developments in literary taste in the early empire: the growth of interest in Xenophon.[24]

To summarize, the pre-Hermogenean lists share the following points in common:

(1) Poetry and prose are distinguished, and prose is divided into the three main genres of history, rhetoric, and philosophy.

(2) Within this arrangement poetry indisputably comes first and the prose categories come later in variable order.[25]

3. THE ORIGIN OF THE CATEGORIES *ΠΟΛΙΤΙΚΟΣ* AND *ΠΑΝΗΓΥΡΙΚΟΣ*

Let us now turn to the question of the relation between the survey of literature in *Peri Ideon* 1. 10–12 and these earlier surveys of literature. If one looks first for similarities, the principal categories in the Dionysian survey can still be made out in Hermogenes' survey. Three of the categories—poetry, oratory, and history—have come through more or less intact.[26] Hermogenes

---

[23] 18. 14–17: Ξενοφῶντα δὲ ἔγωγε ἡγοῦμαι ἀνδρὶ πολιτικῷ καὶ μόνον τῶν παλαιῶν ἐξαρκεῖν δύνασθαι . . . πάντων ἄριστος ἐμοὶ δοκεῖ καὶ λυσιτελέστατος πρὸς ταῦτα πάντα Ξενοφῶντα (I think that Xenophon is the only ancient writer who can suffice for a political man . . . Xenophon seems to me to be the best of all and the most profitable for all these things). See Wegehaupt (1896). In other words Dio seems to convey a profound admiration of Homer, for example *Or.* 2 (*On Kingship* II) and in *Or.* 36 (*Olbian*).

[24] See Münscher (1920), 117 ff.; also Desideri (1978), 140–1; also below, Ch. IV.

[25] It seems likely that this was a widely established pattern. An indication of its longevity is provided by the *fragmentum Coislinianum*, a fragment of a reading list from the Middle Ages. See Usener (1889), 129 ff.; for a fuller treatment, Kroehnert (1897), 4 ff. There are now fifteen categories in all, the first six genres of poetry (epic, iambic tragedy, comedy, elegy, lyric), followed by oratory and history (examples drawn primarily from classical authors). Philosophy comes last, with both classical and post-classical examples, and in between six new categories: grammarians, orthographists, writers περὶ διχρόνων, writers on ethnography, doctors, and commentators on doctors (paragraph 9, specifying what metres various poets wrote in, seems to be out of place).

[26] *À propos* of Hermogenes' section on historians, Nicolai (1992) observes that he starts from the same group of six, i.e. two groups of three (Herodotus, Thucydides, Xenophon; Ephorus, Theopompus, Philistus), that we find in the earlier lists (minus Xenophon), with the anomalous additions of Hecataeus (to the latter triad?) and Hellanicus (to the former). Nicolai's argument that the group of six historians is a selection predating any of the extant sources seems to be entirely convincing.

does not have a category of philosophers (he never even uses the word φιλόσοφος in *Peri Ideon*), although there is a degree of overlap between that and the group of three writers mentioned at the start of the section on πανηγυρικὸς λόγος. As we have seen, in Dio's list too the category philosophical prose has been superseded by a category of prose broader than philosophy ('the Socratics'), which is dominated by Xenophon. This is probably a response to the taste for Xenophon in the early empire (see Chapter V).

One difference between Hermogenes' reading list and the Dionysian list is that whereas in the latter list the major division was between poetry and prose, Hermogenes has shifted the emphasis completely by dividing literature into the categories ὁ πολιτικὸς λόγος and ὁ πανηγυρικὸς λόγος. This antithesis can be interpreted in various ways.[27] Taking the broadest possible view, we might also think of the two categories as reflecting two major performance contexts for oratory in the ideal Greek world: the life of the city, occupied in politics and everyday business, where one might expect to hear political or forensic speeches, and the life of the festival, situated in the *paneguris*, where one would expect to see performances of epideictic oratory, and for that matter poetry and history. The difference is not absolute: politics might well be discussed at a *paneguris*; hence Isocrates, *Antidosis* 46, can refer to a certain type of speech (akin, presumably, to his own political diatribes) as (λόγους) Ἑλληνικοὺς καὶ πολιτικοὺς καί πανηγυρικούς (speeches that are Hellenic, political, and panegyric), and he seems to have in mind a contrast between these and forensic speeches.

Narrowing the focus rather, we can also think of the new categories representing a development from the Aristotelian tripartite division of oratory into forensic, deliberative and epideictic: ὁ πανηγυρικὸς λόγος is epideictic and ὁ πολιτικὸς λόγος seems to represent a synthesis of forensic and deliberative.[28] The use of the adjectives πολιτικός and πανηγυρικός to denote two contrasting rhetorical genres is perhaps not so old; the furthest it can be traced back is to a passage from Book 2 of Philodemus' *Rhetorica* where there seems to be a citation from the *Symposium* of Epicurus (1. 102. 20 ff. = Supp. 49, 18 ff.):[29]

---

[27] For the development of the term πολιτικός see Brandstätter (1894), 184 ff. There is no corresponding study of the development of the term πανηγυρικός.

[28] For the three categories, see Aristotle, *Rhetoric* 1. 3.

[29] Arrighetti (1960), 185 (= 21 (*Sumposion*), 4); Hubbell (1920), 243 ff.)) translates.

ἵνα δὲ παριστῇ διελεγχόμενον ὁ Ἐπίκουρος τὸν νεανίσκον τὸν ἐκ μελέτης
ῥητορικῆς ὡς ἂν δύναμιν ἐπαγγελλόμενον τοῦ σοφιστεύειν τὴν πανηγυρικὴν καὶ
τὴν πολειτικήν, ποιεῖ τὸν Ἰδομενέα μετὰ τὸ "παρρησία ἔστω" μέχρι τῶν
"ἔγγνωστο ὑμεῖν" ἐξαιτούμενον συγγνώμην, εἰ νέος ὢν θρασύνεται, καὶ συνάπ-
τοντά τιν᾽ αὐτὸν τοιαῦτα κατὰ λέξιν.

(In order to represent the young man as being refuted when he claimed
that his rhetorical study gave him power to deliver panegyrics and engage
in politics, Epicurus makes Idomeneus beg pardon for his youthful
presumption (from 'let there be free-speech' until 'it had been known
by you'), and represents someone addressing him thus.)

Here ἡ πολιτική and ἡ πανηγυρική are two contrasting arts that the
power of sophistical education claims to provide.[30]

A different range of meanings for both terms is found in the
works of Dionysius; ὁ πολιτικὸς λόγος is quite a general term for
oratory, as opposed to other genres, for example poetry, history,
and philosophy.[31] The adjective πανηγυρικός is used of an open
style appropriate to festivals, full of ostentatious and pleasant
effects, and contrasted with the ἀληθινός (convincing) style, which
is a mark of political oratory (it is never contrasted with the
adjective πολιτικός, and there is no sign that Dionysius thinks in
terms of an antithesis between these two adjectives). The term is
specially associated with Isocrates, but is also used of Demosthenes, particularly with respect to his use of the γλαφυρὰ
ἁρμονία.[32]

[30] We find this also at 251. 10ff.: καὶ [φήσει τις· εἰ χάρι]ν τοῦ δύη[ασθ]αί τινα
μ[α]θόντα [τ]ὰ ῥητορικὰ κα[ὶ δ]ημη[γ]ορεῖν δυν[ατῶς κα]ὶ δίκ[ας] ε[ὖ] λέγ[ειν ἀφαι]ρήσε[-
τάι] τις τὸ π[ολιτεύε]σθαι τῆς ῥητο[ρικῆς, ὡς τῆς] ῥητορικῆς [οὐκ ὂν ἰ]δι[ον, οὐκ ἂν φθάν[οι
καὶ τὸ] πανη[γυ]ρικὸν αὐτῆς εἶδος ἀφαιρούμενος, ὃ διά τε γραφῆς καὶ χ]ωρὶς γραφῆς οἱ
ῥητορικοὶ π]ερ[αίν]ου[σι]· πολλ[οὶ] γὰρ ἂν καὶ [το]ῦτο μιμήσαιντο, [τὸ παραδεδομ]ένο[ν
μὲ]ν παρὰ σοφιστῶν] οὐκ ἀνει[λη]φότες, εὐ]φυεῖ[ς δ᾽ ὄντες (Someone will say: if for the
sake of ability someone were to take away from someone who learnt rhetoric and to
speak in public well and to plead cases well the political part of rhetoric, on the
grounds that it does not belong in rhetoric, should he not first also take away the
panegyrical form of it, whether rhetoricians accomplish it with writing or without?
For many would imitate this, not by receiving transmitted doctrine from sophists,
but by being clever).

[31] Among its complements are: poetry: *De Compositione Verborum* 22 (98. 6, 11);
history: *Thuc.* 2 (327. 12); *De Compositione Verborum* 22 (98. 6); philosophy: *De
Compositione Verborum* 2 (8. 6); common language: *Lys.* 4 (12. 19); Socratic
dialogues: *Dem. Lex.* 23 (179. 12); ὁμιλίαι ἰδιωτικαί: *Thuc.* 50 (409. 10); ἐριστικά,
φυσικά: *Isoc.* 1 (55. 13); ἐγκώμια, ψόγοι, ἀπολογία, κατηγορία (i.e. the genres of
rhetoric other than the deliberative): *Dem. Lex.* 23 (179. 4). It is also synonymous
with ἐναγώνιος: *Isoc.* 12 (72. 5).

[32] Contrasted with ἀληθινός at *Dem. Lex.* 8 (143. 19), in the description of

Moving closer to Hermogenes, we find the terms πολιτικός and πανηγυρικός designating the stylistic qualities of different patterns of argumentation in *Peri Heureseos*: according to *Peri Heureseos* 3. 13, if you have some arguments that are suggestive of political oratory and some that are panegyrical, you should put the panegyrical ones last, to create an impression of ἀκμή, and according to *Peri Heureseos* 4. 1 arguments should be given a different stylistic expression depending on whether they are πολιτικά or πανηγυρικά, but a good student is expected to be able to handle both types of thought and both the respective appropriate forms of expression, and examples of all of them are to be found in Demosthenes' *De Corona*. What this opposition represents is perhaps the two grander χαρακτῆρες of Demetrius' *Peri Hermeneias*: on the one hand δεινότης, the tightly packed, forceful style; and on the other hand the more abstract μεγαλοπρέπεια associated with historical writing. And we could compare the tight rhetorical period with the looser historical period. Also, perhaps, the opposition between Demosthenes and Isocrates in Dionysius of Halicarnassus.

This strongly suggests that the stylistic application of the categories πολιτικός and πανηγυρικός was not something confined to *Peri Ideon*. The difference is in the force of their application, particularly that of the category πανηγυρικός. Unlike the author of *Peri Heureseos*, Hermogenes does not find anything πανηγυρικόν about Demosthenes, and he uses it as the name of a broad category covering Plato, the 'Socratics', history, and poetry. There is as far as I can see no sign of this extended use of the word before Hermogenes, and I suspect that it may well be a Hermogenean innovation and that it is indissociable from the adaptation of the reading list in *Peri Ideon* 2. 10–12.[33] The extension of the meaning was justified in so far as all the literature he wanted to designate as

Demosthenes' Protean versatility; with ἐναγώνιος at *Dem. Lex.* 4 (136. 8) (of Isocrates); also at *Dem. Lex.* 45 (229. 5) of one of two modes of *harmonia* used by Demosthenes, associated with χάρις; a synonym of θεατρικός at *De Compositione Verborum* 22 (108. 5); also *De Compositione Verborum* 23 (120. 7), with respect to Gorgianic figures; contrasted with δικανικός at *Peri Mimeseos* 31 (212. 1) (of Isocrates).

[33] It could perhaps be argued against this that where Hermogenes innovates with respect to the use of a technical term, he explains himself at great length, most of all, perhaps, in his use of δεινότης in 2. 9, and that there is no corresponding discussion in the case of πανηγυρικός. But the absence of such a discussion is not a sufficient reason for believing that Hermogenes has *not* innovated.

πανηγυρικός had in common a certain ostentatious quality of style which could be distinguished generically from the persuasion-oriented style of πολιτικὸς λόγος.[34]

It may well be that *Peri Heureseos* had a direct influence on Hermogenes in his stylistic use of these terms, especially since we have independent reasons to suppose that *Peri Heureseos* was used by Hermogenes in the composition of *Peri Ideon*.[35] Although *Peri Ideon* shifts the application of these two terms so that Demosthenes and πανηγυρικός no longer intersect to any degree, Hermogenes' analysis preserves the spirit of the distinction. What *Peri Heureseos* called πανηγυρικός comes through into *Peri Ideon* as λαμπρότης, which, as we have seen, is a major component of ἀκμή in *Peri Ideon*, and of course ἀκμή and πανηγυρικός were linked in *Peri Heureseos*.

4. DEMOSTHENES AND PLATO

The arrangement of a reading list, and the emphasis it puts on different authors, can have literary implications, as for example in the case of Dio's reading list with its bias toward Xenophon.[36] What literary implications does the reading list in *Peri Ideon* have? First, it implies that the greatest two prose authors are Demosthenes and Plato. This was a common view, held by the author of *Peri Hupsous*,[37] and by Aelius Aristides (for whom the rival claims of Plato and Demosthenes represent the perennial conflict between philosophy and rhetoric; see Chapter VII). It is also

---

[34] He also may have reasoned that two of the three subcategories of ὁ πανηγυρικὸς λόγος were the sort of thing that might have been delivered at a πανήγυρις (poetry, because Homer's poetry was often thought to have been originally performed at great festivals; and history, because there was a tradition that the first complete reading of Herodotus' *History* took place on the occasion of a festival at Olympia (Lucian, *Herodotus* or *Aetion*, 1), and this may have suggested to him that all history could have been performed under the same conditions.

[35] For the evidence, see App. A.

[36] Another example of a deviant list from the same period might be the one that Aelius Aristides included in his *Peri Tou Paraphthegmatos*, where in order to justify the practice of self-praise in literature, he goes through the whole corpus of classical Greek literature, following roughly the Dionysian categories. See Rutherford (1995).

[37] The importance of Demosthenes comes out most, perhaps, in the section on σχήματα (cc. 16 ff.). This is brought out particularly in Russell (1981a). The effect of the valorization of Demosthenes and Plato is to push Thucydides into the background.

reminiscent of the list of authors preferred by Phrynichus Arabius in his influential work, *Sophistike Proparaskeue*, which starts with Plato and Demosthenes (and the other orators), then proceeds to Thucydides, Xenophon, Aeschines the Socratic, Critias, Antisthenes, Aristophanes, and the tragedians.[38]

Second, the arrangement of Hermogenes' list implies a perspective that is unambiguously rhetorical. Both the major categories are essentially types of oratory, and the implication is that all literature takes its place within the framework of rhetoric. Furthermore, just as ὁ πολιτικὸς λόγος is superior to πανηγυρικὸς λόγος, so Demosthenes is superior to Plato, and is in fact the greatest Greek writer. From the same period, one can compare Galen's estimation of the relative value of Plato and Hippocrates, based not on stylistic grounds, but in terms of their intellectual contribution to the science of medicine; Plato's contribution is considered significant, but flawed in various ways, and the true master is Hippocrates.[39]

Let us look a little more closely at Hermogenes' views about Demosthenes and Plato. His estimation of Demosthenes is no more than a slight intensification of the high regard in which he had been held at least since the first century BCE.[40] Cicero and Dionysius present Demosthenes as a supremely versatile stylist.[41] Hermogenes amplifies this claim in two ways. First, by way of analysing Demosthenic versatility, he shows how each of the seventeen *ideai* are exemplified in his speeches. Second, he argues that Demosthenes' use of all qualities of style is perfect, identifying this ability with the quality δεινότης.[42]

[38] Photius, *Bibliotheca* 158 (101a). The presence of Critias in the list is another parallel; the principal differences are the inclusion of Antisthenes and also Aristophanes. The fact that Phrynichus' work is exclusively about diction perhaps makes some difference.

[39] See De Lacy (1972).

[40] It is not there in Demetrius (probably 1st cent. BCE): see Morpurgo-Tagliabue (1979); also Anastassiou (1966), 54 ff. It is a singular omission that Anastassiou's generally excellent discussion stops short of the 2nd cent. CE (though compare p. 3 n. 3). On δεινότης, see also Rutherford (1994*b*).

[41] Cicero *Or.* 23, 26; Anastassiou (1966), 44 ff.; Dionysius of Halicarnassus, *Dem. Lex.* 8 (cited above, p. 18). I would suggest that it can be inferred from Ps. Longinus' concession that Demosthenes is monotonous that Caecilius of Caleacte criticized Demosthenes for being monotonous.

[42] Dionysius has already said that Demosthenes was δεινός, but he meant something else by the term: for him, δεινότης was an important stylistic virtue, realized either in general skill in rhetoric, particularly with respect to invention, or in forcefulness of style, and it was in the latter that Demosthenes excelled particularly. Hermogenes' concept of δεινότης is a development from the first of

There were those who preferred Plato's style (like the author of *Peri Hupsous*), but Hermogenes puts him second among prose authors. Is he a close second or does Demosthenes win easily? I suspect the latter. For one thing, the category of πανηγυρικὸς λόγος is by definition inferior (the associations with the πανήγυρις, after all, might suggest that this is not a serious form of discourse). Furthermore, in the core Hermogenes pays Plato remarkably little attention. He is presented as a paradigm for the use of themes relating to the gods in the section on σεμνότης, and in the section on γλυκύτης as a paradigm for the use of poetry within prose (παραπλοκή) and for mythical sentiments, for example for the myth of the origin of Aphrodite in the *Sumposion* and the myth of the cicadas in the *Phaidros* (330. 2 ff.). He is mentioned too in the section on ἐπιείκεια, basically for Socratic irony (348. 23), and also in the section on κάλλος for *paronomasia* (302. 4). So he is cited for the use of four of the *ideai*, but only four.[43]

In the post-core in *Peri Ideon* 2. 10 (387. 5 ff.) Hermogenes tries to produce an overall picture of Plato's style, i.e. the most perfect πανηγυρικός language. It consists of the following elements: (*a*) the *ideai* that make up μέγεθος, except for σφοδρότης and τραχύτης; (*b*) ἀφέλεια, which should be present throughout, except when σεμνότης is needed instead; (*c*) γλυκύτης; (*d*) δεινότης κατὰ μέθοδον, but not the more conspicuous sorts of δεινότης, unless one is representing a character making a speech, like Socrates in the *Phaidros*; (*e*) a comparative absence of γοργότης, since it is all ἀφήγησις (narrative);

the two Dionysian senses and is much more general: a perfect skill in the use of all elements of language, which is not much different from possession of the art of rhetoric itself. And, since Hermogenes continues to believe that Demosthenes is a master of δεινότης, it seems to follow that Demosthenes is the only model that the student of rhetorical stylistics needs for complete understanding of the subject.

[43] The spread of dialogues cited in the core is much what we would expect. The most frequently cited is the *Phaidros*, for examples of myths, aesthetically attractive sentiments, personifications, παραπλοκή, and the use of epithets in the section on γλυκύτης (330. 7; 331. 22; 333. 18; 337. 13; 338. 21), both quasi-poetic features; also in the section on σεμνότης for the central myth about the soul, for its allegorical presentation (246. 18), for the theme (245. 6; cf. 251. 16), and for sound patterns (247. 17; 248. 1); a rare example of δεινότης (387. 18). This pattern of citations supports what would have been established from other sources—that the *Phaidros* was an exceptionally popular dialogue during this period (see Trapp (1990)). There are citations from the *Sumposion* in the sections on κάλλος (302. 4), on γλυκύτης (336. 16; 337. 13), and on ἐπιείκεια (348. 23); there are also citations from the *Timaios* in the section on σεμνότης (243. 6ff.; 247. 5), the *Charmides* in the section on ἐπιείκεια (348. 23), from the *Republic* in the section on γλυκύτης (336. 18; 337. 1).

(*f*) in dialogue, you can use τραχύτης and σφοδρότης and conspicuous δεινότης (cf. (*d*)). But the different *ideai* will not be mixed together well (388. 10).

Some of this would be expected on the basis of the core, but some of it is a surprise. In particular, nothing in the core would have led us to suspect that Plato shows ἀφέλεια. This is one of numerous changes of emphasis between core and post-core.[44] That Plato was not regularly associated with ἀφέλεια is suggested by the low frequency of references to him in *Peri Aphelous Logou* (mentioned only once: c. 64). Light on the element of ἀφέλεια is shed by the σύγκρισις between Plato and Xenophon which comes in the discussion of Xenophon's style in *Peri Ideon* 2. 12. It emerges from this that there are two major differences between Plato and Xenophon:

(i) in his *Sumposion* Xenophon goes for pure ἀφέλεια, mentioning the mundane and vulgar details of the *sumposion*, e.g. dancing girls and drinking (he does similar things even in his historical works), while Plato, in his work of the same name, rejects these, and by doing so raises the style in the direction of σμνότης. This repeats point (*b*) in the discussion of Plato's style. What this means is that Plato is better than Xenophon because Plato combines ἀφέλεια with σεμνότης, a form of mixing.[45]

(ii) Plato's characters are not as ἀφελής as those of Xenophon, with the exception of adolescents, such as Theaitetos in the *Theaitetos*.

I would suggest that Hermogenes rethought his views about Plato's style when he came to write 2. 10–12, because his decision to include both Xenophon and Plato in πανηγυρικὸς λόγος required him to compare the two, something he did not consider doing in the core. The way he justified having Plato come out superior to Xenophon was by presenting Plato as possessing the same virtues as Xenophon (e.g. ἀφέλεια), but in addition possessing others (e.g. σεμνότης).

Hermogenes never compares Plato with Demosthenes, but the grounds for his view that Demosthenes is better are clear. For one

---

[44] See above, p. 7; below, p. 75.

[45] In *Peri Aphelous Logou*, by contrast, Xenophon is shown to use σεμνότης (cc. 53 ff.).

thing, there are many *ideai* which Plato does not use well (all those except σεμνότης, κάλλος, γλυκύτης, and ἐπιείκεια, it seems). For another, he does not mix them as much as he could. Thus, in the section on σεμνότης, it seems that, although Plato writes about divine themes well, he does not vary the style by adding elements of γοργότης, as Demosthenes does in *Against Aristogeiton* A' (in fact, there is virtually no γοργότης in Plato!). Again, according to *Peri Ideon* 2. 10, although Plato uses τραχύτης and σφοδρότης in dialogue, he uses these qualities individually, and does not blend them in well with others. His ability to combine σεμνότης with ἀφέλεια seems to be an exception, but this only shows up as a skill when you compare him with Xenophon. If you compare him with Demosthenes, what is more obvious is that Plato is capable of only σεμνότης and not the other *ideai* that make up μέγεθος, particularly the aggressive ones, like σφοδρότης, whereas Demosthenes manages all sides of μέγεθος, and in fact it is here that his δεινότης is most conspicuous (see 2. 9).

Use of δεινότης is in fact another area where Plato is inferior to Demosthenes. He has δεινότης κατὰ μέθοδον, but the showier variety only manifests itself when he is portraying a skilful speaker (like Socrates in the *Phaidros*) or a sophist (like Polus in the *Gorgias*). This deficiency is not wholly distinct from the previous one I mentioned, since for Hermogenes δεινότης means using *ideai* perfectly, and being able to mix them. But this difference is particularly important, because in general δεινότης is one of the key features that distinguishes πολιτικὸς λόγος as a whole from πανηγυρικὸς λόγος; the fact that Plato has any δεινότης at all is thus in itself rather surprising.

Hermogenes' views about the relative importance of Demosthenes and Plato are probably based exclusively on stylistic grounds. This is worth saying because it might be thought that Plato is being put down because he is a philosopher, just as Aelius Aristides attacked Plato's views on rhetoric in two great works, *On Rhetoric* and *In Defence of the Four* (see Chapter VII). However, there is no sign of hostility to philosophy *per se* in *Peri Ideon*.[46]

---

[46] In the section on κάλλος Plato is cited for what he says about symmetric beauty in the *Phaidros* 264c (297. 16); and also in the section on ἐπιείκεια for what he says about that quality *à propos* of the proems that introduce the laws in the *Laws* 6. 757e (345. 13). The precept about speaking through ἔμφασις in the *Timaios*, which is quoted in the section on σεμνότης, is used as a precept for the teaching of rhetoric in the proem to *Peri Ideon*.

5. THE FUNCTION OF THE LIST

What would the function of the list have been? One obvious possibility is to serve as a guide to students, to help them to pin-point which *ideai* they could find in different authors. However, there are two problems with that view.

First, Hermogenes believes that Demosthenes uses every *idea* as it ought to be used, which means that he is the κανών for all styles and all techniques. We find this view stated at 217. 12 ff.:

τὰ γάρ τοι τοῦ Δημοσθενικοῦ λόγου καθαπερεὶ στοιχεῖα καὶ ἀρχὰς εἰ δυνηθείημεν ἀκριβῶς αὐτὰ ἕκαστα ἐφ᾽ ἑαυτῶν πόσα τέ ἐστι δεῖξαι καὶ ὁποῖα καὶ ὅπως γίνεται τίς τε ἡ πρὸς ἄλληλα μῖξις αὐτῶν καὶ τί δύνανται τόνδε ἢ τόνδε μιγνύμενα τὸν τρόπον, τάχα ἂν περὶ ἁπάντων τῶν λόγων εἰρηκότες εἴημεν.

(If we could demonstrate accurately and specifically, in reference to the individual elements and basic principles of composition that make up the style of Demosthenes, how many there are and what effect they produce, combined in this way or that, we should have discussed all the various styles in general.)

In theory, then, Demosthenes is the only author that a student would need to know.

You might even take this a stage further, and ask why a student would need to read the classics at all, even Demosthenes, if the whole point of *Peri Ideon* is that it supplies canonical models for different styles. All students need to do is look up the appropriate section of the work—*Peri Ideon* itself renders obsolete the need for them to hunt through classical texts in order to build up a perfect stylistic facility. Though Hermogenes claims that the perfect model is Demosthenes, in a sense it is the theory of *ideai* itself, given textual form in *Peri Ideon*, which henceforth constitutes the κανών for prose style.

In view of these considerations, one might be driven to the opposite conclusion that the reading list in *Peri Ideon* is not after all intended as a serious and practical guide to students, but is just there as an exercise, to show how the main authors look when *idea*-theory is applied to them.

However, that would be an exaggeration. It might be more accurate to speak of a tension between the pluralism and inclus-iveness promised by the list and the totalitarian authority given to the Demosthenic κανών. In practice, I think, Hermogenes would have conceded that not everything can be perfectly illustrated from Demosthenes. For example, Plato is a better κανών for how to deal with the sacred; while for plain and simple characterization one should model oneself on Xenophon or on Menander; and for various effects associated with γλυκύτης, poetry is probably better. Nevertheless, in general Hermogenes probably had less use for a broad reading list than rhetoricians before him.

IV

The Position of Poetry

Another implication of the reading list concerns the position Hermogenes assigns to poetry. In the earlier lists poetry always comes first, and Homer is said to be the source of all literature.[1] There is partly no doubt a reflex of a general idea that poetry is a more important art than prose.[2] There is also the historical view that prose develops from poetry.[3] But it is also clear that rhetoricians believed that knowledge of poetry was of great importance in building up a stylistic facility.[4] In transferring poetry from first position in the list to last, Hermogenes is perhaps intending to rebut this view, suggesting that poetry is only of limited value in rhetorical training. The last place is not necessarily a dishonourable one (one should perhaps bear in mind the structure of the hypothetical Hellenistic poetry list referred to earlier in which the last place seems to have been reserved for the poet whom one Hellenistic critic at least regarded as the second greatest writer of Greek literature), but it probably is meant to be here, especially since poetry is not even a major category on its own and is discussed relatively briefly in comparison with the prose genres.

From this starting point, I aim in this section to look more broadly at the position of poetry in *Peri Ideon*, beginning with a general survey of the material, moving on to a study of what it has to tell us about the relative positions of poetry and religion, and finally turning to the question of the relative importance of Demosthenes and Homer.

---

[1] So Quintilian, *IO* 10. 1. 46: *hic enim quem ad modum ex Oceano dicit ipse omnium amnium fontiumque cursus initium capere, omnibus eloquentiae partibus exemplum et ortum dedit . . .*

[2] The fact that the reading list is structured in this way may perhaps be a contribution of the grammarians.

[3] Plutarch, *De Pythiae Orac.* 24. 406c–f; Strabo 1. 2. 6; Varro in Isidor. *Etym.* 1. 38. 2. Norden (1898), 1, 31 ff.; Hirzel (1895), ii. 209–10.

[4] See North (1952).

I. POETRY IN *PERI IDEON*

In the core of *Peri Ideon* Hermogenes mentions only a limited range of poets. Homer is mentioned for his Ionic dialect in the section on γλυκύτης (336. 11), for his monosyllabic ἀναπαύσεις, which are 'non-stationary', and generate κάλλος (311. 18); for συνθήκη appropriate to σεμνότης (while *metatheses* of the same verses illustrate the opposite qualities) (252–3); for his ἐπαναστροφή in the section on κάλλος (304. 10) and for his λέξις in the section on καθαρότης (229. 10). The portrayal of Odysseus in Homer is important in the section on δεινότης (2. 9), and many citations from Homer appear in the analysis of poetic style in 2. 10. The only other hexameter poet mentioned is Hesiod, cited in the section on γλυκύτης for his use of dialect (336. 11), and also because a citation of two lines of Hesiod (*Op.* 121–2) by Plato illustrates the technique of παραπλοκή (337. 6; Plato, *Rep.* 5. 468e).

To turn to lyric poets, Archilochus is mentioned because he is γοργός with respect to συνθήκη at 319. 23; Stesichorus is singled out for his use of epithets: 338. 25; Sappho is mentioned on the section on γλυκύτης because she uses λέξις which appeals to the senses (331. 19) and because her personification of the lyre (334. 9) is an example of the technique of personifying lifeless objects. Anacreon is mentioned in the section on ἀφέλεια because of his ἦθος (322. 16, 323. 22); Simonides is introduced as an example of δεινότης with respect to the use of poetic techniques (370. 2);[5] and Pindar is mentioned *à propos* of the λέξις appropriate to σεμνότης (249. 6).

Of the dramatists, Sophocles and Euripides are mentioned in the section on δριμύτης, Sophocles for his use of the adjective φίλανδρος (*TrGF* 4. 1111); Euripides for his use of the noun φιλανδρία at *Andromache* 230 (341. 12) and for the sequence of metaphors at fr. 636N (*Poluidos*) (344. 6). Menander's characterization is mentioned in the section on ἀφέλεια (323. 23 ff.); also he is said to be γοργός with respect to συνθήκη (319. 23). The author of *Peri Aphelous Logou* (64) believes that comedy is a source for the diction of γλυκύτης, but there is no sign of that sentiment in *Peri Ideon*.

---

[5] Hermogenes cites the description of Simonides at Theocritus 16. 44 with the reading δεινὸς ἀοιδός, where the MSS of Theocritus otherwise have θεῖος ἀοιδός; Hermogenes' reading could be the right one: see Barchiesi (1996), 17 n. 28.

Hermogenes refers to two Hellenistic poets. Theocritus is mentioned because of his simple characters in the section on ἀφέλεια (1. 1 at 323. 20; 3. 1 at 322. 19) and because his Doric forms are appropriate for σεμνότης (15. 88: 247. 20). Euphorion is mentioned in the section on δριμύτης (341. 18) because of his use of the adjective ἀτρέα. Finally, three lines in Sotadean metre, perhaps to be attributed to Sotades, are cited in the section on σεμνότης (253. 2 ff.).[6]

There is little tragedy, no Aristophanes. No elegy or epigram (though there is Archilochean *iambos*). No hexameter poetry after Hesiod. No reference to hymns. Some of the absences are perhaps to be explained by the hypothesis that Hermogenes cites poets who are good examples—κανόνες, in fact—in areas where the prose models are not as good. Hence the surprising frequency of citations from Theocritus and Sappho, who illustrate ἀφέλεια and γλυκύτης respectively, *ideai* that are not well illustrated from prose authors. On the other hand, the paucity of citations from Euripides, an author still widely read in the age of Hermogenes, is perhaps to be explained by the fact that he was the κανών for no style in particular, and illustrated no qualities that could not be illustrated as well, or better, from other authors.

On the other hand, it is perhaps also true that much poetry, if not all of it, shows less variety in the use of the *ideai* than prose, and judged by the standard of *Peri Ideon*, this means that poetry is not as good as prose. Homer, it goes without saying, uses them well, but many poets confine themselves to only a few *ideai*. For example, Sappho, Anacreon, Theocritus, Euphorion, and even Menander would perhaps none of them wander very far from a few basic qualities.

In *Peri Ideon* 2. 10 there is a sketch of the types of ἔννοιαι believed to be appropriate to poetry, and the following categories are mentioned: (*a*) stories about Kronos and the Titans, the Gigantes, Zeus, and in general the loves of the gods, their wars, friendships, their births, upbringings, and so on. (A contemporary audience might perhaps have thought of the *Gigantias* of Dionysius, probably of the early second century CE);[7] (*b*) (391. 23 ff.)

---

[6] First cited in Dionysius, *De Compositione Verborum* c. 4; Sotades 4(b) in Powell (1925), 239.

[7] The papyrus fragments of this poem and also of the *Bassaricon* of Dionysius have been edited by E. Livrea (Rome, 1973).

tales of wonder told about men or animals—Kadmos becoming a snake,[8] Alcyon, swallows and nightingales, sex-changes, like those of Teiresias and Kaineus, winged men, mythical beasts, like Pegasus and the Gorgons, Centaurs, Sirens, Tritons, Lastraegonians, Cyclopes, and Perseus; (*c*) fantastic and superhuman deeds, like Achilles leaping a vast distance, or Ajax or Hector lifting a vast stone; (*d*) the idea of objects acting as servants to the gods, like the gates of heaven opening spontaneously, or the earth producing flowers. Cf. also 335. 1 (section on γλυκύτης); (*e*) simple descriptions of nature, even if they have less of the miraculous (392. 16); (*f*) poetical details, particularly with respect to descriptions of death in the *Iliad* (392. 24 ff.).

This is not meant as a complete survey, merely a list of a few features which are characteristic of poetry (though not confined to poetry: Hyperides, *Deliakos* seems to have had a theme corresponding to category (*a*) here, not to mention the narrative about the origin of the Areopagos in Demosthenes, *Against Aristogeiton*). However, the list inevitably creates the impression that the basic stuff of poetry is various species of fantasy: representing gods as human beings, giving men semi-divine abilities, and personifying animals and objects.

There is one μέθοδος—pretending that what you say comes from the Muse (393. 7 ff.). This is allowed also in *panegurikos logos* (perhaps he is thinking of the central speech of the *Phaidros*).[9] So much for the claims of poets to be inspired. In fact, inspiration is not to any degree something which Hermogenes talks in terms of, either on the part of the poet or on the part of the audience (contrast the attitude of the *Peri Hupsous*). So this is in fact a very important absence, in so far as it undercuts the claims of poetry to be a sacred art.

The other area of poetry that is important is, of course, metre. Many of the citations in the core come in the context of ἀνάπαυσις and συνθήκη. In 2. 10 (394. 10), talking about hexameter poetry, he says that poets control the stylistic effect of their lines (*a*) by selecting whichever form of the hexameter they wish to use (and there are thirty-two of these, he adds); and (*b*) by controlling *caesura* and word-break within the line (394. 17 ff.). But these

---

[8] Cf. *Peri Heureseos* 203. 21 ff. (Cadmus changing into a snake, citing Euripides, fr. 930); Horace, *AP* 187: *aut in avem Procne vertatur, Cadmum in anguem.*

[9] 237a; see 338. 21.

things aside, the same aesthetic effects apply in poetry as apply in prose. The difference is simply that the prose writer has a freer rein to produce the effects he desires, whereas the poet has to superimpose them on the verse-pattern that he has chosen.

Only part of the interest of poetry for Hermogenes is its value in its own right, its usefulness in providing a κανών in certain areas. He is also interested in the use of citations of poetry within prose texts. This technique is called παραπλοκή, and it is set out in the section on γλυκύτης. A citation from poetry included in a prose text adds to the stylistic effect of the text as a whole, by providing γλυκύτης. If a citation is to work in this way, it must be integrated into the text, and not be marked off too much (if it is too marked off, if it is cited like a piece of evidence, like decrees are cited in speeches, the effect fails). To produce such an effect, a writer does not have to cite verses from actual poems; he can make them up, as Plato makes up verses in the *Sumposion* and in the *Phaidros*, so in that case we are dealing with a sort of *prosimetrum*, in which the poet chooses to write in both verse and prose.[10] The fact that one of the main functions of poetry that attracts Hermogenes is its stylistic utility when cited in prose texts κατὰ παραπλοκήν seems emblematic of the subordinate position occupied by poetry in his theory with respect to prose.

2. POETRY AND RELIGION

For Hermogenes poetry is not inherently a religious *medium*, a point that can be elicited from the explanation of appeals to the Muses as merely a μέθοδος in 2. 10 (393. 7 ff.). Furthermore, it is not even the best medium to describe sacred things. That emerges from the section on σεμνότης, where Hermogenes discusses ἔννοιαι that concern the gods, and here one might have thought for sure one would find references to religious poetry, but no: the κανών is Plato (for once). He draws a single example from the *Dios Apate* (*Il.* 14. 346), but rejects it on the grounds that it is ἀνθρωποπαθής— anthropomorphic, we would say.[11] And when orators use such

---

[10] Plato, *Sumposion* 197c; *Phaidros* 241d.

[11] The link between poetry and the human comes out also in the section on ἀφέλεια, where Theocritus gets cited as a κανών for the quality of simplicity with respect to ἔννοια (322. 19; 323. 20). Similar also is treating animals and objects as if they have reason, as in the appeal to her lyre in Sappho, 334. 9 (section on

religious themes, they make the same mistake of mythologizing their themes: even Hyperides' *Deliakos* is expressed in a mythical and poetical manner (μυθικῶς καὶ ποιητικῶς: 243. 15).

Plato describes the divine much more effectively. This comes out particularly in certain passages of *Timaios* (243. 13–244. 6), also in what Hermogenes regards as the *allegoria* of the central speech of the *Phaidros* (246. 18), and in the use of suggestive ἔμφασις, illustrated again from the *Timaios*.[12]

This implies a philosophical attitude to the representation of the divine in literature on the part of Hermogenes, which is both like and unlike Plato's in *Republic* 2. Like Plato, he attributes no great value to the anthropomorphic representation of gods in epic (I maintain that such a devaluing is the implication of excluding such representations from the realm of σεμνότης (i.e. μέγεθος) and transferring them to γλυκύτης (i.e. ἦθος)). But unlike Plato, he does not suggest that this is impious or morally wrong. He merely implies that Homer does not describe the divine, and is in fact simply an entertainer—the contrast with the serious concerns of the man involved in political life is perhaps in the background here.

One wonders whether perhaps Hermogenes' attitude is a little unfair on Greek religious poetry. What would he have made of Aratus' *Phainomena*, a very popular poem in antiquity, which, however, is never mentioned in *Peri Ideon*? Or of the poetry of Empedocles and Parmenides? And what about the hymn?

There is an interesting parallel from his own times (or from not long before, at any rate) in Aelius Aristides' *Humnos* in honour of Sarapis, which begins with a literary manifesto justifying the practice of writing hymns in prose.[13] This passage seems to have a possible relevance to *idea*-theory, because we saw earlier that the arrangement of Hermogenes' reading list implies that prose is a more important genre than poetry. If *Peri Tou Paraphthegmatos* could influence *idea*-theory, then surely the *Humnos* in honour of Sarapis could also.

This is how the manifesto breaks down in detail. Aristides γλυκύτης), which is analogous to the appeal to the Muses mentioned in the post-core.

---

[12] Hermogenes himself seems to imitate this passage in describing his own doctrine: 216. 16; 217. 9. This suggests that he sees rhetoric as a quasi-religious doctrine; cf. the implication of Aristides' *Kata ton exorkhoumenon*.

[13] *Or.* 45 in Keil's edn.

begins by criticizing poetic style (1–4); goes on to argue that in view of the fact that prose is used for all other purposes (including giving oracles), it is strange that only poetry is used for writing hymns; claims that prose is more natural and that it developed before poetry (contrary to the traditional view that poetry is prior)[14] (8–9); and he rebuts the claim that metre ($\mu\acute{\epsilon}\tau\rho\text{ov}$) makes poetry the superior form, arguing that the principle of appropriateness that prose writers observe is a measure ($\mu\acute{\epsilon}\tau\rho\text{ov}$) as well (10–13).

Aristides' assertion of the importance of prose *vis-à-vis* poetry has sometimes been derived from Isocrates' defence of poetry as a medium for encomium in the *Evagoras*, but it goes considerably beyond that, and there is no exact analogy for it in earlier literature.[15] The chances are that it is something peculiar to the changed literary taste of the Second Sophistic, where prose seems for the most part to have been more highly regarded than poetry.[16]

Hermogenes may well have known the *Hymn to Sarapis* and he must have been familiar with whatever controversy Aristides' practice of writing hymns in prose had produced. The connection between the description of ideal oratory in *Peri Tou Paraphthegmatos* and *idea*-theory would provide a parallel for Aristides' theory of prose hymns, and his generally high view of prose, influencing Hermogenes. Hermogenes would certainly have agreed with the general point that prose shows a $\mu\acute{\epsilon}\tau\rho\text{ov}$ of its own which is just as good as that of poetry, whether that is understood as a principle of appropriateness or as prose-rhythm.

If there is a difference between their views about the relation between poetry and prose, it might be that Hermogenes' estimation of poetry is lower than Aristides'. There is something dismissive about the way that Hermogenes sums up the themes appropriate to poetry. He is not concerned to justify prose as being as good a medium as poetry; rather, he assumes that prose is superior, and throws the burden of proof on to someone who

---

[14] See in general Höfler (1935), 30; Boulanger (1923), 303 ff.; Sohlberg (1972), 182–3; Russell and Winterbottom (1972), 558 ff.; see now Russell (1990*b*).

[15] Race (1987), 136–7; Plato, *Laws* 669d; 8, 829; Höfler (1935).

[16] For this view see, for example, Bowersock (1969), 116–17: 'the age of the Second Sophistic shows no literary figure of importance, political or otherwise, who was a poet.' One thinks, perhaps, of Aper's general attack on poetry in Tacitus, *Dialogus* 9. A good survey of the somewhat scanty remnants has been provided by Bowie (1990).

wants to show that poetry is as good; that, say, with respect to religious poetry, any poet is capable of writing as well as Plato.

3. HOMER AND DEMOSTHENES

It is not just poetry that has been dethroned from its first position but also Homer, who had come first in the earlier reading lists, and who is praised in Quintilian's reading list as both the greatest of Greek authors and a paradigm for later rhetorical techniques.[17] In view of the overwhelming importance of Demosthenes in the system, I would like to be able to infer that for Hermogenes Demosthenes has displaced Homer as the supreme Greek author. We cannot go quite as far as that because there are other indications in *Peri Ideon* that Homer is ultimately the greater: in a digression on the mixing of *ideai* in the section on περιβολή, Hermogenes says that no one is better than Demosthenes at mixing *ideai*, with the qualification that Demosthenes is second to Homer;[18] and he goes further in 2. 10 where he says that Homer is not just the greatest poet but the greatest of all prose writers and orators.[19] There would seem to be a parallel for this in a passage of Aristides' *Peri Tou Paraphthegmatos*, where he sketches the ideal of the perfect orator, which seems to mean himself, but allows that Homer may be an exception.[20]

However, it is perhaps legitimate to draw a distinction between the absolute value of an author and his value as a model in rhetorical education, and almost every page of *Peri Ideon* bears witness that for Hermogenes, Demosthenes is the supreme model. Furthermore, if we look closely at the passages in *Peri Ideon* 2. 10, the possibility suggests itself that Hermogenes is not talking about Homer's use of the *ideai* of language in general, but at something more specific: his ability with respect to the imitation of the language of other people, be it other poets (390. 3) or men of war. There is probably a reference to *Peri Ideon* 2. 9, where—as a

---

[17] Quintilian, *IO* 10. 1. 47 (cited above. n. 1); also *Peri Mimeseos* 204. 8–9: τῆς μὲν οὖν Ὁμηρικῆς ποιήσεως οὐ μίαν τινὰ τοῦ σώματος μοῖραν, ἀλλ' ἐκτύπωσαι τὸ σύμπαν (Imitate not just one part of the body of the works of Homer, but all of it); see what Hermogenes claims for Demosthenes in the proem at 217. 12 ff.

[18] 279. 25–6: δυσχερὴς δὲ ἡ μῖξις, καὶ σχέδον οὐδεὶς οὕτω καλῶς οὐδὲ τῶν ἀρχαίων αὐτῇ κέχρηται ὡς ὁ ῥήτωρ, μετά γε Ὅμηρον (Mixing is difficult, and virtually nobody, even among the ancients, employs it as well as the orator, after Homer, at least).

[19] 389. 26 ff.; 390. 16 ff.

[20] See p. 92 and n. 6.

preamble to his demonstration that true δεινότης involves not just rhetorical force but a lower style too when that is appropriate— Hermogenes shows that Homer presents Odysseus sometimes as using a forceful style, for example during his embassy to Antenor in *Iliad* 3. 221–2 and his words are compared to winter snow-flakes, and sometimes as using a more restrained style, as when he addresses the Phaeacians in *Odyssey* 8. 172 and 9. 5. The justification of this move in the argument is clearly that poetry is traditionally defined as μίμησις. But Hermogenes seems to mean by this not the broader concept of μίμησις as used by Aristotle, which covers narrative as well as impersonation of character, but only the latter, as used in Plato, *Republic* 3. 392e. And with respect to that he can grant the first prize to Homer, without risk of compromising his more broadly based high estimation of Demosthenes, because impersonation of character is not a particularly important technique in political oratory.

There is little sign that Homer shows any unusual ability in the area of mixing *ideai*, which of course is where Demosthenes excels. I find an isolated instance of Homeric excellence in this area in the section on γλυκύτης (332. 9), which concerns Homer's description of Zeus grabbing Hera (*Il.* 14. 346); ἦ ῥα καὶ ἔμαρπτε ἀγκὰς Κρόνου παῖς ἦν παράκοιτιν (So he spoke, and the son of Kronos seized his wife in his arms). The natural γλυκύτης of the sentiment is balanced, according to Hermogenes, by τραχύτης with respect to the diction (ἔμαρπτε and ἀγκὰς), and this balancing is also an instance of the application of propriety for reasons of morality, since excessive γλυκύτης would be sexual explicitness and obscenity. But this is not common, and Hermogenes makes no real effort to demonstrate that Homer is good at mixing *ideai*.

It is interesting that the view that Demosthenes is at least as good as Homer is paralleled in a source which is probably more or less contemporary with *Peri Ideon*. The *Encomium of Demosthenes* is included in the Lucianic corpus, and though there are solid factors that suggest that it is not actually by Lucian, the chances must be that it dates from approximately the same era.[21] There are

---

[21] For the two opposing views see the introduction of Bauer (1914), 1 ff. The opinion that the dialogue is not authentic goes back to antiquity (H. Rabe, *Scholia in Lucianum* (Leipzig, 1906), 224: οὗτος ὁ λόγος ἐνδεῖ τῆς τοῦ Λουκιανοῦ ἰδέας καὶ ἀγχινοίας); for modern formulations, see R. Helm, *RE* 26, 1735–6, s.v. *Lukianos*; Hirzel (1895), ii. 282 ff.; Alpers (1910), draws attention to numerous linguistic features that seem to be inconsistent with Lucianic authorship (right at the end of

two main characters in this dialogue: the narrator, who is name-
less, and a poet called Thersagoras who admires Homer, but
condescends to acknowledge the merits of Demosthenes. The
narrator meets Thersagoras who announces his intention of
honouring Homer with an encomium, and the narrator points
out that he himself is an admirer of Demosthenes and complains
that Thersagoras is only interested in poetry. Thersagoras defends
himself with the argument that even if Homer and Demosthenes
are of roughly equal quality, an encomium in honour of Homer is
a greater accomplishment than one in honour of Demosthenes
because in the case of Homer material for many of the conven-
tional encomiastic *topoi* is lacking (for example birth, home-
country, accomplishments in life), so that one has no option but
to praise him on the basis of the poetry alone. In conceding that
Homer and Demosthenes are of roughly the same quality,
Thersagoras presents a rapid σύγκρισις of the two authors,
comparing passages with parallel themes in c. 5 and in c. 6
speaking of various techniques that they share, for example
pathos, disposition, tropes, variation, resumptions, comparisons.[22]
He admits that Demosthenes shows greater propriety in invective
and shows greater skill in sustaining intensity in describing the
misfortunes of the Greeks than Homer. He also makes the point
that the style of Demosthenes is in some respects poetic just as the
style of Homer to some extent approaches the quality of prose.
And it is easy to imagine that the narrator of the dialogue, who is a
more trenchant defender of Demosthenes than Thersagoras,
would have been sympathetic to Hermogenes' position.[23]

his monograph Alpers seems to return to the possibility that the author was
Lucian); in favour of authenticity are Bauer (1914) and Drerup (1923), 151 ff.

[22] On the σύγκρισις, see Bauer (1914), 9–10.

[23] Another interesting case is Phrynichus Arabius, *Ecl.* 394 (Fischer), according
to which a certain Balbus of Tralles, of unknown date but probably not much
earlier than Phrynichus, had the daring to suggest that Menander was better than
Demosthenes. This suggests that Demosthenes was the bench-mark of literary
excellence, though Balbus may of course have believed that Homer was better than
either Menander or Demosthenes.

V

Xenophon: *Kanon* of *Apheleia*

I. STYLISTIC READINGS OF XENOPHON

In this chapter I survey some of the views about Xenophontic style that were circulated in the early Empire. There are five stages.

(a) Dionysius. *Xenophon's Inappropriate Simplicity*

Dionysius includes Xenophon twice in his reading list in *Peri Mimeseos*, both as a historian and as a philosopher. That in itself is interesting, and symptomatic of the uncertainty felt by early critics about how to classify Xenophon. Even this two-way classification leaves out some works, of course: the *Kunegetikos*, for example, a popular work later on. What Dionysius said about Xenophon the philosopher has not survived (though cf. *Peri Mimeseos* 2. 120. 6), but we do have his account of Xenophon the historian (*Peri Mimeseos* 2. 208. 6 ff.):

ἐκλεκτικὸς μὲν γὰρ καὶ καθαρὸς τοῖς ὀνόμασι, καὶ σαφὴς καὶ ἐναργής, καὶ κατὰ τὴν σύνθεσιν ἡδὺς καὶ εὔχαρις, ὡς καὶ πλεῖον ⟨ἔχειν⟩ ἐκείνου· ὕψους δὲ καὶ μεγαλοπρεπείας καὶ καθόλου τοῦ ἱστορικοῦ πλάσματος οὐκ ἐπέτυχεν· ἀλλ' οὐδὲ τοῦ πρέποντος τοῖς προσώποις πολλάκις ἐστοχάσατο, περιτιθεὶς ἀνδράσιν ἰδιώταις καὶ βαρβάροις ἔσθ' ὅτε λόγους φιλοσόφους, λέξει χρωμένος διαλόγοις πρεπούσῃ μᾶλλον ἢ στρατιωτικοῖς κατορθώμασι.

(He is selective and pure in diction, and clear and vivid, and in respect of composition he is sweet and pleasant, so as to exceed him (Herodotus), but he does not achieve sublimity, grandeur or in general the historical style. In fact, he often misses decorum with respect to character, giving philosophical words to private individuals and barbarians, and using diction that suits dialogues rather than what would be right for military victories.)

Xenophon is simple in respect of diction, completely fails to achieve the grandeur needed in history, and often puts into the mouths of ordinary people and barbarians words that are not suited to them, particularly philosophical reflections. The reference to philosophy suggests that Dionysius' view of Xenophon the philosopher might have been similar: perhaps he would have said that in those works Xenophon put inappropriately mundane speeches into the mouths of philosophers. Notice that the strategy of classifying Xenophon in two ways could indicate his failure to write appropriately in either. The idea of the inappropriateness of Xenophontic style is a long-lived one, and later critics return to it again and again, though not so much to censure him for it as to make a virtue out of it.[1]

(b) Dio. A Political Xenophon

Dio of Prusa discusses Xenophon at some length in his *Peri Askeseos Logou* (*Or.* 18), arguing that his style provides excellent reading for the man of political life (ἀνδρὶ πολιτικῷ). And certainly Xenophon is among the authors that Dio's own style of writing seems to be indebted to.[2] Dio sums up Xenophon's style in the following words (*Or.* 18. 14):

τά τε γὰρ διανοήματα σαφῆ καὶ ἁπλᾶ καὶ παντὶ ῥᾴδια φαινόμενα, τό τε εἶδος τῆς ἀπαγγελίας προσηνὲς καὶ κεχαρισμένον καὶ πειστικόν, πολλὴν μὲν ἔχον πιθανότητα, πολλὴν δὲ χάριν καὶ ἐπιβολήν, ὥστε μὴ λόγων δεινότητι μόνον, ἀλλὰ καὶ γοητείᾳ ἐοικέναι τὴν δύναμιν.

(For not only are his ideas clear and simple and easy for everyone to grasp, but the character of his narrative style is attractive, pleasing and convincing, being in a high degree persuasive, with much charm also and effectiveness, so that his power suggests not cleverness, but actual wizardry (tr. Cohoon).)

So Xenophon is simple, but persuasive. Dio is particularly keen on the speeches in the *Anabasis*, which he believes function as a kind of standard (κανών- *Or.* 18. 15) for a man faced with such situations in real life. Dio makes no reference to Xenophon having a problem with inappropriateness, and it seems unlikely that he would have agreed with Dionysius about this.

The qualities that Dio attributes to Xenophon are those that Dionysius attributes to Lysias, who seems to be simple, but is in fact δεινός with respect to εὕρεσις. We could think of Dio's Xenophon as a Lysianic Xenophon or a Xenophon who is δεινὸς περὶ τὴν εὕρεσιν.

---

[1] See pp. 65, 66; also *Peri Hupsous* 4. 4 (*Resp. Lac.* 3. 5).

[2] See Russell (1992), 2.

Quintilian's account of Xenophon in *IO* 10. 1, from about the same time, is similar in spirit to Dio's: Xenophon is simple, but persuasive. He has unaffected charm (*iucunditatem inadfectatam*). The goddess Persuasion sits on his lips. Again, there is no trace of Dionysius' criticisms.[3]

(c) Ἀφέλεια *and* Peri Aphelous Logou

Against this background we now have to try to place Ps. Aristides B' '*Peri Aphelous Logou*', which sets out to describe the style of Xenophon, more precisely to show how the ἀφελὴς λόγος differs from the πολιτικὸς λόγος of the orators.

The basic meaning of ἀφελής seems to have been 'plain, lacking rough-ground (φελλεύς)'.[4] We find it first as an aesthetic term in a fragment of Antiphanes' *Mystis* (*CPG* 2. 161. 8), in which a cup is praised τῆς συμμετρίας καὶ τῆς ἀφελείας (for its symmetry and its plainness).[5] An early usage is in an elegy of Theognis, in which it is used of direct and even rude humour.[6] To move to rhetorical applications, we find it of simple *kolon*-structure in Aristotle's *Rhetoric*.[7] According to the Stoic Chrysippus, one of the most important elements in rhetoric was ὁ ἐλευθέριος καὶ ἀφελὴς κόσμος (adornment that is liberal and plain).[8] Dionysius uses it of the

---

[3] *IO* 10. 1. 82: *quid ego commemorem Xenophontis illam iucunditatem inadfectatam, sed quam nulla consequi adfectatio possit? ut ipsae sermonem finxisse Gratiae videantur et, quod de Pericle veteris comoediae testimonium est, in hunc transferri iustissime possit, in labris eius sedisse quandam persuadendi deam* ('Why should I speak of the unaffected charm of Xenophon, so far beyond the power of affectation to attain? The Graces themselves seem to have moulded his style, and we may with the utmost justice say of him, what the writer of the old comedy said of Pericles, that the goddess of persuasion sat enthroned upon his lips' (tr. Butler).)

[4] First at Aristophanes, *Eq.* 527: διὰ τῶν ἀφελῶν πεδίων (across the stoneless plains); but see Forssman (1982), who connects it with ἀφελεῖν, suggesting that it means 'without a flaw', having at some time been part of a more complex expression amounting to: '(additions being taken away) and without flaw'. The tradition that there was an altar of Apheleia at Athens (Heyschius, 1791; Eustathius on Hom. *Il.* 22. 451) reflects confusion with Philia: see F. Eckstein, *LIMC* 1. 1. 351–3.

[5] The fragment is cited in Athenaeus, 15. 446bc. Kock has doubts about the reading (elsewhere—494cd—the text has ἀσφαλείας), and suggests ὠφελείας, but I do not see the need for that.

[6] Theognis 1211: ἀφελῶς παίζουσα; the word is attested also for Sophocles, fr. 723, but the force of the application is uncertain; another fairly early reference is: ἀφελής καὶ μέστος παρρησίας at Demosthenes, *Ep.* 4. 11, though the date of this is uncertain; it is associated with Spartans at Phylarchus, 81 *FGrH* 44.

[7] 1409[b]16: ἀφελῆ δὲ λέγω τὴν μονόκωλον ('I call the *monokolon* plain').

[8] Plutarch, *Stoic repugn.* 28. 1047a (= *SVF* ii. 297); I owe this reference to

style of Lysias.[9] Plutarch, as usual a rich source for moral terminology, uses it of simplicity of character, though sometimes also of simple language.[10] According to Ps. Longinus, *Peri Hupsous* 34. 2 Hyperides λαλεῖ μετὰ ἀφελείας (talks with plainness).[11]

Peri Aphelous Logou falls into the following sections.[12] An introduction (2–27) explains how individual strata—ἐννόημα, σχῆμα, ἀπαγγελία, ῥυθμός, plus μεταχείρισις—can make a difference between the two styles. After that, there is a lengthy discussion of ἦθος (28–53), which in Xenophon usually comes down to the appearance of a simple and excellent character. This is followed by the most structured part of the work, discussions of the *ideai*: σεμνότης, περιβολή, γλυκύτης, κάλλος, ἀλήθεια (54–76). The second half is made up of discussions of a wide range of rhetorical topics, among them οἰκονομία (77), παραδείγματα (79–80), ἐπιχειρήματα (81–2), and beginnings (84–7), a second comparison with πολιτικὸς λόγος (90–4), a section on diction (95–101), and numerous miscellaneous techniques. There is much repetition. Sometimes the author seems not so much to be presenting techniques as commenting on passages of Xenophon. The loose organization of the work seems to reflect the genre itself, which encourages an appearance of disorganized arrangement (see below).

The author has a broad interest in Xenophon's works, both the historical and the philosophical. However, a relative lack of interest in the historical may be indicated by the absence of references to the *Hellenika*. In the *Anabasis* a passage that particularly interests him is the atypical mythical narrative of Apollo and Marsyas (1. 2. 8).[13] Many of the minor works are ignored, but *Agesilaos* is a favourite, cited over twenty times—a high proportion of citations, considering its size.[14] The *Kunegetikos* is also cited a handful of times.[15]

Elizabeth Asmis. One thinks of Horace's *simplex munditiis* (*Odes* 1. 5. 5). The Stoic formulation is reflected in Quintilian, *Inst. Orat.* 8. 3. 87.

[9] e.g. *Lysias* 6. 14. 14; 8. 15. 21; 17. 28. 14; 24. 36. 1; *Isaeus* 2. 57. 9; 3. 58. 23; 11. 71. 10; 20. 91. 2; *Isocrates* 7. 100. 5 ff.; 8.101. 20; 9. 103. 7; 11. 107. 10–11; 16. 115. 5; *Dem. Lex.* 9. 145. 9; 39. 212. 25; *De Compositione Verborum* 22. 97. 12; *Peri Mimeseos* 9. 215. 15. Generally it is used as a synonym for ἀποίητος and ἀνεπιτήδευτος.

[10] Of language at *Phoc.* 19. 1; *Mor.* 748a3; cf. Diodorus Siculus, 33. 7. 7. 6.

[11] For the association of λαλός and ἀφέλεια, see *Peri Aphelous Logou*, cc. 80 and 82.

[12] On this work, see in general Schmid (1917); Reardon (1971), 102.

[13] 127 ff.; cf. Achilles Tatius, 3. 15.

[14] For these references see Schmid (1926), 130–1. I list references for the

[See p. 68 for n. 14 cont. and n. 15]

Two main themes stand out. The first, perhaps the most important theme in the whole work, is ἦθος. Xenophon creates an impression of ἦθος by avoiding emphatic statements of opinion or value-judgements, moral imperatives (53), and even direct statements of fact. He tends to frame his statements with moderate expressions of emotion (36), or expressions of doubt and reserve. Attributing statements to other people can serve the same purpose (38). He has a special interest in portraying character, particularly good character (37, 41). He includes low and important themes, for example, what great men do in jest (35), and everyday places and things (97–8). Sometimes he deliberately lowers and disguises grandeur or rhetorical force (92–3). Most of the interest that the author shows in the historical works seems to be because of the light they shed on ἦθος.

The second major point is that he gives the impression of writing without a definite purpose in view, so that the effect seems to be one of the points being thrown together at random (82). The language gives the impression of not being like a strategic approach (ἐπιβολή), and in fact its purpose is hidden (4). This is especially true of the beginnings of works, for which *Peri Aphelous Logou* has a special penchant (one can compare the apparently artless and purposeless introduction to prose works known as the προλαλιά) (85).[16] However, in fact there always is a definite purpose to it, and in fact the impression of simplicity is always an impression, because everything is brought about by technique or handling (μεταχείρισις is his word for it).

Both themes have a sort of model in the passage toward the end of the *Kunegetikos* (13. 6), where Xenophon anticipates criticism from sophists on the grounds that his writings, which are actually καλῶς καὶ ἑξῆς γεγραμμένα (well and methodically written), are in fact nothing of the sort, and he defends himself in advance by saying (13. 7) that his aim in writing has been to make men σοφοὺς καὶ ἀγαθούς (wise and good). Sophists, he goes on, are hunters of

Agesilaos: from Bk. 1: 1 (93), 3-4 (107), 5–6 (18), 7 (59), 8 (72), 14(109), 19 (20, 96), 20 (138), 25 (70?), 30 (96), 33 (118), 35 (110), 36 (93); from Bk. 2. 5 (133), 6 (112), 7 (117); from Bk. 5: 5 (111); from Bk. 6: 7 (67). As Dr D. C. Innes suggests to me, the interests of *Peri Aphelous Logou* might perhaps have been occasioned by the fact that *Agesilaos* was a good model for a prose-encomium.

[15] 1, 1 (40, 65); 1, 4 (57); 1, 18 (43); 10. 1 (66).

[16] See Mras (1949). The idea of lack of order is exactly paralleled in the account of λαλιά in Menander Rhetor: Russell and Wilson (1981), 125.

men, while the form of hunting which he advocates serves a useful social function.

The attitude to Xenophon shown in *Peri Aphelous Logou* is quite unlike Dio's sketch of the political Xenophon, though there is perhaps a trace of the political Xenophon of Dio in the idea that Xenophon does everything by μεταχείρισις—he is not as disingenuous as he looks. But it is only a trace.

Peri Aphelous Logou differs from Dio in that the author does not think that Xenophon's style is πολιτικός, at least not on the surface. On the other hand, he thinks that Xenophon's writings have an organization and a purpose which is concealed under a show of being strung together at random. Furthermore, ἀφέλεια defined by *Peri Aphelous Logou* would be quite a persuasive style, because you go out of your way to project the character of a good man, and to communicate in the simple terms that people will understand. So from this point of view the difference between *Peri Aphelous Logou* and Dio is not so great.

It is also interesting to see how *Peri Aphelous Logou* continues the idea from Dionysius of inappropriate language in Xenophon. *Peri Aphelous Logou* supposes that Xenophon deliberately lowers the tone, making complex language simpler. Instead of matching the thought, the style conceals it. It is implied that it is a good thing for the style to be inappropriate, at least judged by the standard of the speech (there are obviously many other respects in which such techniques are appropriate, judged by the standard of the audience, for example, or the character of the writer). This comes out most clearly in the analysis of Tissaphernes' speech, where the application of μεταχείρισις generates inappropriateness. To put it more generally, all characters in ἀφέλεια literature talk like ἀφελεῖς men. But what for Dionysius was inappropriateness has for the author of *Peri Aphelous Logou* become a feature of the genre.

(d) *Xenophon in* Peri Ideon

Hermogenes discusses the style of Xenophon and ἀφέλεια at two points: in the core in the sections on ἀφέλεια, γλυκύτης, and δριμύτης, and in the post-core in his discussion of πανηγυρικὸς λόγος. Both times he associates Xenophon with two other writers, who form a little sub-group of ἀφελεῖς. One is Aeschines the Socratic, the other is Nicostratus.[17]

[17] See pp. 38–9.

In the post-core Hermogenes mentions the following features of Xenophon's style: (*a*) ἀφέλεια (404. 22 ff.): this is the most important thing: Xenophon is totally ἀφελής; (*b*) γλυκύτης (404. 24 ff.): he derives some γλυκύτης by intensification of ἀφέλεια (as in the *Kunegetikos*) and some independently, e.g. from mythical narratives (as in the stories of Abradates and Pantheia and of Tigranes and his wife in the *Kuropaidia*); (*c*) other *ideai* (405. 11 ff.): he uses μέγεθος with respect to ἔννοια, but makes it ἀφελής by μέθοδος and λέξις. He is καθαρός and εὐκρινής; he uses δριμύτης and ὀξύτης (which is related to ἀφέλεια and γλυκύτης), and he uses ἐπιμέλεια; (*d*) comparison with Plato (405. 18 ff.): Xenophon is more ἀφελής, partly in respect of theme. For example, Plato excludes dancing girls from his *Sumposion*, whereas Xenophon includes them in his. And he makes references to quasi-symposiastic activities (like drinking) even in his historical works; (*e*) simplicity of character (406. 7 ff.): Xenophon's characters (e.g. the young Kuros) are simpler than Plato's; and finally (*f*) occasional poetical vocabulary (406. 15 ff.).

This is not greatly different from the picture of Xenophon that emerges from the core, except that there Hermogenes concentrates on ἀφέλεια, γλυκύτης, and δριμύτης. There are a few additional points: Xenophon illustrates arguments drawn from animal behaviour (325. 21); the technique of attributing human traits to animals, a feature of γλυκύτης, with parallels in poetry, is well illustrated from the *Kunegetikos* (335); and later personification of the animate, giving προαίρεσις to something that is ἀπροαιρετικόν, is illustrated from *Kuropaidia* 7. 3. 8: ἡ χεὶρ ἐπηκολούθησεν (the hand followed him) (360. 7).[18] Xenophon also quotes poetry (337. 5). He sometimes subtly misuses words for effect, for example the word φιλανθρωπία applied to dogs at *Kun*. 3. 8 (340. 24).[19]

Of special interest is the basic technique of δριμύτης, which is said to be putting complex propositions in a simple way.[20] This

[18] The hand of the dead Abradates, having been severed, comes away when Kuros touches it. The passage is cited at 360. 7 as an example of *pathos*; in *Peri Aphelous Logou* 32 the same words had been cited to illustrate ἦθος—an interesting inversion; though in *Peri Aphelous Logou* 39 the story of Abradates and Pantheia as a whole illustrates *pathos*.

[19] Cf. *Peri Aphelous Logou* 20, where the author comments on *Agesilaos* (1. 19): *he made many men lovers of his friendship*, which seems to involve an analogous transference of a word.

[20] Since the first technique Hermogenes mentions seems to involve a lack of τὸ πρέπον, I wonder if we should see in this a reflection of the view of Dionysius of

corresponds to the lowering and simplifying of complex propositions in *Peri Aphelous Logou*. More importantly, it corresponds to
the idea of Xenophontic inappropriateness in Dionysius, with a
slightly different emphasis: Dionysius sees Xenophon as giving
philosophical thoughts to simple people, Hermogenes sees him as
putting complex things simply. What links the two is the idea of a
conflict between the complexity of the ideas and the simplicity of
the style or the speakers.

The relationship to *Peri Aphelous Logou* is multi-faceted. There
are many parallels. Xenophon is a κανών of ἀφέλεια and ἦθος. He
has qualities of grandeur, but disguises them. He likes to represent
animals in human terms (for the correlate to this in *Peri Aphelous
Logou*, see c. 66). On the other hand, there are also subtle
differences:

1. With respect to complexity: although Hermogenes concedes
that Xenophon's language is sometimes more complex than it
seems, that he can disguise μέγεθος (405. 11), and that he often
puts complex propositions in a simple way (that is the essence of
δριμύτης), the picture is still a lot simpler than the one in *Peri
Aphelous Logou*. Hermogenes does not entertain the possibility
that Xenophon's organization of points can be strategic (to allow
him ἐπιχειρήματα concerning animals is no great concession); he
does not mention that his characters are not always simple and
naïve, but sometimes just good; and he does not mention the
possibility that the speeches in Xenophon's historical works are
worth imitating rhetorically.

2. With respect to works cited: the most frequently cited works
are the *Kuropaidia*, cited eight times (among other things for the
stories of Abradates and Pantheia and the episode of Tigranes and
his wife),[21] and the *Kunegetikos*, cited six times, but usually for
γλυκύτης; never for ἀφέλεια.[22] The *Anabasis*, the *Hellenika*, and
Sumposion are each referred to once.[23] The *Agesilaos*, much cited

---

Halicarnassus that Xenophon lacks τὸ πρέπον, and a reaction to the view of Dio and
the author of *Peri Aphelous Logou* that he does show τὸ πρέπον.

[21] Abradates and Pantheia (7. 3. 8 ff.) at 360. 7; 405. 6; Tigranes and his wife (3.
1. 36 ff.) at 405. 8. Also 1. 3. 2 at 323. 15; 3. 3 at 406. 9; 4. 19 at 323. 16; 6. 17 at 406.
18; 2. 3. 9 at 325. 23.

[22] A general reference at 405. 3; otherwise on p. 335: 3. 6 (line 10); 3. 7 (lines 10–
12); 4. 3 (line 10); 5. 33 (line 20; also cited by Arrian, *Kunegetikos* 16. 6); also 3. 8 at
340. 21 (δριμύτης).

[See p. 72 for n. 23]

in *Peri Aphelous Logou*, is not mentioned at all, nor is the *Memorabilia*. So this is an even plainer, less historical Xenophon than the one presented in *Peri Aphelous Logou*.

(e) A Modern Kanon for Ἀφέλεια

We have seen that Hermogenes associates ἀφέλεια not only with Xenophon but also with the classical writer Aeschines the Socratic and the modern writer Nicostratus. In fact stylistic emulation of Xenophontic ἀφέλεια was a widespread trend in the early empire.[24] The author of Ps. Dionysius *Rhetorica* Β′ (μέθοδος γαμηλίων) recommends the ἀφελής style of Xenophon and Nicostratus.[25] A similar statement is made by Menander Rhetor,[26] and we hear that Metrophanes of Epicarpia wrote a study of the works of Plato, Xenophon, Philostratus, and Nicostratus, and the common fact here will be ἀφέλεια.[27]

Something of a secondary model for the ἀφέλεια style seems to have developed in Titus Aurelius Nicostratus, a native of Macedonia.[28] In *Lives of the Sophists* Philostratus uses the style of Nicostratus as one of two parameters to specify the style of Aelian:[29] ἡ μὲν ἐπίπαν ἰδέα τοῦ ἀνδρὸς ἀφέλεια προσβάλλουσά τι τῆς

---

[23] *Anabasis* 4. 5. 32–3: 406. 2; *Hell.* 7. 2. 9: 328. 18 (κλαυσιγέλως; a word that found its way into Demetrius, *De Eloc.* 28); *Sumposion*: 405. 22.

[24] See Münscher (1920), who collects the data, but offers nothing by way of an interpretation. On Xenophon in the early empire, see also Reardon (1971), 350–1, citing Perry (1930), 96; see also Baumgarten (1932), 1 ff.

[25] 2. 9. 266. 13.

[26] *Peri Epideiktikon* 389–90: μεστὴ δὲ καὶ ἡ ἱστορία Ἡροδότου γλυκέων διηγημάτων· ἐν οἷς ἡδονὴ παντοδαπὴς παραγίνεται τῷ λόγῳ, οὐ μόνον ἀπὸ τῆς ξένης τῶν διηγημάτων ἀκοῆς, ἀλλὰ καὶ ἀπὸ τῆς ποιᾶς συνθέσεως, ὅταν μὴ τραχείᾳ χρώμεθα τῇ ἐξαγγελίᾳ, μηδὲ περιόδους ἐχούσῃ καὶ ἐνθυμήματα, ἀλλ᾽ ὅταν ἁπλουστέρα τυγχάνῃ καὶ ἀφελεστέρα, οἷα ἡ Ξενοφῶντος καὶ Νικοστράτου καὶ Δίωνος τοῦ Χρυσοστόμου καὶ Φιλοστράτου τοῦ τὸν Ἡρωικὸν καὶ τὰς Εἰκόνας γράψαντος ἐρριμμένη καὶ ἀκατασκεύαστος (The history of Herodotus is full of sweet narratives in which there are all sorts of pleaasure, not only from the foreign dialect of the narratives, but also from the individual composition, when we do not make use of diction that is either rough, or which has periods and enthymemes, but when it is simpler and smoother, like the random, unornamented diction of Xenophon, Nicostratus, Dio Chrysostomus, and Philostratus, the athor of the *Heroicus* and the *Eikones*). See Russell and Wilson(1981), 297–8.

[27] According to Suda, s.v. Metrophanes' work was entitled: Περὶ Τῶν Χαρακτήρων Πλάτωνος, Ξενοφῶντος, Νικοστράτου, Φιλοστράτου. There are some signs that Nicostratus was thought of as belonging to a canon of modern prose writers: see Ch. VII; ἀφέλεια of Heliodorus: Photius, *Bibl.* 73. 50a6.

[28] For evidence for the life of Nicostratus, see Stegemann (1936), 551–2.

[29] *Vit. Soph.* 624 (123. 12 ff. Kayser).

Νικοστράτου ὥρας, ἡ δὲ ἐνίοτε πρὸς Δίωνα ὁρᾷ καὶ τὸν ἐκείνου τόνον
(The general *idea* of the man is ἀφέλεια, adding something of the
beauty of Nicostratus, while it sometimes looks toward Dio and
his tension). Nicostratus and Dio (presumably Dio of Prusa) are
used as bench-marks for different types of ἀφέλεια, Nicostratus'
style being more florid, and Dio's having more muscularity and
tension.[30]

Another important figure in this movement, though he is not
explicitly associated with ἀφέλεια, is Arrian of Nicomedia, whose
literary output bridged philosophy and history, like Xenophon's
own. Arrian makes several explicit references to the *Anabasis* in his
own *Anabasis of Alexander*; a particularly interesting point is where
Alexander in a protreptic speech to his army before the battle of
Issus reminds them of Xenophon and his Ten Thousand (2. 7).
The model for this may be the protreptic speech that Xenophon
makes in the *Anabasis* (2. 3); one is reminded of Dio's claim that
Xenophon's *Anabasis* is an excellent model for the man involved in
public life. Earlier on in the *Anabasis of Alexander* Arrian includes a
brief digression about Midas and the Gordian Knot (2. 3); this is
reminiscent of *Peri Aphelous* 124, where the example comes from a
digression about Midas in Xenophon's *Anabasis* (1. 2. 4).

Perhaps the most interesting work of all is his *Kunegetikos*,
which included frequent references to Xenophon's work of that
name.[31] One thinks of course of the references to Xenophon's
Kunegetikos in *Peri Aphelous Logou* and *Peri Ideon*. One passage,
Kunegetikos 5. 33, about catching hares,[32] is cited both by

---

[30] For Dio's style, see *Vit. Soph.* 487 (6. 30 ff. Kayser): Δίωνα δὲ τὸν Πρυσαῖον οὐκ
οἶδ' ὅ τι χρὴ προσειπεῖν διὰ τὴν ἐς πάντα ἀρετήν, Ἀμαλθείας γὰρ κέρας ἦν, τὸ τοῦ λόγου,
ξυγκείμενος μὲν τῶν ἄριστα εἰρημένων τοῦ ἀρίστου, βλέπων δὲ πρὸς τὴν Δημοσθένους ἠχὼ
καὶ Πλατῶνος, ᾗ, καθάπερ αἱ μαγάδες τοῖς ὀργάνοις, προσηχεῖ ⟨ὁ Δίων⟩ τὸ ἑαυτοῦ ἴδιον ξὺν
ἀφελείᾳ ἐπεστραμμένη (As for Dio of Prusa, I do not know what one ought to call
him, in view of his all-round excellence; for, as the proverb says, he was a 'horn of
Amaltheia', since his style (?) was created out of the noblest of all that has been most
nobly expressed. He looks toward the sonority of Demosthenes and Plato, but his
own quality sounds in harmony with it with a tense simplicity, as the bridge
enhances the tone of musical instruments). Dio imitates the high style of Demosthenes and Plato, but he reduces the volume, increases the pitch and improves the
timbre, like the bridge (μαγάς) on a string instrument. On the evaluation of Dio of
Prusa, see Brancacci (1985).

[31] For Arrian's interest in Xenophon, see Reardon (1971), 210 ff.; on the
Kunegetikos, see Stadter (1980), 57; id. (1976), 157 ff. On the significance of the
name Flavius Arrianus Xenophon, see id. (1980), 2–3; also id. (1967), 155 ff.

[32] οὕτω δὲ ἐπίχαρί ἐστι τὸ θηρίον, ὥστε οὐδείς ὅστις οὐκ ἂν ἰδὼν ἰχνευόμενον,
εὑρισκόμενον, μεταθεόμενον, ἁλισκόμενον, ἐπιλάθοιτ' ἂν εἴ του ἐρῴη (The beast is so

Hermogenes as an example of an ἔννοια appropriate to γλυκύτης
(335. 21), and also by Arrian, who generally praises the *Kune-*
getikos, but criticizes this sentence on the grounds that watching
the hare being caught is not a pleasant sight (*Kunegetikos* 16. 6).
Another work including the same theme is Dio of Prusa's
Euboikos, which is largely concerned with the life-style of
Euboean hunters, and bore the alternative title *Kunegetikos* in
later antiquity.

Another work that Arrian may have made use of is the
Agesilaos, this in his monographs on Dio of Syracuse and
Timoleon (both lost)—an interesting point of contact with *Peri*
Aphelous Logou.[33]

Arrian wrote no novels, but the novel was another growth area
where the style of Xenophon was cultivated. Here the key model
was the *Kuropaidia*, particularly the story of Abradates and
Pantheia (mentioned, we recall, both in *Peri Aphelous Logou* and
in *Peri Ideon*). The work entitled *Araspes, the Lover of Pantheia*,
attributed by Philostratus to a certain Celer (it was also attributed
to Dionysius of Miletus) (*Vit. Soph.* 524), was perhaps an instance
of an imitation of the *Kuropaidia* moving in the direction of the
novel.[34]

2. HERMOGENES' APPROPRIATION OF ᾿ΑΦΕΛΕΙΑ

Since the idea that Xenophon's style contrasts with political
language is already in Dionysius, the date of *Peri Aphelous*
Logou could be pushed back into the first century CE, although
nothing would rule out a much later date. The most promising
method of dating would seem to be to try to establish a chronology
relative to *Peri Ideon*. It ought to be possible to do this because of
the existence of a number of parallels between the two.

Several positions are possible on the question of the relative
date of *Peri Ideon* and *Peri Aphelous Logou*.

1. *Peri Aphelous Logou* might draw on *Peri Ideon*. This possibility might be supported by the argument that the analysis of

charming that anyone who sees it being tracked, discovered, pursued, and caught
would forget anything he was in love with).

[33] See Bowie (1970), 26 (= 193).
[34] On the authorship, see Bowie (1985), 686.

ἀφέλεια is in the end more complex, since ἀφέλεια in *Peri Aphelous Logou* is a broad category incorporating a number of *ideai* of its own.

2. *Peri Ideon* might draw on *Peri Aphelous Logou*. That might seem to be supported by the complex way in which *Peri Ideon* itself exploits ἀφέλεια, presenting it as a style of use in πολιτικὸς λόγος also (which might have been derived from *Peri Aphelous Logou* 100–1), and showing that Demosthenes makes extensive use of it. It is only the analysis of Xenophontic ἀφέλεια which is simpler.

3. The orthodox view on the subject is probably that of Schmid, who supposed that when Hermogenes wrote the main section of *Peri Ideon* ('the core') he was under the influence of *Peri Politikou Logou* but did not know *Peri Aphelous Logou* (but that he had got to know *Peri Aphelous Logou* before writing the 'post-core').[35] This strange view seems to have been based on the fairly extensive analysis of ἀφέλεια and the styles of three ἀφελεῖς authors (Xenophon, Aeschines the Socratic, and Nicostratus) in the section περὶ τοῦ ἁπλῶς πανηγυρικοῦ in the post-core (403. 20 ff.). But there is also a discussion of ἀφέλεια in the core and the same three authors are mentioned in the course of the discussion (329. 8 ff.). One could argue that the discussion of ἀφέλεια in the core was also an afterthought, but it seems likelier that we should abandon the attempt to use the supposed influence of *Peri Aphelous Logou* as a criterion to separate core and post-core.

4. *Peri Ideon* and *Peri Aphelous Logou* are not directly related, but each presupposes some other simpler treatment of Xenophontic ἀφέλεια as an independent quality of style.

Of these possibilities, (3) can be rejected outright. The most significant difference between core and post-core on the subject of ἀφέλεια is probably that in the post-core Plato turns out to have ἀφέλεια also, and Hermogenes shows how their styles can be distinguished on this point (see Chapter III).

Of the other options, it might be safest to go for (4). But it is worth saying that if there is a closer relationship between the two, it is much likelier to be (2) than (1). My reason has to do with their positions on πολιτικὸς λόγος. The author of *Peri Aphelous Logou* believes that πολιτικὸς λόγος is a comparatively simple foil for

---

[35] Schmid (1917), 137 ff., esp. 148; also Boulanger (1923), 237.

ἀφέλεια; this is very much like the view represented in *Peri Politikou Logou*. But the whole thesis of *Peri Ideon* is that πολιτικὸς λόγος is much the more subtle and complex form of prose. It is not impossible that *Peri Aphelous Logou* was written by someone who had read *Peri Ideon*, but it is much less likely.

My suspicion is that it was the other way round, and that Hermogenes may have drawn some of his stylistic contrasts and methodologies from *Peri Aphelous Logou*. I will show how this may have worked in the following sections. See further, Appendix C.

What I have no doubt about is that Hermogenes knew some view of the form: 'Xenophontic ἀφέλεια is an important form of style'—this remains so, even if the form he knew it in was not *Peri Aphelous Logou*—and he wanted to argue that in fact this is a form of style that Demosthenes uses just as well as Xenophon, if not better. To put it in a form that is paradoxical, but contains some of the truth, he wanted to argue that Demosthenes writes like Xenophon better than Xenophon.

He constructed the argument like this. He analyses the Xenophontic κανών as essentially consisting of a sub-group of three *ideai*: ἀφέλεια, γλυκύτης, δριμύτης.[36] These amount to simplicity of character (ἀφέλεια), poetic naïvety (γλυκύτης), and the effect of putting complex propositions in a simple form (δριμύτης). Analysed in these terms, the Xenophon that emerges is a simple Xenophon, the Xenophon of the *Kuropaidia* and the *Kunegetikos*, somewhat simpler than the Xenophon of *Peri Aphelous Logou*, and simpler than the one of Dio of Prusa.

Hermogenes breaks each of these *ideai* down into constituent elements, and shows that they are exemplified both by Xenophon, by other prose writers like Aeschines the Socratic and Nicostratus, and by poets (ἀφέλεια by Theocritus, γλυκύτης by lyric poets, and παραπλοκή, δριμύτης by tragedians). But he also shows that at least some of the techniques associated with each *idea* are used by Demosthenes. Once he has established that, he can always imply that the Demosthenic uses are so brilliant, that they represent an out-Xenophoning of Xenophon.

To carry out his manifesto, Hermogenes has to show that Demosthenes uses these rather un-Demosthenic qualities as well

---

[36] γλυκύτης is an intensification of ἀφέλεια (329. 21); δριμύτης is related to ἀφέλεια and γλυκύτης: 339. 16.

as Xenophon, and indeed better than him. He deals with this in different ways in the different sections.

Let us take the section on ἀφέλεια first. Most of the effect of ἀφέλεια in *Peri Ideon* resides in five categories of ἔννοιαι: (*a*) he suggests ἀφελεῖς ἔννοιαι are the same as καθαραί ones, which he has already illustrated from Demosthenes (322. 5 ff.); (*b*) the proper ἔννοιαι of ἀφέλεια are those of unsophisticated characters (322. 12 ff.), but he cites no examples of these from Demosthenes. In fact the models cited are Theocritus, Xenophon, and Menander; (*c*) another type of ἀφελὴς ἔννοια is that close to the 'vulgar' (324. 11 ff.), and here most of the examples he cites come from the private speeches of Demosthenes (there is also one from a public speech); (*d*) a further type of ἀφελὴς ἔννοια involves deriving syllogisms from animals or plants, and again this is illustrated from Xenophon (325. 20 ff.); (*e*) the last technique is proving by oaths and not through facts (326. 23 ff.); simple oaths, that is, such as the opening of *De Corona* (18. 1), not complex ones, where a factual proof is disguised as an oath, such as the Marathon Oath (*Or.* 18. 208). It is worth mentioning here that in the section on ἀλήθεια Hermogenes develops a more formalized distinction between emotional expressions that suggest ἀφέλεια (because you say that you are feeling the emotion in advance) and ones that do not (because you do not say it, and the effect is more spontaneous), and examples of both types are to be found in πολιτικὸς λόγος. The other strata are not so important; there is an overlap with καθαρότης, and there is no explicit reference to Demosthenes.

Hermogenes acknowledges that if ἀφέλεια is an independent quality, it is to be found principally in the utterances of simple people (category (*b*)), and that no such utterances are found in the works of Demosthenes. The same probably goes for (*d*). But with categories (*c*) and (*e*) he attempts to claim the category for Demosthenes: (*e*) is fairly uncontentious, but a problem with (*c*) would perhaps be that though there are examples of quasi-vulgar ἔννοιαι in the private speeches, it is much harder to find these in the public speeches. In the case of (*c*) Hermogenes twice cites passages which, on his own admission, were obelized in his day, and neither in fact shows up in our editions. In the case of one (from *De Corona*), he seems prepared to admit that the obelization is justified, whereas in the other (from *Against Neaira*) he seems to suggest that the obelizers might have erred because their awareness of the versatility of Demosthenes' style is inferior to his own (see p. 83).

So Hermogenes' attitude to ἀφέλεια in Demosthenes is: on the one hand, it is a quality that is easier to illustrate from other prose authors and from poets; but on the other hand, if you look closely there are many examples in Demosthenes.

The situation is similar with respect to the other two *ideai* related to ἀφέλεια. Γλυκύτης turns out to consist of the following techniques. First, ἔννοιαι of the following kinds: (*a*) those having mythical content (330. 2 ff.), e.g. *Or.* 23. 66; (*b*) narratives (330. 20 ff.); (*c*) narratives with a mythical material (330. 23 ff.); (*d*) reference to things that can be sensed, principally a poetic device (331. 6 ff.); (*e*) personification of inanimate objects (333. 15 ff.).

Besides ἔννοιαι, three types of λέξις are said to be appropriate to γλυκύτης: (*a*) poetic vocabulary, and also the Ionic dialect (336.1 ff.);[37] (*b*) παραπλοκή: interspersing poetry in prose (336. 15 ff.), as Plato often quotes lines of Homer (Xenophon is also said to do this) and as Demosthenes occasionally cites poetry in his public speeches, e.g. Euripides, *Hecuba* 1 and fr. 122 at *Or.* 18. 267, and Sophocles, *Antigone* 175 at *Or.* 19. 247; (*c*) the use of many epithets (338. 19 ff.; e.g. Stesichorus).

This is not an *idea* that is well represented in Demosthenes, but Hermogenes has made special efforts to find examples where he can. He points out that Demosthenes can include mythical narratives, such as the passage about the origin of the Areopagus in *Against Aristocrates* 66 (330. 9 ff.) (ἔννοιαι (*c*)). More important is the technique of παραπλοκή: Demosthenes sometimes cites poetry (λέξις (*b*)), although it might be objected that citations of verse are not an integral component of prose style.[38]

The *idea* δριμύτης is mainly a matter of verbal wit. Hermogenes says it consists of the following techniques: (*a*) ἔννοιαι that are 'superficially profound' (339. 20 ff.; cf. 328. 24 ff.), i.e. which involve putting something complex in a very simple way. Such techniques are found particularly in Xenophon; (*b*) misapplication of a word like φιλανθρωπία in Xenophon, *Cyneg.* 3. 8 (339. 25 ff.); (*c*) the use of two similar-sounding words in succession, as in Demosthenes, *Or.* 8. 27 (342. 3 ff.); (*d*) a normal use of a term

---

[37] For the use of the Ionic dialect in the 2nd cent. CE, see Smyth (1894), 110 ff., 115 ff.

[38] For παραπλοκή, see pp. 49, 55, 58.

followed by a metaphorical use (342. 19 ff.), as in Demosthenes, *Or.* 9. 17 and *Or.* 19. 289; (*e*) a mild trope followed by a harsh trope drawn from the same semantic field (343. 14 ff.), as in Demosthenes, *Or.* 2. 10.[39]

The basic technique of putting complex propositions in a simple way (*a*) is not one that Demosthenes seems to be able to exemplify. Demosthenes is involved only because he is a source for examples of some types of word-play ('*c–e*').

The strategy is clear: break the Xenophontic *ideai* down into the constituent techniques, and show that Demosthenes uses at least some of them well. This is to appropriate the quality of Xenophontic ἀφέλεια for Demosthenes, and can be used to justify the overall claim that Demosthenes uses these *ideai*, as all others, perfectly. Whether this is a plausible strategy is another matter.

[39] For this technique, see App. A. 3.

VI

The Demosthenic Canon

I. THE CANON EXTENDED

Hermogenes cites from over half the Demosthenic speeches that have come down to us, particularly from the public speeches, but also from private speeches, and from the *Epistles* (not from the *Erotikos* or the *Epitaphios*).[1] If one compares his citations with those of other rhetoricians, such as the author of *Peri Politikou Logou*, no really striking differences emerge, with the possible exception that an unusually high proportion of citations come from *De Corona*, cited over 120 times, three times more than the nearest rival, and a source of examples for almost all of the *ideai*.[2] This was probably not an untypical view; Aelius Aristides even dreams about the speech.

Many of the passages cited in *Peri Ideon* had been cited by generations of rhetoricians before him. The overlap with passages cited in *Peri Politikou Logou* is particularly high, but there is a degree of uniformity even if one looks as far back as Demetrius, who cites Demosthenes frequently in his discussion of the quality δεινότης. For example, *De Corona* 71, which is a key passage in the discussions of ἀκμή in *Peri Ideon* and *Peri Heureseos*, had been cited by Demetrius (*De Eloc.* 279) to illustrate an effective rhetorical question.[3] Similar patterns of imitation and adaptation of

---

[1] Rabe suggested that there might be an allusion to the *Erotikos* at 373. 13 (Demosthenes on Pericles), but why can that not be an allusion to 3. 21? (I cannot understand Wooten (1987), 104, who seems to refer to '6. 44–5'). Dionysius, *Dem. Lex.* 44, believed that the *Epitaphios* was a forgery, also mentioning an *Encomium of Pausanias* which is not in our texts.

[2] Exceptions are καθαρότης, τραχύτης, δριμύτης. Only the second is perhaps significant: τραχύτης is the style for attacking important people, but there is no room for this in *On The Crown*.

[3] For the citations in *On Ideas* and *On Invention*, see App. A.1. Cited also as an example of γοργότης at 317. Here are the other examples: *Philippic* 3. 56 was an example of παράλειψις in Demetrius (*De Eloc.* 263) and is used in much the same way in *Peri Ideon* 351. The first sentence of *Against Leptines* is often cited by Demetrius for its periodic effect and clausula; and we find a similar use by

the same basic examples emerge if we compare Dionysius[4] or the fragments of Caecilius.[5] All of which suggests that key passages of Demosthenes were regarded as of particular importance, even as constituting a sort of canon, which any rhetorician claiming to understand Demosthenes would have to take account of.

More than any rhetorician who preceded him (or followed), Hermogenes is committed to the view that Demosthenes uses all *ideai* with perfect skill. This project requires that examples be drawn from throughout the Demosthenic Corpus, because different speeches illustrate different styles better. This pattern is already established in Dionysius (who cites from a special set of speeches to illustrate the middle style), but it goes further in *Peri Ideon*. For example, we have already seen that the private speeches tend to be cited under ἀφέλεια. And in the section on κάλλος there is a tendency to cite speeches with a neat, antithetical style, like *Against Leptines* and *Against Androtion*. Another example, which I would like to spend a little more time on, is the use of *Epistles* 2 (*On the Sons of Lycurgus*) and 3 (*On his Return*) in *Peri Politikou Logou* and *Peri Ideon*.[6] The style normally associated with

Hermogenes (311. 1); also *Peri Politikou Logou* 64. 6 (συνθήκη). Demetrius also cites *De Corona* 188 (τοῦτο τὸ ψήφισμα . . . (*De Eloc.* 273)) and this is also a favourite passage in *Peri Ideon*. On The False Embassy 259 (νόσημα γάρ . . .) is cited by Demetrius (*De Eloc.* 280) as an example of ἐπιμονή, Dionysius of Halicarnassus cited it as an example of the middle style (*Dem. Lex.* 14); and Hermogenes cites it as an example of the *lexis* appropriate to ἀκμή (270. 4), where the force of the application is somewhat similar to that of Demetrius (cited also at *Peri Politikou Logou* 14. 12 (σεμνότης); 47. 17 (ἔμφασις); 63. 7 (συνθήκη)); another example is the 'climax' at *De Corona* 179, cited at *Peri Hermeneias* 270, and also by Hermogenes at 304. 19.

[4] *Phil.* 3: beginning: Hermogenes treats it as περιβολή and γοργότης/συστροφή; Dionysius had treated it as an example of ἐξηλλαγμένος λόγος in 9; Hermogenes reanalyses it as language that cuts, but does not seem to cut. *Peri Politikou Logou* 11. 13: πλαγιασμός, but σεμνότης. *Against Meidias* 69: complex sentence structure in Dionysius, *Dem. Lex.* 9. Hermogenes reanalyses it as βαρύτης: 364; *De Corona* 60: *Dem. Lex.* 14 (middle style): *Peri Ideon* 290. 22 (περιβολή).

[5] The 'Marathon Oath' passage from the *De Corona* (208), which had been show-cased perhaps from the time of Caecilius of Caleacte, as an example cast in the form of an oath. Hermogenes cites it twice: in the section on λαμπρότης (266. 24 ff.); and in the section on ἀφέλεια as an example of an oath that is not ἀφελής (327. 15) (see p. 72). Similarly, Caecilius (Tiberius, in Sp. 3. 79. 15 ff.) cited the passage concerning the arrival of the news of the capture of Elateia (*De Corona* 169) to illustrate διατύπωσις; and Hermogenes cites this several times (291. 19; 316. 10; 320. 7) to illustrate points of sentence structure, a different reason.

[6] In the section on τραχύτης he discusses *thoughts* that imply criticism of important people, and examples include passages from *Epp.* 2 and 3 in which the 'important people' are the Athenian *demos* (*Ep.* 3. 42 (256. 5 ff.; also 258. 20–1); *Ep.*

epistolography was plain and dialectical, rather like ἀφέλεια, in fact.[7] But the Demosthenic *Epistles* are not a good example. Purporting to have been written by the exiled Demosthenes from the island of Calaureia, they are written in a tone of remonstration and injured pride much admired in declamation of this period, a tone for which the *idea*-theorists used the term βαρύτης. Passages from *Epistles* 2 and 3 are cited in both *Peri Politikou Logou* and *Peri Ideon* to illustrate βαρύτης; *Peri Ideon* also uses reproachful sentences from them to illustrate τραχύτης, a related quality.

Indignant and self-reproaching speeches of this sort, often dramatizing quasi- or wholly fictional episodes from the end of Demosthenes' life, and often using the technique of figured language, were extremely popular with declaimers and their audiences during this period.[8] Rhetoricians naturally looked around for examples in the works of Demosthenes, and their search lead them to the *Epistles*, bestowing new importance on this tail-end of the Demosthenic canon. Though the author of *Peri Politikou Logou* finds βαρύτης in a wide range of Demosthenic speeches, we already find two citations from *Ep*. 3. Hermogenes agrees with him about *Ep*. 3 (with the qualification that he thinks that some of his examples really belong to τραχύτης), but he thinks that *Ep*. 2 is an even better example, since there the effect starts right from the first sentence, in which Demosthenes complains of the ingratitude which has been shown him by the Athenian *demos* (364. 15):

ἐνόμιζον μὲν ἀφ' ὧν ἐπολιτευόμην, οὐχ ὅπως μηδὲν ὑμᾶς ἀδικῶν τοιαῦτα πείσεσθαι, ἀλλὰ κἂν μέτρι' ἐξαμαρτὼν συγγνώμης τεύξεσθαι . . .

---

2. 8 (257. 1, 6); *Ep*. 3. 37 (257. 7). In the section on βαρύτης he recommends *thoughts* in which one says that one has been badly treated, or one has not received the favours one deserves, or has, on the contrary, been repaid by punishment, and says that there are many examples in *Epp*. 2 and 3 (364. 12), and that in the case of *Ep*. 2 the effect starts right from the first sentence, in which Demosthenes complains of how the Athenian *demos* has behaved toward him (364. 15). The association of the *Epistles* with βαρύτης was made already in *Peri Politikou Logou*, which cites as examples of it two of the illustrations that Hermogenes uses to illustrate τραχύτης (3. 42 at 19. 9 and 3. 37 at 19. 21), but Hermogenes seems if anything to strengthen the association.

[7] Demetrius, *De Eloc.* 223 ff.; cf. J. Sykutris, *RE Supp.* 5. 185 ff., s.v. *Epistolographie*.

[8] See p. 28.

(I used to believe on the basis of my political activities that not only would I not be treated like this unless I had wronged you, but that I would meet with forgiveness even if I committed minor offences . . .)

And the implication seems to be that *Ep.* 2 as a whole instantiates the quality, a fact which would make it the best example of βαρύτης in the whole Corpus.

Hermogenes is not uninterested in questions of genre relating to speeches in the Demosthenic canon, so it is remarkable that he never comments on the genre of the *Epistles*, especially since epistolography normally seems to have been associated with a different style. His view, I suspect, was that important generic differences, at least within πολιτικὸς λόγος, were grounded in differences of function, subject matter and addressee. Thus, there is a great deal of difference between public and private speeches, where all three factors are different, but little or none between public speeches and the *Epistles*, where all three are the same.

Hermogenes' quest for unusual effects in Demosthenes leads him on one occasion to treat as genuine a passage which other ancient rhetoricians regarded as spurious.[9] I am thinking of a discussion from the section on ἀφέλεια (325. 11 ff.):

ἐκεῖνα μέντοι διὰ τὸ ἄγαν εὐτελὲς καὶ ὠβέλισάν τινες καὶ ὑπεξείλοντο, ἴσως ὀρθῶς ποιοῦντες, λέγω τὸ "κυάμους ἐφθοὺς βοῶσα καὶ κατὰ πᾶν τὸ θέρος ἐπλανᾶτο" καὶ τὰ ἑξῆς· ταῦτα γὰρ καὶ τὰ τοιαῦτα ἐν μὲν ἰδιωτικοῖς λόγοις ἴσως ἂν ἁρμόσειεν, ἐν δημοσίῳ δὲ καὶ τηλικοῦτον ἔχοντι ἀξίωμα λόγῳ ἢ προσώπῳ ἢ πράγματι πῶς ἂν ἁρμόττοι; τοιοῦτόν ἐστι καὶ τὸ ἐν τῷ Κατὰ Νεαίρας ὠβελισμένον ὑπό τινων τὸ "ἀπὸ τριῶν τρυπημάτων τὴν ἐργασίαν πεποιῆσθαι" λέγειν. λίαν γὰρ εὐτελές ἐστι, καὶ εἰ σφοδρὸν εἶναι δοκεῖ.

(There is another passage that some critics have obelized or removed because it is so trivial, and perhaps they are right to do so: 'She wandered around all summer shouting "baked beans"' etc. Such passages as this might be appropriate in private speeches, but in a public speech, or one that should be as dignified as a public speech because it deals either with a person or a topic of public interest, they have no place. Similar too is the passage from the speech *Against Neaira*, which has also been questioned by some critics: 'She plied her trade through three openings.' This is extremely vulgar, even though it seems to be vehement (tr. Wooten).)

---

[9] On questions of authenticity, see Lossau (1964), 67 ff.; Speyer (1971), 118.

In fact neither passage occurs in our editions.[10] The tone of the
first of these is puzzling. Hermogenes seems to be agreeing with
the obelizers that such a passage has no place in a public speech.
But in that case, why does he mention it at all? Perhaps just
because he realizes that there is going to be a high degree of
overlap between passages of this sort of low quality and passages
which textual critics obelize because of their vulgarity, and
conflict, in other words, between the belief that Demosthenic
language contains infinite stylistic variety, and the belief that the
text of Demosthenes contains interpolations which can be identified because of their stylistic abnormality. The only way of
pinpointing inauthenticity for sure would be if a passage contains
really glaringly inappropriate language. But that is not really true
of the sentence about baked beans cited at 325. 13, and I wonder if
Hermogenes does not secretly think that the obelizers might be
wrong about this one also.

Hermogenes does not seem to recognize the possibility that
Against Neaira as a whole might be inauthentic, but this possibility had been raised by Dionysius of Halicarnassus, who (*Dem.
Lex.* 57) had listed this as one of a number of speeches he regarded
as spurious on the grounds that they were ἀηδεῖς καὶ φορτικοί in
respect of style.[11] The others he mentioned are *Against Aristogeiton* (either both or just the second: see below), *The Defence on a
Charge of Bribery*, *On the Sheltering of Harpalus*, and *On the
Treaty with Alexander*, *The Defence . . .*, and *On the Sheltering . . .*
did not make it into our editions, and they are likely to have been
spurious (it is probably no coincidence that their themes are
among those most popular in the declamation-schools, as Kohl's
list of historical themes that show up in declamation illustrates).[12]

The speeches *Against Aristogeiton* raise a special problem.
Photius reports the view that they are both spurious, attributing
it to Dionysius, but stating that he himself believes that they are
genuine.[13] We seem to have the passage of Dionysius in *Dem. Lex.*
mentioned earlier, but the numerical symbol Β′ there could refer
either (as a cardinal) to both speeches *Against Aristogeiton* or (as

---

[10] The obelized passage attributed to the *De Corona* was placed after section 129
of that speech by W. Nitsche, *BPW* 5 (1885), 708 (cited in Rabe's apparatus).

[11] For the spuriousness of *Against Neaira*, see also Photius, *Bibl.* 265. 492a23 =
Caecilius, fr. 147, and Libanius, *argumentum*.

[12] Kohl (1915).

[13] Photius, *Bibl.* 265. 491a29 = Caecilius fr. 143.

an ordinal) to the second only.[14] General agreement about the spuriousness of the second *Against Aristogeiton* seems to be indicated by the absence of citations from it in the rhetoricians. But if Dionysius believed that the first was spurious as well, then he was not followed by the authors of *Peri Hupsous* (c. 27. 3) or of *Peri Politikou Logou* or of *Peri Ideon*. Certainly, some passages of the first speech are unusually crude. It might be thought surprising, for example, that Hermogenes did not question the authenticity of a passage as manifestly undignified as c. 62, cited as an example of the λέξις appropriate to καθαρότης or τραχύτης (229. 11, 258. 10), which concerns Aristogeiton getting into a fight with a man from Tanagra and eating his nose: καὶ ὅτι ταῦτ᾽ ἀληθῆ λέγω, κάλει μοι τὸν ἄνθρωπον οὗ τὴν ῥῖν᾽ ὁ μιαρὸς οὗτος ἐσθίων κατέφαγεν (To prove that I am telling the truth, call the man whose nose this abomination devoured). But in fact he cites from the speech frequently. It is one of the prime exhibits in the section on τραχύτης, and one passage in particular, part of a digression on law, serves as one of his prime examples of *idea*-mixing.[15]

In the same context we can mention works not apparently regarded as spurious in antiquity but widely regarded as spurious today. One thinks of the numerous passages from *Epistles* 2 (*For the Sake of his Return from Exile*) and 3 (*On Behalf of the Children of Lycurgus*) that are cited in *Peri Ideon* and *Peri Politikou Logou*,

[14] *Dem. Lex.* 57 (251. 1). Blass emended the MSS τῇ κατ᾽ Ἀριστογείτονος β′ to τοῖς κατ᾽ Ἀριστογείτονος β′. Usher (1965) prints Blass's text, but translates 'in the second speech *Against Aristogeiton*'.

[15] cc. 15 ff. is used in the section on σεμνότης as an example of the sort of *thought* appropriate to that *idea* (245. 9–10), i.e. a *thought* concerning a divine subject which has to do with the world of men. And it is clearly an unusually straightforward presentation of an abstract intellectual topic, so much so that the passage has been supposed to incorporate a sophistic treatise (Pohlenz (1924), but see Gigante (1956), 268 ff.; Guthrie (1969), 75–6). Hermogenes is particularly interested in the *figuration*—the way that the clause κἂν μεγάλην πόλιν οἰκῶσι κἂν μικράν breaks up the effect of σεμνότης (251. 3, 381. 18), and also in the *rhythm* (251. 17, 254. 3). *Peri Politikou Logou* had already cited this passage as an example of σεμνότης, because it illustrated the use of the ἀποφαντικὸν σχῆμα (6. 16). So it looks as if Hermogenes' main contribution was to refine the respects in which the passage illustrated the *idea*. He also cites a passage about the brother of Aristogeiton (c. 80) (261. 8, 263. 15); similar passages from the speech—but not this one— had been used to illustrate σφοδρότης in *Peri Politikou Logou* (46 at 44. 6, 46. 16; 52 at 44. 4). It seems that Hermogenes was following the extensive use of the speech which had been made by the author of *Peri Politikou Logou*, who had found it a useful source of illustrations for a number of *ideai*, citing it no less than ten times (besides those mentioned: 2 at 37. 4 (ἀξιοπιστία); 4 at 37. 6 (id.); 10 at 17. 8 (βαρύτης); 15 at 6. 16 (σεμνότης); 28 at 45. 13; 45 at 17. 15 (βαρύτης); 58 at 8. 15 (σεμνότης)).

mainly as examples of βαρύτης.[16] There is also the case of *On Halonnesus*, cited in *Peri Ideon* to illustrate τραχύτης. Libanius is the first to report the views of ancient scholars who believed that this speech was wrongly attributed to Demosthenes, suggesting Hegesippus as an alternative author, but the view that it was stylistically anomalous goes right back to Dionysius.[17] Other speeches cited by Hermogenes but now generally recognized as spurious are *Philippic 4*, *Against Nicostratus*, and *Against Conon*.

Hermogenes' discussion of the styles of the two Antiphons (399. 18 ff.) shows that he was acquainted with the idea that there might be questions, based both on stylistic grounds and on historical grounds, about the authorship of texts. However, even there, I have suggested that stylistic analysis might be part of a strategy (δεινότης κατὰ μέθοδον) serving the purpose of showing that the Antiphon who wrote *Peri Aletheias* is likely to have been the one who influenced Thucydides, which is not to Thucydides' credit.[18] Certainly, in the case of Demosthenes, there is no sign of such an approach. While the lack of citations from certain speeches—for example the *Epitaphios*—may be a sign that he regarded these as inauthentic, Hermogenes shows no interest in investigating the historical background of speeches with a view to solving questions of authenticity, and any idea of abstracting a formula for Demosthenic style against which questions of authenticity can be judged seems to have been eclipsed by the thesis that there is no stylistic quality that Demosthenes does not accommodate and exploit.

Related to this is the feeling to which Hermogenes gives vent that previous scholars of Demosthenes have erred because they did not understand the style. This point is made in the introduction (216. 17 ff.). But it emerges particularly clearly from a passage in the section on ἀλήθεια (362. 21 ff.) where, having given a substantially correct interpretation of the μέν-*solitarium* at the start of Demosthenes, *Against Timocrates*, he continues:

καί παρέσχε μυρία τοιαῦτα πράγματα ζητοῦσι περὶ αὐτοῦ τοῖς ἰαλέμοις τούτοις, οἵ φασιν ἐξηγεῖσθαι τὸν ῥήτορα καὶ δὴ καὶ βιβλία καταλιπεῖν ἐτόλμησαν τῶν εἰς

---

[16] Goldstein (1968) argues for the authenticity of *Epistles* 1 and 4, but not these.
[17] Libanius, *arg.* 7. 45 Foerster; cf. Dionysius, *Dem. Lex.* c. 9, 148. 6; 13, 157. 3–4; Libanius condemns *Or.* 7. 45 which Hermogenes cites as genuine: 255. 27; 258. 8.
[18] See p. 24.

αὐτὸν ἐξηγήσεων, ἃ καὶ νῦν ἐξελίττοντες οἱ πολλοὶ τῶν διδασκάλων οἴονταί τινες εἶναι καὶ τοὺς συνόντας πείθουσιν, ὅμοιοι, φασίν, ὁμοίους.

(It has given countless trouble to those wretched students of his, who say that they are explaining the orator, and have dared to leave books of commentaries on him, which most teachers unroll and think that they are someone and try to persuade their pupils—birds of a feather, as they say.)

We see the same pattern in the discussion of the obelized passages in the section on ἀφέλεια. In the case of the obelized passage of *De Corona* he believes that the obelizers probably got it right (though perhaps there is an implication that the passage could be defended on the grounds of stylistic variety). In the case of the obelized passage from *Against Neaira*, on the other hand, the obelizers got it wrong because Hermogenes' perfect understanding of the full variety of Demosthenic style was not at their disposal.

There had been a change in attitude since the days of Caecilius and Dionysius, who devoted a large part of their scholarly activities to determining whether or not speeches were genuine. Hermogenes seems willing to entertain such an approach in the case of Antiphon, but in the case of Demosthenes he holds back. To some extent this reflects a change in attitude as to the nature of Demosthenic style—if he is a true chameleon, capable of taking on any stylistic colour to suit the circumstances, how could you ever show that something was un-Demosthenic? But one cannot help feeling that it may also reflect a change in the relationship between critic and author. Caecilius and Dionysius could condone or condemn the works of Demosthenes because they had a more or less rational attitude toward the task. But Hermogenes, like Aristides before him, believes that perfect rhetorical skill is an accomplishment beyond the range of ordinary mortals, so that his attitude to Demosthenes, whom he believes embodies it, is more like that of a worshipper to a god.[19] His task is to give an account of the divine orator's excellences. But the criticism and condemnation of works by the master has no part in such a project.

---

[19] Demosthenes as divine: *Peri Ideon* 379. 4.

2. CONTEMPORARY RELEVANCE FOR A DEMOSTHENIC SPEECH?

Different works by great authors take on different significance at different times. We have already seen variations in the works of Xenophon preferred by different critics: from the *Anabasis* in the case of Dio, to the *Agesilaos* in the case of *Peri Aphelous Logou*, to the *Kunegetikos* in the case of Arrian and Hermogenes. The same was no doubt true of Demosthenes' works. For example, the speeches directed against Philip took on a new significance for Cicero when he was working on his own *Philippics*.[20]

A clue as to where Hermogenes' special interests in Demosthenes may have lain is provided by a statement he makes to the effect that he wrote studies of individual speeches. As one might have predicted, one of those was *De Corona* (354. 6). We also hear of a work on *Against Leptines* (308. 10) and another on *Against Androtion* (299. 20). I would interpret these references as indications that these were speeches in which Hermogenes was particularly interested, and *à propos* of which he had something new to say.

We saw that the *De Corona* is far and away the favourite speech of Hermogenes (you might think that would be true of all rhetoricians but it is not; in *Peri Politikou Logou* the *De Corona* is less frequently cited than *Peri Tes Parapresbeias* or *Against Leptines*). We can only guess what sort of things would have been discussed in the work on *De Corona*. One of them was apparently the ἀφέλεια in the opening prayer—that is why he mentions the work in the first place. He probably would have wanted to show that the speech illustrates almost all the *ideai*—and in case of those *ideai* not illustrated by the speech (like τραχύτης), to show why they are not. Special attention would have been devoted to the use of ἀκμή, which is a technique Hermogenes is particularly concerned with in the core, and which has no analogue in *Peri Politikou Logou*.

Let us now turn to *Against Leptines*, or to use its ancient title, *Peri Tes Ateleias* ('On the exemption'). It emerges from the references to it scattered through *Peri Ideon* but clustered in the section on κάλλος that he sees this speech as an example of a special

[20] See Wooten (1983).

style. This view can be seen as an extension of the view already
established in Dionysius that *Against Leptines* belongs to the
middle style (*Dem. Lex.* 14). But Hermogenes works this out in
much greater detail. There are three aspects to this.

(a) Sentence Structure and Κῶλα

Hermogenes says that κάλλος is produced primarily by long κῶλα,
but also by shorter κῶλα, when they are interconnected in such a
way that they are not complete in themselves but rather the
sentences as a whole have a sense of unity.[21] This effect is
illustrated by two passages from *Against Leptines*: first, section 41:

οὐ τοίνυν μόνον μὴ Λεύκων ἀδικηθῇ δεῖ σκοπεῖν, ᾧ φιλοτιμίας ἕνεκα ἡ περὶ τῆς
δωρεᾶς σπουδὴ γένοιτ' ἄν, οὐ χρείας, ἀλλὰ καὶ εἴ τις ἄλλος εὖ μὲν ἐποίησεν ὑμᾶς
εὖ πράττων, εἰς δέον δὲ νῦν γέγονεν αὐτῷ τὸ παρ' ὑμῶν λαβεῖν τότε τὴν ἀτέλειαν.

(So to save Leucon from injustice is not the only thing to consider—for
whom honour would be the source of his concern about his privilege, not
need—but also whether another man on the one hand served you well
while he was doing well, but now on the other hand has come to need the
exemption that he received from you then.)

The second passage is from the very beginning:

ἔστι δὲ οὐκ ἄδηλον, ὦ Ἀθηναῖοι, τοῦθ', ὅτι Λεπτίνης, κἄν τις ἄλλος ὑπὲρ τοῦ
νόμου λέγῃ, δίκαιον μὲν οὐδὲν ἐρεῖ περὶ αὐτοῦ, φήσει δ' ἀναξίους τινὰς ἀνθρώπους
εὑρομένους ἀτέλειαν ἐκδεδυκέναι τὰς λῃτουργίας, καὶ τούτῳ πλείστῳ χρήσεται
τῷ λόγῳ.

(It is not, Athenians, unclear that Leptines, and anyone else who speaks
on behalf of the law, will on the one hand say nothing just about it, but on
the other hand will say that certain people, by finding exception, have got
out of public services, and that he make most use of this argument.)

The interruptions (ἐπεμβολαί) do not seem to be interruptions but
rather to follow naturally, and because of that the overall effect is
that of a single unified sentence. He contrasts this effect to that of
Olynth. 2. 5:

καί δυοῖν ἕνεχ' ἡγοῦμαι συμφέρειν εἰρῆσθαι, τοῦ τ' ἐκεῖνον, ὅπερ καὶ ἀληθὲς
ὑπάρχει, φαῦλον φαίνεσθαι, καὶ τοὺς ὑπερεκπεπληγμένους ὡς ἄμαχόν τινα τὸν

---

[21] Hermogenes described this as a κόσμον . . . κομματικόν (not κωμματικόν, as in
Rabe's text: 307. 8), which is a pun, referring to ornament that has to do with
rhetorical κόμματα, but suggesting ornament that has to do with embellishment (cf.
κομμόω).

Φίλιππον ἰδεῖν ὅτι πάντα διεξελήλυθεν οἷς πρότερον παρακρουόμενος μέγας ηὐξήθη.

And I think it is worth telling on account of two things: the fact that he—*which is actually true*—is shown to be worthless, and those who are overwhelmed at Philip's apparent invincibility see that he has exhausted all the deceptions on which his earlier greatness was founded.)

In this case there is some κάλλος, on account of the balancing clauses and the composition, but the parenthetic clause (underlined) makes the effect γοργός.

Against Leptines also comes up in the discussion of μερισμός (the μέν . . . δέ construction) in the section on περιβολή. If the δέ clause follows at a long interval, the effect is said to be περιβολή; if it follows at a short interval, the effect is γοργότης. But if both μέν and δέ clauses contain balancing pairs of clauses, the effect is κάλλος, and to illustrate that he cites this Isocratean passage from *Against Leptines* (26):

παρὰ μὲν γὰρ τὰς τῶν χορηγιῶν δαπάνας μικρὸν ἡμέρας μέρος ἡ χάρις τοῖς θεωμένοις γίνεται, παρὰ δὲ τὰς τῶν εἰς τὸν πόλεμον παρασκευῶν ἀφθονίας πάντα τὸν χρόνον ἡ σωτηρία τῇ πόλει.

(On the one hand the result of the expenditures of the *khoregoi* is for a small part of the day the gratification for the spectators, on the other hand the result of generosity in the area of equipment for war is for all time security for the city. Trans. Vince (1930))

Hermogenes would presumably say (though he does not) that this is saved from being overly Isocratean by variation in the παρίσωσις (cf. 299–302).

(b) Ἀνάπαυσις

The opening sentence comes up in the discussion of ἀνάπαυσις in the section on κάλλος (310–11):

ἄνδρες δικασταί, μάλιστα μὲν εἵνεκα τοῦ νομίζειν συμφέρειν τῇ πόλει λελύσθαι τὸν νόμον, εἶτα καὶ τοῦ παιδὸς εἵνεκα τοῦ Χαβρίου, ὡμολόγησα τούτοις, ὡς ἂν οἷός τ᾽ ὦ, συνερεῖν.[a] ἔστι δ᾽ οὐκ ἄδηλον, ὦ ἄνδρες Ἀθηναῖοι, τοῦθ᾽ ὅτι Λεπτίνης,[b] κἄν τις ἄλλος ὑπὲρ τοῦ νόμου λέγῃ,[c] δίκαιον μὲν οὐδὲν ἐρεῖ[d] περὶ αὐτοῦ, φήσει δ᾽ ἀναξίους τινὰς ἀνθρώπους εὑρομένους ἀτέλειαν ἐκδεδυκέναι τὰς λῃτουργίας,[e] καὶ τούτῳ πλείστῳ χρήσεται τῷ λόγῳ.[f] ἐγὼ δ᾽ ὅτι μὲν τινῶν κατηγοροῦντα πάντας ἀφαιρεῖσθαι τὴν δωρειὰν τῶν ἀδίκων ἐστίν, ἐάσω[g].

(Gentlemen of the jury, on the one hand particularly because of the belief
that it is the city's advantage for the law to be broken, then also for the
sake of the son of Chabrias, I made an agreement with these men, in so far
as I am able, to support their cause.[a] It is not, Athenians, unclear that
Leptines, [b] and anyone else who speaks on behalf of the law, [c] will on the
one hand say nothing just about it, [d] but on the other hand will say that
certain people, by finding exception, have got out of public services, [e] and
that he make most use of this argument.[f] The point that to take away the
privilege from all because of an accusation against some is unjust I will
pass over.[g])

Hermogenes distinguishes *clausulae* that are 'steady' (βεβηκώς)
from *clausulae* that are 'unsteady' (οὐ βεβηκώς) or 'suspended'
(ἀνηρτημένος). Modern equivalents might be 'resolved' versus
'unresolved' or 'closural' *versus* 'anticlosural' (to use the aesthetic
terminology developed by Barbara Herrnstein Smith).[22] The
former tends to be associated with long syllables, and regular
patterns, the latter with short syllables and irregularity. It is the
latter which suggests κάλλος, while the former suggests σεμνότης.
The proem of *Against Leptines* seems to be dominated by
unresolved *clausulae*, for example *a, b, c, d* (apparently at the
end of a clause in Hermogenes' text), and *g*. But to provide
variation Demosthenes includes a few resolved *clausulae* also,
namely the perfect iambic *e* and the double cretic *f*.

(b) *Ἦθος with Respect to Criticizing your Opponent*

Another aspect of the *Against Leptines* that interests Hermogenes
is ἐπιείκεια: Demosthenes goes easy with Leptines, and deliberately draws attention to this technique, as in this manipulative
parenthesis (section 102): καὶ μοι μηδὲν ὀργισθῇς· οὐδὲν γὰρ ἐρῶ σε
φλαῦρον (And do not be angry at me, for I will not say anything
bad of you). Intuitively, one can see that this point is consonant
with those that precede. Although *Against Leptines* is a political
speech, the degree of aggression is very much limited.[23]

[22] Smith (1968).
[23] In section 13: Athenian national character is honest and good, whereas . . . τὸ
δὲ τοῦ θέντος τὸν νόμον, τὰ μὲν ἄλλ' ἔγωγ' οὐκ οἶδα, οὐδὲ λέγω φλαῦρον οὐδὲν οὐδὲ σύνοιδα,
ἐκ δὲ τοῦ νόμου σκοπῶν εὑρίσκω πολὺ τούτου κεχωρισμένον ('. . . as to the character of
the proposer of this law, I have no further knowledge of him, nor do I say or know
anything to his prejudice; but if I may judge from his law, I detect a character very
far removed from what I have described'). Another feature of this speech is that,
like the so-called *sumbouleutikoi* (i.e. *On the Symmories, For the Megalopolitans, On*

Hermogenes' work on the speech may have dealt with aspects of invention, and there may be a trace of one of these in the *Peri Methodou Deinotetos* (441. 8 ff.), which contains the statement that whereas Phormio, who preceded Demosthenes, used the headings: 'just', 'expedient', 'good', 'merit', Demosthenes changes the order of the points.[24] The author claims to have discussed this in his discussion of the speech. Although Hermogenes is not the author of *Peri Methodou Deinotetos*, is this perhaps a genuine fragment of Hermogenes that made its way into *Peri Methodou Deinotetos*?

Rhetoricians had been interested in the speech for a long time: Demetrius cited the opening; Cicero and Dionysius both mention it as an example of the middle style; *Peri Politikou Logou* often cites it.[25] The reason for Hermogenes' interest in the speech was that it exemplified a consistent style different from the later political style of *De Corona* and the political speeches, and somewhat like that of Isocrates (which was more consistently καλός), but subtly distinct from it. We can only guess how he would have explained the difference. One factor may have been that *Against Leptines* was an early speech, delivered, like *Against Androtion*, in 355 BCE. Hermogenes might have argued that this style was an early style, and, specifically perhaps, that he imitated it from Isocrates.[26] However, Syrianus, in his commentary, reports the views of Apsines and Aspasios, which may continue some of Hermogenes' observations. The basic point is that the case was difficult: Leptines was popular, unlike Ktesippos, on whose behalf it was delivered. Furthermore, the law of Leptines was very much to the people's advantage. And finally, the statute of limitations on the law had been passed. For all these reasons, a really forceful treatment was ill-advised, and Demosthenes elected a more diplomatic approach.[27]

Behalf of the Freedom of the Rhodians), there is ἐπιείκεια in so far as the speaker plays down what he could say against his opponent, and shows ἦθος (350).

[24] On the structure of the speech, see Kennedy (1963), 221.

[25] *Peri Politikou Logou*: 1: 64. 6; 11 ff.: 11. 1; 12: 26. 19; 21: 38. 11; 33: 42. 22; 41 ff.: 21. 6; 32. 4; 51: 32. 7; 52: 40. 3; 56: 64. 4; 64: 16. 3; 68: 27. 15; 71: 32. 12; 72: 21. 1; 73 ff.: 61. 18; 75: 41. 23; 76: 30. 14; 77: 47. 5; 80: 47. 10; 84: 40. 15; 89: 13. 19; 96: 27. 3; 100: 42. 7; 134: 40. 22; 141: 36. 13; 146: 22. 2; 153: 47. 23; 155: 41. 22; 157: 42. 25; 45. 5.

[26] For Demosthenes as a pupil of Isocrates see *Vit. Soph.* 504.

[27] Syrianus, 66. 7 ff.: ἠθικώτερον γὰρ μᾶλλον καὶ δι' ἐπιμελείας τε καὶ κάλλους

A similar style seems to have been believed to have been used in the proem of *Against Androtion* (1), the subject of an independent work by Hermogenes:

ὅπερ Εὐκτήμων, ὦ ἄνδρες δικασταί, παθὼν ὑπ' Ἀνδροτίωνος κακῶς, ἅμα τῇ τε πόλει βοηθεῖν οἴεται δεῖν καὶ δίκην ὑπὲρ αὐτοῦ λαβεῖν, τοῦτο κἀγὼ πειράσομαι ποιεῖν, ἐὰν ἄρ' οἷός τ' ὦ.

(Just as Euktemon, men of the jury, finding himself wronged by Androtion, thinks that he should help the city and obtain satisfaction on his own behalf, that I too will try to do, if I am able.)

Rhetoricians were understandably struck by the anomalous sequence of infinitives ending in - εῖν in the first sentence. The explanation that was applied in the case of *Against Leptines* does not work here, because the rhetorical situation was not a particularly sensitive one. Later commentators on *Peri Ideon* scratch their heads to second-guess Hermogenes. Most explanations start from the tradition that Androtion was a pupil of Isocrates, so that Demosthenes might be parodying him, or demonstrating that this style is easy to imitate, or perhaps just adapting his style to suit the character of the addressee.[28]

πεπλεγμένον Ἀψίνης καὶ Ἀσπάσιος ἀπεφήναντο τὸν πρὸς Λεπτίνην, τραχύτητος δὲ καὶ σφοδρότητος ἄμοιρον διά τε τὸ πρὸς ἔνδοξον πρόσωπον ὑπὲρ ἀδόξου τοῦ Κτησίππου ποιεῖσθαι τοὺς λόγους καὶ διὰ τὸ ἐξήκειν αὐτῷ τὸν χρόνον τῆς γραφῆς, ἣν ἐγράψατο πρότερον Βάθιππος ὁ Ἀψεφίωνος πατὴρ τὸν Λεπτίνου νόμον ἔτι μὴν διὰ τὸ συμφέρειν τῷ δήμῳ τὸν νόμον ἐπὶ τοὺς πλουσίους μετάγοντα τὰς λειτουργίας· ὥστε καὶ πρὸς ὀργὴν ἔτρεψεν ἂν τὸν ἀκροατήν, εἰ πρὸς καταφορὰν ἐχώρησεν ὁ ῥήτωρ τοῦ τὰ λυσιτελοῦντα νομοθετοῦντος. εὐθέως γοῦν ἐκ προοιμίων διὰ τῶν ἐξ ἐπιπλοκῆς βραχείας πεπλεγμένων κώλων τὴν περὶ τοῦ δικαίου τέθεικεν ἀντίθεσιν, καθ' ἣν σαθροτέροις ἦν ὁ Λεπτίνου νόμος— τῷ γὰρ συμφέροντι μᾶλλον ἔρρωτο—ἰσχυρὰν δὲ αὐτὴν δῆθεν ἐπιδεῖξαι βουλόμενος ἐπήνεγκεν ὡς εἰδὼς ἀκριβῶς "καὶ τούτῳ πλείστῳ χρήσεται τῷ λόγῳ". καίτοι δῆλον ὅτι τοῖς σαθροτέροις ἐπ' ἐλάχιστον οἱ ῥήτορες χρῶνται (Apsines and Aspasios showed that *Against Leptines* has more ἦθος, and is interwoven with ἐπιμέλεια and κάλλος, but is free of τραχύτης and σφοδρότης because it is directed against a popular individual and is on behalf of an unpopular one—Ktesippos—and because the time for the indictment brought by Bathippos, father of Apsephion, against the law of Leptines, had expired, and again because the law which directed liturgies toward the rich was to the advantage of the *demos*. Consequently, Demosthenes would have angered the audience, if he had attacked a man who passed a law in favour of the people. Right from the proem he cast the antithesis about justice in the form of *kola* interwoven with short interruptions, an antithesis in respect of which the law of Leptines was weak (it rested more on the argument from expediency), but pretending to want to show that this point was a strong one, he added that in full knowledge of it 'he will make much use of this argument'. But obviously orators do not rely on weak points like that). See also John of Sicily, 6. 347W.

[28] Syrianus, 64. 4 ff. John of Sicily, 6. 329–30W, gives quite an involved explanation: Androtion was a pupil of Isocrates, and so were the jurors, such

There may have been another reason for interest in *Against Leptines* in this period also. Immunity (ἀτέλεια) was an important issue in the cultural world of the second century. The emperor Hadrian had provided that certain categories of cultural experts, including ῥητόρες, should be immune from the obligation of providing services for their local communities, something that many of them might well have otherwise been asked to do, since they often came from distinguished backgrounds. However, the grant of immunity was not sacrosanct, and sophists who were asked to take on burdensome public services might find themselves obliged to make a case in defence of their personal immunity. In such circumstances we might expect them to have had recourse to Demosthenes' great speech on this theme, and indeed it was a popular theme at this period. For example, Leptines' law was the subject of a declamation by Lollianus of Ephesus;[29] and of several declamation themes mentioned by Apsines.[30] Aristides also wrote at least one declamation on this theme,[31] and this is particularly interesting because Aristides is also the most celebrated example of a sophist who successfully defended his grant of immunity after it was challenged. He had been asked by the Smyrnaeans to take on a series of offices, and he was forced to make a formal claim of ἀτέλεια before the Roman authorities several times, a terrible burden on a personality already overwhelmed by neurosis and self-doubt. In view of

---

was the influence of Isocrates (!); Demosthenes shows how easy the style is, especially since Diodorus was a private citizen; and, by starting with this style but moving away from it, Demosthenes shows how easy it is. For the idea that Demosthenes adapts his style to the speaker, I wonder if it is worth mentioning that a similar relation exists between Aristotle, whose speeches were abusive (257. 22) and the Ps. Demosthenic, *Against Aristogeiton* A´ which is abusive in tone. This idea of adapting the style to suit the character of the addressee will be grounded in the account of ἦθος in Plato's *Phaidros*.

[29] *Vit. Soph.* 527: Polemo denounces Leptines on account of his law, because the supply of corn has not reached Athens from Pontus: ὧδε ἤκμασεν· κέκλεισται τὸ στόμα τοῦ Πόντου νόμῳ καὶ τὰς Ἀθηναίων τροφὰς ὀλίγαι κωλύουσι συλλαβαί, καὶ ταὐτὸν δύνανται Λύσανδρος ναυμαχῶν καὶ Λεπτίνης νομομαχῶν ('His climax was as follows: "The mouth of the Pontus has been locked up by a law, and a few syllables keep back the food supply of Athens; so that Lysander fighting with his ships and Leptines fighting with his law have the same power"').

[30] Kohl (1915), 264 = Apsines 252. 16H.

[31] We know this from *Against Capito*. Two surviving declamations for and against Leptines' law have sometimes been ascribed to Aristides. See Boulanger (1923), 291–2, who is agnostic; Harry (1894), arguing in favour of authenticity.

that, it seems likely that his declamation on the Leptines theme was composed when his own ἀτέλεια was on his mind.[32]

The same speech and the subject of ἀτέλεια also come together in an anecdote reported by Philostratus concerning the sophists Heracleides of Lycia and Apollonius of Athens. Heracleides, who had recently been deprived of his immunity by the emperor after he lost in a debate with Apollonius, quipped to Apollonius that he ought to read *Against Leptines* if he was going to Egypt to see the emperor (who was born at Leptis); Apollonius replied: 'So should you—it's about immunity!'[33]

All of this suggests that well-publicized cases concerning ἀτέλεια encouraged an interest in *Against Leptines* at this period, and in devoting a special study to the speech, Hermogenes may have been catering for this interest. Certainly, the basic rhetorical lesson that the rhetoricians drew from the speech—that you cannot afford to be forceful or indignant in defending what is after all not a right but a costly privilege, so go easy, and do not provoke your benefactors—is one which may have been useful also to sophists defending their tax-exemptions before the Roman authorities in the second century CE.

---

[32] See Bowersock (1969), 36 ff.; the story is told in *Hieros Logos* 4.

[33] *Vit. Soph.* 601: πρεσβεύων δὲ παρὰ Σεβῆρον ἐν Ῥώμῃ τὸν αὐτοκράτορα ἀπεδύσατο πρὸς Ἡρακλείδην τὸν σοφιστὴν τὸν ὑπὲρ μελέτης ἀγῶνα, καὶ ἀπῆλθεν ὁ μὲν τὴν ἀτέλειαν ἀφαιρεθείς, ὁ δὲ Ἀπολλωνίου δῶρα ἔχων. διαδόντος δὲ τοῦ Ἡρακλείδου λόγον οὐκ ἀληθῆ ὑπὲρ τοῦ Ἀπολλωνίου, ὡς αὐτίκα δὴ βαδιουμένου ἐς Λιβύην, ἡνίκα ἦν ὁ αὐτοκράτωρ ἐκεῖ καὶ τὰς ἐξ ἁπάσης γῆς ἀρετὰς συνῆγεν, καὶ πρὸς αὐτὸν εἰπόντος "ὥρα σοι ἀναγιγνώσκειν τὸν πρὸς Λεπτίνην" "σοὶ μὲν οὖν, ἦ δ᾽ ὁ Ἀπολλώνιος, "καὶ γὰρ δὴ καὶ ὑπὲρ τῆς ἀτελείας γέγραπται." (While he was on an embassy to the emperor Severus at Rome, he engaged in a contest against the sophist Heracleides over declamation, and the result was that Heracleides lost his tax-exemption, while Apollonius received gifts. Heracleides spread a false story about Apollonius that he was about to set out to Libya, when the emperor was staying there and was gathering about him the talented from all over the world, and he said to Apollonius: 'It is time for you to read the speech *Against Leptines*.' 'No, it is time for you to read it, ' said Apollonius, 'After all, its subtitle is "On Behalf of the tax exemption"!').

VII
Aelius Aristides

The figure of Aelius Aristides looms large in the background of literary rhetoric of the second century CE. There are three main connections between him and *idea*-theory: (*a*) he is one of only two contemporary authors mentioned in *Peri Ideon*, and is cited twice; (*b*) excerpts from his works appear in *Peri Politikou Logou*—hence the former attribution of *Peri Politikou Logou* and *Peri Aphelous Logou* to Aristides;[1] (*c*) a passage from *Peri Tou Paraphthegmatos*, which happens to be one of the passages cited in *Peri Politikou Logou* and which I have already discussed in Chapter II, does in fact have a great deal in common with *idea*-theory.

I should also repeat (*d*) that, as I mentioned in Chapter IV, there is an intriguing parallel between the encomium of prose in the *Hymn to Sarapis* and the implication of Hermogenes' reading list that prose is a superior medium to poetry.

I. ARISTIDES AND THE RHETORICAL IDEAL

Of the excerpts from works by Aristides included in *Peri Politikou Logou* two are from *Peri Tou Paraphthegmatos* and one from *Kata Ton Exorkhoumenon*. The citation from the last is a fairly run-of-the-mill passage defining the power of rhetoric as persuasion.[2] More interesting, perhaps, is that *Kata Ton Exorkhoumenon* defends the thesis that orators should not have to lower their standards to suit the debased tastes of their audience, and that its title implies that oratory is a sacred mystery. Rhetorical skill has

---

[1] The passages are: *Or.* 28 (*Peri Tou Paraphthegmatos*) 119 ff. at 54. 16 ff.; *Or.* 28. 145 at 55. 15 ff.; *Or.* 34 (*Kata Ton Exorkhoumenon*) 33 at 65. 5; also *Or.* 45 (*Pros Platona Peri Rhetorikes*) 128D at 55. 15 ff.; *Or.* 29 (Sic. 1) 65. 13 ff. On these borrowings, see Boulanger (1923), 242–3.

[2] The citation is followed by a sentence asserting that speech is a demonstration of φιλανθρωπία and εὔνοια. This sentence does not occur in our texts of Aristides, although, as Schmid notes, it is in the same spirit. It could conceivably be from some lost work of Aristides.

come to be seen as something of absolute and sacred worth—a tenet typical of Aristides and entirely in the spirit of *idea*-theory. The premiss of *Peri Tou Paraphthegmatos*, the source for the other two citations in *Peri Politikou Logou*, is that Aristides has been criticized for praising himself by making a remark in passing (παράφθεγμα) in the course of a prose hymn in honour of Athena. The speech is a defence of that παράφθεγμα, and most of it is given over to a catalogue of illustrations of self-praise on the part of Greek authors, but it also includes passages describing the abilities and functions of the ideal orator. The second passage cited by *Peri Politikou Logou* (145) justifies the practice of self-praise as part of the virtue of the ideal man (an intelligent man sees the truth, a just man pays to himself and others their due, a brave man is not afraid to speak it, a man who criticizes such conduct is bad). In the first passage cited by *Peri Politikou Logou* (119 ff.) Aristides describes the orator's skill in mixing different qualities of language and combining various techniques:

ὅταν οὖν τις ἀγώνισμα ποιήσηται διὰ πάντων τῶν καλῶν τούτων διεξελθεῖν καὶ πάσας μίξεις μῖξαι περὶ τοὺς λόγους, καὶ πρῶτον μὲν τὰ ἤθη πρέποντα τοῖς καιροῖς ἀποδοῦναι, ἔπειτα τὰς συζυγίας, οὗ μὲν ἀκριβείας δεῖ, ἐνταῦθα ὥραν προστιθείς, οὗ δ᾽ ἐργασίας, ἐνταῦθα τάχος, τῷ δὲ περιττῷ σαφήνειαν, χάριν δὲ οὗ σεμνότης, οὗ δὲ εὕρεσις, ἐνταῦθα διαχείρισιν, οὗ δὲ τολμήματα, ἐνταῦθα ἀσφάλειαν, ἐφ᾽ ἅπασι δὲ ῥαστώνην καὶ δρόμον, καί μοι παρείη περὶ τούτων ἄμεινον σοῦ καὶ τῶν σοὶ προσομοίων ἐπίστασθαι, σκοτοδινιᾷ δὴ πᾶς ἐνταῦθα ἀκροατὴς καὶ οὐκ ἔχει τίς γένηται, ἀλλ᾽ ὥσπερ ἐν παρατάξει κυκλούμενοι θορυβοῦνται, καὶ ὡς ἕκαστος ἔχει φύσεως ἢ δυνάμεως οὕτως ἐπαινεῖ, ὁ μὲν τῆς λέξεως τὴν ἀκρίβειαν, ὁ δὲ τοῦ νοῦ τὴν λεπτότητα, ὡς ὡραῖα.

(Whenever someone takes on the challenge to proceed through all these kinds of beauty and to use all the oratorical mixtures, and first of all to present a character suitable to the occasion, and next to preserve a balance: where there is need of precision, here adding charm, and where there is need of elaboration, here adding brevity, and adding clarity to redundance, and grace where there is gravity, and where there is use of content, here adding that of arrangement, and where there is boldness, here adding caution, and, to top it all, an easy and fluent delivery—and permit me to understand these matters better than you and your like—at this point every member of the audience grows dizzy and does not know who he becomes, but as if they were enclosed in a battle line, they are bewildered, and each offers praise according to his own natural endowments or faculties, one for precision in the vocabulary, another for charming delicacy of thought, and another for beauty.) (Trans. Behr, 1981)

The first passage is reminiscent both of the picture of the rhetorical ideal in Cicero's *Orator* and of Dionysius' image of Demosthenes, as Proteus, but also suggestive of some passages of *Peri Ideon*, so suggestive, in fact, that its relevance would have been noticed even without the citation in *Peri Politikou Logou*.[3] Most of the techniques the orator operates with here are stylistic qualities, some of them identical or similar to qualities found in *idea-theory*.[4] However, some seem to be more like moral qualities (e.g. 'boldness' and 'safety'). Invention and arrangement also play a smaller part. After this Aristides goes on to describe the orator's reactions upon not being appreciated correctly. In traditional oratory, the aim is to influence the audience by getting them on your side. Here, the orator aims to show off his skill, and if the audience are not up to appreciating it, the problem is theirs. The ostensible aim of *Peri Tou Paraphthegmatos* is to prove that this attitude is well established in Greek literature, but even if it was, it had never been given the attention it received from Aristides.[5]

For Aristides, the ideal is realized only in the works of Homer (not a real exception, since he was not an orator) and perhaps also in his own. Most other orators have not attempted to handle all the forms of language, but have mastered only a few, and Demosthenes is by implication one of these.[6] All of this is reminiscent of

---

[3] 2. 529–30 Dindorf. This passage made its way somehow into the text of *Peri Politikou Logou* (= 141–3), and Hermogenes may have known it from there, as did a passage from *Kata Ton Exorkhoumenon* describing the power of rhetoric to persuade. The presence of these passages in the text of Aristides might be used to strengthen the argument for links between Aristides and *idea-theory*, but unfortunately we have no idea of the date when the interpolations were made.

[4] σεμνότης is the same, as is σαφήνεια; ὥρα recalls ὡραῖος (= γλυκύς) in *Peri Ideon*; τάχος suggests γοργότης.

[5] The earliest trace of the idea of the theme is in Aristotle's discussion of the ἀλαζών and the εἴρων in *EN* 4. 7. We find the question of to what extent it is permissible in a speech for the speaker to praise himself better developed in Plutarch's *Peri Tou Heauton Epainein Anepiphthonos*. Radermacher showed convincingly that this topic had a background in the rhetorical schools: we find examples in Alexander Noumeniou, Quintilian, *IO* 11. 1, in the Ps. Dionysian *Peri Ton Eskhematismenon Logon*, also in the *Peri Methodou Deinotetos* 441. 16 ff.). This tradition is so well established that there can be no question but that Aristides will have been familiar with it. See the introduction to the Loeb 5. 110 ff. (De Lacy and Einarson); Radermacher (1897); also Pohlenz (1913), 358 ff.

[6] οἷόν τι λέγω, ἔστι κάλλη περὶ λόγους, ὡσαύτως δὲ περὶ ποίησιν, καί τινες ἰδέαι καὶ πόρρω καὶ ἐγγὺς ἀλλήλων, ἃς ἅμα μὲν πάσας λαβεῖν οὐ ῥᾴδιον, μέρος δὲ ἕκαστος

the situation in Cicero's *Orator*, where again the ideal of oratorical perfection is one that not even Demosthenes has reached.[7] Since in the case of *Peri Tou Paraphthegmatos* the true subject is explicitly Aristides, it looks as if he regards himself as superior to any classical author, including Demosthenes. From the point of view of *Peri Ideon* that is an incredible claim, but confirmation is to be found in *Hieros Logos* 4. 19, where he recounts a dream in which Rhosander, a philosopher, said to him: 'you have surpassed Demosthenes in dignity, so that not even the philosophers can scorn you.' Aristides mentions that he was greatly encouraged by this dream (no doubt believing it to have been sent by Asclepius, who had encouraged him to return to declamation after his illness). For Aristides, classical models were there to be surpassed, not worshipped.[8]

So there has been an interesting change of emphasis: the image of Demosthenes as ideal orator in *Peri Ideon* is similar to, and perhaps modelled on, this passage of *Peri Tou Paraphthegmatos* (or similar ones); for Aristides this was a standard that had eluded any one classical writer (except Homer), though modern writers and orators might yet attain it, and Aristides himself seems to have believed that he had done so. What Hermogenes did was to appropriate an abstract ideal grounded in the aspirations of contemporary writers, and apply it to Demosthenes, arguing that it was not after all a theoretical abstraction, but that in the works of the greatest of the Attic orators it had achieved a lasting textual realization.

Aristides shared the common view that Demosthenes was one of the two greatest classical writers, the other being Plato.[9] As a sophist and orator, one might have expected him to prefer Demosthenes, whom in one passage he calls an image of a Hermes.[10]

ἀποτεμνόμενος κατὰ τοῦτο ηὐδοκίμησεν· Ὅμηρον δέ, εἰ βούλει, ποιητῶν ἐξαίρει λόγου (What do I mean? There are kinds of beauty in oratory, and just as in poetry, there are also certain *ideai*, some of which are far separated, others closely related to one another; and it is not easy to acquire all of them together, but each writer has taken for himself one style and become distinguished for this. But if you wish, except Homer in the case of poets from the discussion) (Or. 28. 119).

[7] Demosthenes has not reached the standard: *Orator* 104.

[8] See *In Defence of Oratory* 120. It seems to me incidentally that it is this attitude of Aristides toward the classical model that makes it quite impossible that he could be the author of *Peri Politikou Logou* or *Peri Aphelous Logou*.

[9] *To Capito* 6.

[10] *In Defence of the Four* 663.

There is a sort of comparison between them in *In Defence of the Four*, where he is concerned to defend the reputations of four great democratic leaders attacked by Plato in the *Gorgias*, and he compares Plato's tone with that of *De Corona* 314, where Demosthenes says to Aeschines: 'you have compared my policy with that of past generations. And rightly so.'[11] Aristides calls this passage φιλάνθρωπον ἅμα καὶ γενναῖον ('kind and noble'), and he contrasts it with the more violent language of Plato. He goes on to say that when, in the passage immediately following this, Demosthenes defends himself against the charge, he could have been a lot more forceful in his defence. So at least here Aristides seems to be saying that Demosthenes has a flexible style, and that, in this respect at least, he is better than Plato.

Aristides' argument here points forward to *Peri Ideon*: in Hermogenean terms, it amounts to saying that the passage generates ἐπιείκεια and ἦθος by self-deprecation (ἐλάττωσις).[12] And in the same way, I believe that the presentation of Demosthenes in *Peri Ideon* as a perfect model, which perhaps borrows something from Cicero's *Orator* and from the image of Proteus in *Peri Tes Demosthenous Lexeos*, owes still more to the passage of the *Peri Tou Paraphthegmatos* cited earlier. This provides a striking precedent to the concept of δεινότης in *Peri Ideon* which presupposes that skill is something that the ideal speaker should both possess and manifest, while avoiding excessive flamboyance.

But although the way they describe the rhetorical ideal is similar, there is a major difference in their deployment of the concept. Hermogenes looks back to the great orators of the past, and he believes that the ideal has already been realized in Demosthenes. For Aristides no writer of the past comes close to the ideal with the possible exception of Homer, and the implication is that he himself is a candidate for this role.

---

[11] 500 ff.; 2. 347 Dindorf; Demosthenes says: εἶτα τῶν πρότερον γεγενημένων ἀγαθῶν ἀνδρῶν μέμνησαι. καὶ καλῶς ποιεῖς (Then you recall the heroes of past generations. And you do this fairly).

[12] Again, in *Hieros Logos* 5. 63 Aristides dreamt that he was at a temple of Plato, when someone said: 'there should be three temples of Plato' and Aristides replied: 'eighty of Demosthenes, and certainly of Homer, I think.' This indicates the belief that Demosthenes and Homer are better writers than Plato.

2. ARISTIDES, HERMOGENES, AND THE CANON

What did Hermogenes think of Aristides? On the one hand, the fact that he cites him at all, and not just once but twice, suggests that he held him in high esteem. Furthermore, the citations come in distinguished places: in the section on σεμνότης and in that on ἀλήθεια. Both citations come from declamations on historical themes. It is clear, then, that it is as a writer of πολιτικὸς λόγος that Hermogenes sees Aristides as making a contribution. Well, that is interesting, because a millennium later Aristides' reputation was as a writer in the ἀφελές style. Theodorus Metochites knew the *Hieroi Logoi*, and believed that Aristides' title to greatness was principally on this basis.[13] Hermogenes might have mentioned him for these, or for his *Hymns*, or for the Panathenaic oration, or for his writings in defence of rhetoric against Plato. But it is in the area of πολιτικὸς λόγος that Aristides had made his contribution, according to Hermogenes. And one suspects that this would have been a contemporary view, and one held by Aristides himself. The *Hieroi Logoi* had been commissioned by Asclepius, it is true; but, on the other hand, Asclepius had also encouraged Aristides to pursue declamation, so here too Aristides' literary activity had been sanctioned by the god.

Although Hermogenes recognizes Aristides' outstanding abilities as a declaimer, he does not go along with Aristides' own view that he is better than the classical models. This point becomes clear, I believe, in the section ἀλήθεια, where Hermogenes says that a certain prayer from Aristides' declamation: *Epi Tou Pempein Boetheian Tois En Sikelia* (40), is ἀληθέστερον ('more veracious') than one in *De Corona*, but stresses that he does not believe that the passage from Aristides is better ('I would be mad if I said that') (354. 1).[14] Hermogenes also cites from Aristides' *Against Kallixenos* in the section on σεμνότης. He cites an *ekphrasis* of a storm, which is part of an attempt to excuse the conduct of the generals at Arginousai (244. 23 ff.):[15]

---

[13] See the edition of Gigante (1969). Theodorus solves the problem by making Aristides into a master of ἀφέλεια by concentrating on the desultory *Hieroi Logoi*. For more on the *Hieroi Logoi* as instances of ἀφέλεια, see Menander Rhetor, 391. 19 ff. (dreams and λαλιά), Baumgart (1874), 103; Schmid (1887–97), i. 190.

[14] For this speech of Aristides, see Pernot (1981).

[See p. 102 for n. 15]

σκηπτὸς ἦν, ὦ Καλλίξενε, σκηπτὸς ὁ ταῦτα κωλύσας οὔτε λόγῳ ῥητὸς οὔτε ἔργῳ
φορητός· ἄρτι μὲν γὰρ συνιούσης τῆς ναυμαχίας ὤδινεν ἡ θάλασσα καὶ κατέβαινεν
Ἑλλησποντίας λαμπρός.

(It was a sudden storm, Callixenus, a sudden storm that prevented this,
that cannot be described in words, and that could not be resisted in
action. Almost as soon as the battle had begun, the sea began to swell and
a strong wind blowing from the Hellespont swooped down on them.)

This need not show that Aristides had unusually great abilities
either, because the reason Hermogenes cites it is to illustrate the
use of an *ekphrasis* dealing with a storm, a type of ἔννοια for which
there are no examples in Demosthenes. Although Hermogenes
does not make this explicit, his own view might very well be that
Aristides erred by including a thought of such comparatively
unmitigated σεμνότης, especially in a speech on a political subject.[16] The absence of such passages in Demosthenes is not an
accident; Demosthenes could never have gone in for such a
sustained use of such a theme.[17]

It seems to have been commonly felt in the Second Sophistic
that modern writers could surpass those of the past. We have seen
that Aristides felt this way about himself. There are signs that
Arrian, loyal follower of Xenophon as he was, also felt that he was
superior to his model. Herodes Atticus also attracted such comments: according to a passage from *Lives of the Sophists* his
associates flattered him with the observation that he belonged in
the canon of the ten orators, and Herodes modestly replied that he
was at any rate better than Andocides (Andocides is tenth in the
canon of ten).[18] On another occasion Herodes was compared to
Demosthenes, a comparison he declined.[19] Again, Atticus, the
father of Herodes, had admired Scopelian of Clazomenae so much
that he had given orders that statues of the orators of classical

[15] Aristides had a special talent for describing storms; there are many such
descriptions in the *Hieroi Logoi*.

[16] I am also suspicious of the clausula: οὔτε λόγῳ ῥητὸς οὔτε ἔργῳ φορητός. Could
Hermogenes have cited this without being aware, or intending us to think, that it is
an intolerable jingle?

[17] For the storm *topos* in declamation, see Innes and Winterbottom (1988), 171
on Sopatros, *DZ* case 37, 224. 20 (trial of generals at Arginousai), citing among
other things P. Yale 1729 (*ArchPap* 24/25 (1976), 55–84) with Stephens (1983).

[18] *Vit. Soph.* 564–5 (72. 11 Kayser). Andocides was one of the worse among the
Attic orators also according to Quintilian, *IO* 10. 21.

[19] Rohde (1900), 350 n. 2; *Vit. Soph.* 539 (49. 25 Kayser).

Athens be pelted with stones because they had corrupted his son's eloquence.[20]

We have seen that Hermogenes includes Nicostratus in his canon of three ἀφελεῖς writers. Nicostratus also belonged to a modern canon of ten 'secondary' (ἐπιδεύτεροι) orators, according to Suda, but that was a much more modest achievement.[21] Equally Hermogenes might have included Aristides in his survey of literature (most likely in the section on πολιτικὸς λόγος). But he omits him. Why? He thought highly enough of him to mention him in the core; Aristides' extremely high opinion of himself might also be thought to justify inclusion.

In principle, Hermogenes ought to have been able to include a modern orator in the canon. He could not, I think, have allowed that anyone could surpass Demosthenes, who is perfect. But a modern orator could have come close. Certainly, he would not have accepted that some general decline in politics or morals prevented such a development, because for him the only essential component in rhetoric is technique.[22] Nor was it a question of a fixed canon of ten, which would admit no additions, because Hermogenes himself alters the canon of ten by including Critias.[23]

The omission was noticed by Schmid, who suggested that Hermogenes might have written *Peri Ideon* at a point when Nicostratus was already dead and Aristides still alive.[24] There is, unfortunately, no way of determining the relative dates of Aristides and Nicostratus,[25] but even if we allow that Nicostratus died sometime before Aristides, there is another problem: surely if his being alive was a sufficient reason for not mentioning a writer, Hermogenes would not have mentioned him in the main part of *Peri Ideon* either.

The only explanation that makes sense is one of quality: Hermogenes did not think that Aristides was up to it, nor *a fortiori*

---

[20] *Vit. Soph.* 521 (34. 7 ff. Kayser).

[21] ἐτάχθη δὲ ἐν τοῖς κριθεῖσιν ἐπιδευτέροις δέκα ῥήτορσι (he was ranked among the ten secondary orators selected) and H. Rabe (ed.), *Scholia in Lucianum* (Leipzig, 1906), 189. 11 ff. A comparable secondary canon from the Alexandrian period is the Pleiad of tragedians (see *TrGF* 1, Cat A5).

[22] Cf. the comparison with Ps. Longinus in II.

[23] Cf. IV.

[24] Schmid and Stählin (1924), II. ii. 817 n. 4.

[25] For evidence for the life of Nicostratus, see Stegemann (1936), 551–2. Suidas says that he was a contemporary of Dio of Prusa (40–118 CE) and Aristides (117–89?), but this is more than a little vague.

was any other modern orator. And, as we have seen, his comments about the style of Aristides in the core are not unambiguously positive.[26] So in the end we see that Hermogenes is a classicist by the standards of his time: believing not that ancient levels of eloquence are unattainable because of some political or moral decline (like Ps. Longinus), but rather that they are still attainable if the right techniques are learnt, although in fact modern orators have not succeeded in this.[27]

It would perhaps be misleading to end by giving the impression that there is a gulf between *idea*-theory and contemporary literature. Certainly, the rhetoricians play little explicit homage to writers of their own times, and instead display an admiration for classical models which sometimes borders on the uncritical. But this is only one side of a more complex picture. Looking back over this study as a whole, I hope to have demonstrated that *idea*-theory has two voices. On the one hand, it is grounded in the literary models of the past, and continues the traditional categories of Greek stylistic theory. But at the same time, some features of it have a contemporary resonance, such as its stylistic vocabulary, enriched by the critical terminology of sophistic declamation, its high estimation of prose *vis-à-vis* poetry, and its appreciation of Xenophon; in these respects, and in others, the *idea*-theorists can be seen to engage with and respond to the cultural values of the Antonine Age.

---

[26] In Rutherford (1992) I suggested that in not including Aristides in his survey Hermogenes may have believed that there was something unique and primary about the great Attic orators of the 5th–4th cents. BCE that qualified them to be models for future writers in ὁ πολιτικὸς λόγος, and that whatever standard of excellence might be achieved by Aristides or any other contemporary orator, it would always be a derivative of these models and never deserve to be imitated by others in its own right. In this respect Hermogenes' view about the canon of οἱ ἀφελεῖς would be significantly different: here he suggests that the canon is, so to speak, an open one and that talented modern writers such as Nicostratus can not only excel in it but excel in an original way so that they become models for others.

[27] Hermogenes' view ends up looking like Messala's in Tacitus' *Dialogus* (28–35); while Ps. Longinus' position is more like that of the final speaker (whether Julius Secundus or Maternus), who sees the decline of oratory as principally a matter of changed political conditions (c. 40). Aristides' view, by elimination, has something in common with the view of Aper.

APPENDIX A

The Relationship between *Peri Ideon* and *Peri Heureseos*

I have referred to this thesis already (pp. 46–7). There are three parts to the argument.

I. AKME LOGOU

We saw earlier that in *Vitae Sophistarum* we find the words ἀκμή/ἀκμαῖος/ ἀκμάζω in a rhetorical sense. The words ἀκμή/ἀκμαῖος/ἀκμάζω seem to refer to a climax in a declamatory performance, or, of a declamatory theme, the quality of accommodating such a performance.

A close analogue in rhetorical theory is found in *Peri Heureseos*.[1] The following passages are important.

1. At 2. 7 (125. 3 ff.), ἀκμή of διήγησις is said to come about if (*a*) an event, (*b*) one's opinion about it, or (*c*) the reason for that opinion is stated several times in different words, each statement corresponding to a κῶλον. The author also specifies that there is more ἀκμή if (*c*) comes last.

2. At *Peri Heureseos* 3. 13 (162. 19 ff.) the author draws a distinction between ἐπιχειρήματα that are ἀποδεικτικά (demonstrative) and require 'political' expression, and ones that are πανηγυρικά (panegyrical), and he advises that if you have some of both, you should keep the πανηγυρικά ones till last, in order to increase the ἀκμή, and to suggest that the heat of the speech has forced this upon you. The focus on the end of the speech can be compared to passage (1); the association with the appearance of emotional climax matches some passages in *Lives of the Sophists*.

3. The discussion of σχήματα λόγου in *Peri Heureseos* 4 (a strange topic for a work on invention)[2] begins (c. 1 (170. 20 ff.)) with a division

---

[1] For *Peri Heureseos* in general, see Kennedy (1972), 626 ff..; id. (1983), 87 ff.; Radermacher (1912), 877.

[2] *Prima facie* there is some reason for thinking that *Peri Heureseos* was not conceived as a whole and that *Peri Heureseos* 4 or possibly *Peri Heureseos* 3–4 together (both of which are each much longer than *Peri Heureseos* 1 and 2) have replaced an earlier book on the *epilogue*. I would want to reserve judgement on this, for one cannot be sure that works on εὕρεσις from this period always included a treatment of the *epilogue* and in any case this author may well have had grounds for omitting it, perhaps feeling that it was covered sufficiently in other works; see e.g.

between ἐπιχειρήματα or ἐργασίαι that are πολιτικά, which are ἀποδεικτικά and ones that are πανηγυρικά (whether they are examples of drawn from παραβολή, 'comparison'). The former should be expressed στρογγύλως (roundly) with ἀντίθετα (antitheses) and περίοδοι (periods); while the latter should be extended πνευματικῶς καὶ ἀκμαίως (in the manner of *pneuma* and peak).[3] A different stylistic treatment is recommended for a third element of argumentation, the ἐνθύμημα.[4] One side of this—the idea that political arguments should be expressed roundly and with antitheses and periods—corresponds to the rounded, tightly constructed rhetorical period, traditionally distinguished from the so-called historical period, which was regarded as loose and slack and generally unsuitable for use in intense public oratory.[5] What is new about the application of the round style in *Peri Heureseos* is that it is the only one of two alternative modes of expression available to the political orator. The other mode, that involving πνεῦμα and ἀκμή, probably has no such ancestry.

4. The main account of ἀκμή is in 4. 4 (183. 10 ff.), a long chapter, devoted to πνεῦμα, which seems to mean a long sentence, longer than a περίοδος.[6] The way to produce a πνεῦμα is to sustain the same σχῆμα λόγου

Apsines 1. 292. 12 ff. Sp.-H.; *Anon. Seg.* 1. 387. 22 ff. Sp.-H.). In addition, common elements link *Peri Heureseos* 1–2 and *Peri Heureseos* 3–4: first, they share rare technical terms, e.g. ὑποδιαίρεσις and ἀξίωσις; again remarks about style are found not only in *Peri Heureseos* 4 (where it is the main theme) but in other books also, e.g. δριμύτης is mentioned not only in *Peri Heureseos* 4 but in *Peri Heureseos* 3; ἀκμή in *Peri Heureseos* 2–3, as well as in *Peri Heureseos* 4; περιβολή, once in *Peri Heureseos* 4, once in *Peri Heureseos* 1; πλατύνω in *Peri Heureseos* 2–3, e.g. 120. 3; πολιτικός and πανηγυρικός in *Peri Heureseos* 1–2 as well as in *Peri Heureseos* 3–4 (107. 10 and 184. 6). Odd, then, that toward the beginning of *Peri Heureseos* 1 the author apologizes for the fact that style is *not* his subject (94. 22 ff.). This might indicate *either* that he had no intention of dealing with style at any point, which would strengthen the case against *Peri Heureseos* 4 having been part of the original plan, *or* that he could have been its author, since it shows awareness of the need for stylistic elaboration in addition to the bare framework of the thought; how better to complete his work, than to add an appendix on σχήματα λόγου.

[3] The terms πολιτικά and πανηγυρικά, here applied to two classes of argument available to the political orator, are used in the same sense in *Peri Heureseos* 3 (162. 18 ff.) and also in *Peri Heureseos* 1, in this case forms of proem (106. 20 ff.; 108. 10 ff.).

[4] I draw attention to a minor case of crossed categories: example and comparison are associated with epicheiremes and developments alike in the panegyric class, whereas in *Peri Heureseos* 3 they were listed among the sources for developments: see 148. 23.

[5] Though Dionysius hints at *Dem. Lex.* 43, 227. 6 ff. that Demosthenes uses both types.

[6] Πνεῦμα is defined at 183. 13–16: πνεῦμα is a composition of language, rounding off a thought in *kola* and *kommata*, measured against sustained breath in accordance with the voice of the speaker. The term occurs only in *Peri Heureseos* 4 and 3. 10, and also in *Peri Aphelous Logou* at 79. 8; occasionally in a more general sense in

(186. 3 ff.), where σχῆμα λόγου means a type of speech act such as the declaration, question, refutation, demonstration, address, denial, prohibition. A certain amount of variation is possible and desirable. For one thing (187. 21), given the same structure, you can vary the number, gender, case, and inflection of the constituent words; you can also vary the particular adverbs and pronouns employed (188. 14).[7] You can also vary the σχῆμα, and this is where ἀκμή comes in. You can either vary the σχῆμα within the same πνεῦμα, for example changing it right at the end of the πνεῦμα, as in *De Corona* 71 ('But here was a man annexing Euboea . . . by these acts was he, or was he not, committing injustice, breaking treaty, and violating the terms of the peace?'). This is called ἀκμὴ λόγου. Or you can vary it from one πνεῦμα to another, and that is called ἀκμὴ νοημάτων.

> πολλάκις γὰρ τοῦτο οὕτω περικαλλῆ τὸν λόγον ἐποίησεν, ὥστε καὶ εἰς τρίτον σχῆμα μεταβαίνοντα ἀναστῆσαι τοὺς ἀκούοντας, ὥσπερ ἀκμαζούσης τῆς τοῦ λέγοντος φορᾶς, ἣν παρίστησι τοῖς ἀκούουσιν ἡ τοῦ σχήματος μεταβολή.

(Often this makes the language so beautiful that, changing[8] to a third figure, it make the audience rise up. It is as if the speaker's impetus, which the change of figure conveys to the audience, is at a peak.)

To illustrate ἀκμὴ νοημάτων, the author cites *De Corona* 44–9. The first πνεῦμα seems to correspond to the description of Philip gaining power in the North in c. 44; the second to the string of genitive absolutes concerning traitors in c. 45. The third one comes somewhere in cc. 46–9, and my guess it that it is meant to be the famous description of the traitors in c. 48: ('Lasthenes was hailed as a friend—until he betrayed Olynthus; Timolaus, until he brought Thebes to ruin; Eudicus and Simos of Larissa, until they put Thessaly under Philip's heel').

Peri Heureseos 4. 4 concludes with advice on the order of points (190. 20 ff.): greater ἀκμή is produced if the better points are placed last.

5. The last reference to ἀκμή in *Peri Heureseos* comes in 4. 9, the chapter on ἐπιφώνημα (198. 1 ff.), where the idea is that when you have a long πνεῦμα with many κῶλα, an effect of ἀκμή can be generated by a final κῶλον which sums up what precedes, as Homer, *Il.* 16. 102 ff. ('Ajax no longer remained . . .') is completed by line 111 ('. . . Everywhere evil was piled on evil.').

To summarize: ἀκμή in *Peri Heureseos* is a sort of culminating effort, associated with the heat of debate (163. 3), with amplifying the language (162. 22, 191. 3), with the impetus of the speaker which makes the audience rise (189. 9 ff.). The author of *Peri Heureseos* associates it

Dionysius, for which see Geigenmüller (1908), 63; several times, also in a more general sense, in *Vit. Soph.* (503, 564, 580, 627).

[7] This is what traditional theory called ἐξαλλαγή or ἄλλαξις.

[8] I read μεταβαίνοντα for μεταβαίνοντας at 189. 9.

particularly with panegyrical ἐπιχειρήματα (3. 13), and with the πνεύματα with which he thinks these should be expressed (4. 1, 4. 4). Κῶλα and κόμματα play an important part in the πνεύματα that produce ἀκμή (183. 17 ff.). Κῶλα also play an important part in ἀκμή of narration in *Peri Heureseos* 2. 7. The relationship to *Lives of the Sophists* is close. Compare τὰς ἀκμαιοτέρας τῶν ὑποθέσεων at c. 519 and ἀκμὰς τῶν ὑποθέσεων at c. 537 with ἀκμὰς τῶν ὑποθέσεων in *Peri Heureseos*. At c. 537 notice the parallels between Polemo's jumping up from his chair and the effect the speaker's impetus has on the audience in *Peri Heureseos*; and between Polemo's rounding off the κῶλον without effort and the idea of ἐπιφώνημα associated with ἀκμή according to *Peri Heureseos* 4. 9.

In *Peri Ideon* ἀκμή is unique in being wholly a combination[9] of elements that belong primarily to two other *ideas*: from τραχύτης and σφοδρότης it borrows aggressive ἔννοιαι and direct μέθοδοι, from λαμπρότης long κῶλα; from all three of the above *ideas* it derives λέξις (mild tropes from λαμπρότης, harsh ones from τραχύτης and σφοδρότης) and also σχήματα (ἀπόστασις and the like from λαμπρότης; aggressive ἐρωτήσεις and ἀποστροφή from τραχύτης and σφοδρότης).[10] As a mixture, ἀκμή represents the mutual reinforcement of two areas of μέγεθος—aggressive attack and amplifying exposition.[11] Ἀκμή is thus essentially a maximization of different strengths within μέγεθος and, though Hermogenes never makes this explicit, the word ἀκμή seems to connote this maximization.

Σχήματα seem to be important, particularly one derived from λαμπρότης—ἀπόστασις (270. 13 ff.)—which means 'separation' or 'asyndeton', a technique mentioned a few times in *Lives of the Sophists*:[12]

κατὰ μέν γὰρ λαμπρότητος σχῆμα ἀκμή γέγονεν ἐν τῷ ἐξέστητε, ὦ Ἀθηναῖοι, τῆς τάξεως, ἐφ' ἧς ὑμᾶς οἱ πρόγονοι κατέλιπον καὶ πάλιν πλεονέκτημα, ὦ Ἀθηναῖοι, μέγα ὑπῆρξε Φιλίππῳ· ἐξ ἀποστάσεως γὰρ εἰσῆκται. κἀκεῖνα δὲ τοιαῦτα· μή μοι σωζέσθω μηδ' ἀπολλύσθω μηδείς, ὃν ἂν ὁ δεῖνα ἢ ὁ δεῖνα βούληται καὶ τὸ πολλὰ ἂν εἰπεῖν ἔχοιεν Ὀλύνθιοι νῦν, ἃ τοτ' εἰ προείδοντο, οὐκ ἂν ἀπώλοντο καὶ ἕως ἂν σώζηται τὸ σκάφος, ἄν τε μεῖζον ἄν τ' ἔλαττον ᾖ, τότε

---

[9] Hermogenes sometimes calls ἀκμή a mixture (270. 4; 273. 4, 16), sometimes a result of *sharing* (276. 21; 277. 13; and also the introduction, 225. 19, 22; 226. 4 ff.). Lindberg (1977), 64 ff., attaches special importance to this fact. It makes little difference: if it is a *mixture*, then it is an effect produced by the orator; if it is a *sharing*, it might be seen as an integral part of the grammar of the system.

[10] Compare especially the introduction to the section on τραχύτης which looks forward to the group τραχύτης, σφοδρότης, λαμπρότης, and ἀκμή (254. 22 ff.).

[11] So Voit (1934), 57–8, analyses δεινότης as a combination of *das Überwältige* on the one hand and *das Erhabene* on the other. For reinforcing mixtures, see Lindberg (1977), 61.

[12] Asyndeton is associated with Gorgias at *Vit. Soph.* 493 (ἀπόστασις and προσβολή); Critias at *Vit. Soph.* 503; also with Antipater of Hierapolis at *Vit. Soph.* 607.

χρὴ καὶ ναύτην καὶ κυβερνήτην καὶ πάντα ἄνδρα ἑξῆς προθύμους εἶναι, ἐπειδὰν
δὲ ἡ θάλαττα ὑπέρσχῃ, μάταιος ἡ σπουδή. ταῦτα δὲ καὶ πλέον ἔχει τι· οὐδὲ γὰρ
ἐξ ἀποστάσεως εἰσῆκται ὥσπερ τὸ πλεονέκτημα, ὦ Ἀθηναῖοι, μέγα ὑπῆρξε
Φιλίππῳ καὶ τὸ ἐξέστητε, ὦ Ἀθηναῖοι, τῆς τάξεως, ἀλλ' ἀπροσδοκήτως ἐξ
ἐπεμβολῆς. διὸ καὶ μειζόνως ἐκλάμπει καὶ πλέον ἔχει τὸ φαιδρὸν ἡ ἀκμή·
κυρίως γὰρ τοῦτ' ἂν ἀπόστασις εἴη, ἐὰν δὲ καταστήσας εἰς ἀρχὴν ἀνάγῃς τὸν
λόγον, ἧττον ἐμφαίνεται τὸ ἀποστατικόν, οἷον τοσοῦτον ὑπειπών. πλεονέκτημα, ὦ Ἀθηναῖοι καὶ τὰ ἑξῆς· προσδοκήσασι γὰρ ἡμῖν ἐνταῦθα ἡ
ἀπόστασις ὤφθη· ἐκεῖ δὲ οὐ πάνυ τι τὸ ἀποστατικόν, οἷον νὴ Δία, ἔδει γὰρ
τὸ καὶ τὸ γενέσθαι καὶ τὸ μὴ γενέσθαι· πολλὰ ἂν εἰπεῖν ἔχοιεν Ὀλύνθιοι καὶ
τὰ ἑξῆς.

(These are examples of ἀκμή being produced from σχῆμα of λαμπρότης:
(a) [*Or.* 10. 46] ('Men of Athens, you have deserted the position in
which your ancestors left you'; and again (b) [*Or.* 18. 61] 'Philip, men of
Athens, started with an enormous advantage.' Both are introduced by
ἀπόστασις.[13] These too are similar (c) [*Or.* 19. 296] 'Let no one be
delivered and no one destroyed who is merely the object of this or that
man's whim'; or (d) [*Or.* 9. 68] 'Many things could be named by the
Olynthians today which, had they foreseen then, would have saved
them from destruction'; again (e) [*Or.* 9. 69] 'While the vessel is safe,
whether it be a large one or a small, then is the time for a sailor and
helmsman and everyone in it to show his zeal . . . But when the sea has
overwhelmed it, zeal is useless.' These examples (c–e) have an extra
element; for not only have they been introduced by ἀπόστασις like: (b)
'Philip started . . .' and (a) 'Men of Athens, you have deserted . . .', but
with ἐπεμβολή, quite unexpectedly. For this reason, the ἀκμή shines
more strongly and has a brighter gleam. For strictly speaking, though
example (b) has ἀπόστασις, if after a κατάστασις you bring the speech
back to a beginning, there is less suggestion of ἀπόστασις: 'prefacing
only this much[14] Philip started with an enormous advantage.' In this
case, we were expecting the ἀπόστασις to appear. But, in the other
example (d) the effect of ἀπόστασις is complete, is it not?'[15] 'For of
course we ought to have done this and that and not so and so. Many
things could be named by the Olynthians today'.)

The effect of ἀπόστασις is reduced if there is a preceding κατάστασις
(introductory statement), which signals that ἀπόστασις is about to

---

[13] Ἀπόστασις means little more than initial asyndeton. We find it here and in the
section on λαμπρότης (see below); in *Peri Politikou Logou* of σεμνότης (6. 19–20; 7.
19; 8. 13; 9. 3); also in *Vit. Soph.* 492.

[14] Rabe prints this as if it were part of Hermogenes' comment and not part of the
text of Demosthenes.

[15] Text: οὐ πάνυ τι τό ἀποστατικόν, οἷον . . . The sense demanded is that there *is* an
effect of *separation*. The easiest emendation is to make of it a question soliciting the
answer 'yes'.

ensue.[16] It is better if there is no κατάστασις, in which case it can be described as ἐπεμβολή (interruption). None of this has all that much to do with ἀκμή, but the aesthetics of ἀπόστασις seem to have been a special interest of Hermogenes, who makes a related point about it in the section on λαμπρότης.[17]

After σχήματα derived from λαμπρότης Hermogenes turns to σχήματα derived from σφοδρότης (271. 15 ff.). These are σχήματα in which you accost your enemy, such as ἀποστροφή and ἔλεγχος. Here again he develops a pet theme, this time that the grandeur of ἀκμή is not incompatible with ἦθος.

Comparing all of this with the discussion of σχήματα and ἀκμή in *Peri Heureseos*, what strikes one is that whereas *Peri Heureseos* is concerned mainly (though not only) with long sentences in which the same σχῆμα is repeated several times, or even longer stretches of narrative, involving several such 'polyschematic' sentences, *Peri Ideon* focuses on much smaller components: sometimes individual sentences, sometimes just the beginning of a sentence, together with the end of the preceding one.

The section on ἀκμή in *Peri Ideon* ends with an investigation of problems arising from two passages of *De Corona*, in which ἀκμή and λαμπρότης seem to be combined (273. 15 ff.). The two passages are: c. 48: 'Just so far Lasthenes was hailed a friend—until he betrayed Olynthus ...'; and c. 71: 'But here was a man annexing Euboea and making it a base of operations against Attica ...'. Hermogenes wants to say that these texts embody both ἀκμή and λαμπρότης: the general form (σχήματα, κῶλα) is of the sort one would associate with λαμπρότης, but σφοδρότης/τραχύτης is present in the implied criticism (of traitors in the case of 48, of Philip in the case of 71), and this makes him think that they instantiate ἀκμή. However, he realizes that it might be objected that these qualities amount to the same thing. In defence of his analysis he points out (274. 25 ff.) that some λαμπρά strata, namely ἔννοιαι and μέθοδοι, have no part in producing ἀκμή. But he also believes more generally that there is a difference between a styleme's being λαμπρός and its contributing, *qua* λαμπρός, to the effect of ἀκμή (274. 7–8), because ἀκμή, uniquely, is a product of two *ideai*, and is not grounded in linguistic elements like ἔννοιαι, σχήματα, or κῶλα.[18]

---

[16] κατάστασις always means 'introductory statement' in the core of *Peri Ideon*. There is another, perhaps more common, sense: *narration* (see Ernesti, s.v.), which we find in *Peri Ideon* only at 369. 6; this sense is found also in the heading to *Peri Heureseos* 2. 1, though in the text we find only the compound προκατάστασις.

[17] It can be compared to the discussion of σχήματα in the section on λαμπρότης (267. 14 ff.) where he makes the related point that ἀπόστασις preceded by κατάστασις is not λαμπρός unless a genitive absolute or similar construction occurs early on in the sentence.

[18] This position is summed up in the statement that ἀκμή has no γένεσις, which

Let us now try to compare the accounts in *Peri Ideon* and *Peri Heureseos*. There are several similarities.

1. In both cases ἀκμή means a maximization of rhetorical effect. In the case of *Peri Ideon* it represents the combination of the emotional and the epideictic sides of μέγεθος, while the author of *Peri Heureseos* says that the effect of changing σχῆμα within a πνεῦμα 'makes the audience rise up, as if the speaker's impetus, which the change of impetus conveys to the audience, is at a peak'. There is a slight difference in that whereas *Peri Heureseos* seems to see ἀκμή as a sort of crescendo grounded in sentence structure, *Peri Ideon* takes it as a maximized combination of ideas from the genus μέγεθος.

2. The techniques are to some extent similar. Σχήματα λόγου are important in both accounts, as are κῶλα.[19] But *Peri Heureseos* concentrates on sustained application of the same figure, whereas Hermogenes focuses on single applications of a σχῆμα, especially ἀπόστασις.[20] In *Peri Ideon* the sustained application of the same σχῆμα is associated not so much with ἀκμή, but with περιβολή (in virtue of the size of the sentence) and with γοργότης (because a large number of points are dealt with swiftly).[21]

3. Also, the passages of Demosthenes that the two authors use to illustrate ἀκμή coincide: the author of *Peri Heureseos* illustrates ἀκμή νοημάτων with *De Corona* 71 and ἀκμὴ νοημάτων with three πνεῦμα-type sentences contained in *De Corona* 44–9 (44, 45, and (on my interpretation) 48 (. . . Lasthenes . . .), while the two problem passages discussed by Hermogenes in the appendix to his section on ἀκμή are *De Corona* 48 and 71. This strongly suggests that the two accounts are related. I would interpret Hermogenes' discussion of these passages as a sort of commentary on *Peri Heureseos* (or its source), in that, whereas the author of *Peri Heureseos* believes that these passages instantiate ἀκμή, Hermogenes adopts the more sophisticated view that they are on the borderline between ἀκμή and λαμπρότης.

Which account is likely to be earlier? Most likely the one in *Peri Heureseos*, which is a blueprint for a type of rhetorical exercise or performance which is surely designed for declamation, or the teaching of declamation. Hermogenes, on the other hand, is interested in ἀκμή

probably means 'foundation for generation', i.e. it is not such that it can produce itself: see Ch. I, pp. 16–17.

[19] In *Peri Ideon*, long κῶλα are one of the things that ἀκμή borrows from λαμπρότης: 256. 18 ff.; 268. 21 ff.; 272. 12; 273. 1; 274. 3; 275. 25 ff.; 277. 8.

[20] Refutation and apostrophe, both listed among the σφοδρὰ σχήματα that produce ἀκμή (271. 16 ff.) and also among those by repetition of which πνεύματα are constituted in *Peri Heureseos* 4. 4 (186. 24; 187. 9); the σχῆμα δεικτικόν produces σφοδρότης according to Hermogenes (263. 3 ff.) and is also among the figures from which πνεύματα are produced according to *Peri Heureseos* 187. 3 ff.

[21] 285. 21 ff.; 318. 2 ff.

purely as a textual phenomenon, and mainly as a challenging case of *idea*-interaction, and it would be difficult to apply the principles he recommends in practice. My hypothesis, then, is that the concept of ἀκμή was developed in the declamation schools along lines similar to what we find in *Peri Heureseos* (and in practice in *Lives of the Sophists*) and that Hermogenes adapted it to suit the terms of his own theory. If *Peri Heureseos* was not a direct or indirect source for *Peri Ideon*, I would postulate the existence of a common source.

I would suggest that ἀκμή started off as a description of a feature of declamatory performance of the sort catalogued in *Lives of the Sophists*. The term was then reapplied in a more specific and textual way in *Peri Heureseos*, and it is finally confined to purely textual features in *Peri Ideon*, where it is reinterpreted as the culminating force generated by a combination of two *ideai*. We can represent this in the following model:

(*a*) Declamatory context   *Vit. Soph.*
(*b*) Analysis as performance   *Peri Heureseos*
(*c*) Analysis as text   *Peri Ideon*

For the meaning of a term to shift from an aspect of a literary performance to a textual feature is a pattern that can be paralleled many times in the history of Greek literature (one thinks of terms denoting lyric genres, which were defined in terms of performance criteria long before they came to denote formal types) and in the history of Greek literary criticism (one thinks of a term like σχῆμα, which seems to start off meaning 'gesture', 'stance', and is only later transferred to the meaning 'figure of speech').

2. PROKATASKEUE

The technique προκατασκευή, discussed in *Peri Heureseos* 3. 2, is a matter of setting out in advance the topics to be dealt with in the *probatio* (κατασκευή), and the order in which they are going to be presented. There are two ways of doing it: either you do what you promised to do in the προκατασκευή (this is illustrated by Demosthenes, *Against Aristocrates* 18) or you forget the προκατασκευή and do something different (this is illustrated by *On the False Embassy* 4).[22] If we turn to *Peri Ideon*, we

---

[22] The two passages are cited at 126. 20 ff. and 127. 11 ff. The point that in the first case Demosthenes does and in the second case does not go on to do what he promised to do is made at 128. 7 ff., where the author says (1) that Demosthenes sometimes puts the προκατασκευή directly after the proem, as in *On the False Embassy*, and sometimes after the διήγησις, as in *Against Aristocrates*, and (2) that when it follows the proem he is not going to deceive but when it follows the διήγησις he is.

find something very similar: among the techniques that Hermogenes regards as capable of producing εὐκρίνεια are: (1) saying you are going to deal with points in a certain order and then confusing them; and (2) making clear the order in which you are going to deal with points and keeping to it. To illustrate these, he uses the same passages that are used to illustrate honest and dishonest προκατασκευή in *Peri Heureseos* 3. 2.[23] Although a terminological parallel is lacking in this case, the argument for Hermogenes having borrowed from *Peri Heureseos* in this point still seems strong.

Let us look at this in more detail. The techniques that illustrate εὐκρίνεια in *Peri Ideon* include:

1. (235. 8 ff.) saying you are going to deal with points in a certain order, then confusing and reversing the order, illustrated by Demosthenes, *Or.* 19. 4.

2. (236. 21 ff.) ἔννοιαι that set out the points that are going to be made and their order, illustrated by Demosthenes, *Or.* 23. 18, where he asks the audience which order they want to hear the points in.

These techniques are as much a matter of invention or of disposition as of style. As it happens, similar techniques are described in *Peri Heureseos* 3. 2, 126. 17 ff., in a chapter of προκατασκευή (prior elaboration), the function of which is to set out in advance headings and issues. This is illustrated by the same passages from Demosthenes that are used in *Peri Ideon*: by *Or.* 23. 18 (where he follows the order of points which he lays down for himself, and it) and by *Or.* 19. 4 (where he ignores it). Again, in the former case it comes after the narration, while in the latter it comes after the proem, and the author bases on this a generalization that when Demosthenes is going to follow the order of points he lays down, he puts it after the narrative, but when he is going to confuse it, he puts it after the proem.

Does the way that Hermogenes handles these passages bear any resemblance to the two types of *promise*? Inevitably yes. In (1) Hermogenes stresses that Demosthenes is going to confuse the material, and this implies that he is going to disregard the order in which he undertakes to present it. He says less in (2), but it would be agreed, I think, that it represents an honest equivalent to (1), and that the expression 'ἔννοιαι that set out clearly the points that are going to be made and their order' (236. 21 ff.) implies that this order is actually followed.

---

[23] The first at 235. 9 ff., illustrated by *On the False Embassy* 4 (235. 13 ff.), the second at 236. 22 ff., illustrated by *Against Aristocrates* 8.

3. SEQUENCE OF TROPES AT *PERI IDEON* 343. 14 FF. AND *PERI HEURESEOS* 4. 10, 199. 4 FF.

Δριμύτης in *Peri Ideon* is effected mainly through various types of word-play. The last of these is produced when a mild trope is followed by a harsher one drawn from the same semantic field, illustrated by Demosthenes, *Or.* 2.10, and Euripides (fr. 636N (*Polyidus*). Hagedorn gives plausible parallels from earlier theories of verbal wit for other types of δριμύτης, but not for this one.[24]

There is an account of trope sequences in some respects similar in *Peri Heureseos* 4. 10, a chapter that Stanford for different reasons regarded as of unique importance for understanding the development of Greek theories of metaphor.[25] The author distinguished two forms of sequences of similar metaphors (199. 23 ff.). Sometimes two instances follow in close succession, as in the sequence ἠσκήσαμεν . . . ἰσχυρός at *Or.* 3. 28; in other cases, the second instance follows at a great interval, and only an expert can detect it; as in the case of the metaphor μεθύει of Philip at *Or.* 4. 49, which picks up προπέποται τὰ πράγματα ('the interests of the state have been poured out like a toast') at *Or.* 3. 22 (i.e. in a different speech!); in such cases, the thought is that the second instance of the metaphor is 'rather comic', so the orator has disguised it by placing it at a remove from the first.

The hypothesis that *Peri Heureseos* is a source for *Peri Ideon* raises new questions about the creation of the *Corpus Hermogenicum*. Although unlikely to be identical with the author of *Peri Ideon*, the author of *Peri Heureseos* was from the same school of rhetoricians. Perhaps this was a popular work on εὕρεσις dating from a generation or so before Hermogenes, and generally familiar to students and teachers of the time. Why Hermogenes' own work on εὕρεσις was not included in the *Corpus Hermogenicum* is not clear. Perhaps it was never written, despite what is claimed in *Peri Ideon*. Or perhaps, although it existed, it was extraordinarily difficult and unsuitable for school use.

[24] Hagedorn (1964), 76.
[25] Stanford (1936), 14 ff.

APPENDIX B

Methodos and its Background

Hermogenes says in his introduction that μέθοδος is the same as the category 'figure (σχῆμα) of thought' (222. 21–2). A figure of thought would usually have meant a stylistically significant pattern not reducible to a superficial lexical pattern but inhering in a syntactic formula.[1] *Prima facie*, this claim seems to be undercut by the paucity of figures of thought, understood in the traditional sense, among the μέθοδοι (there are in fact rather more of them among the σχήματα). Where they do correspond, the figures of thought have been well assimilated into the framework of μέθοδος so that they can be analysed as modes of presenting or adapting ἔννοιαι. For example, ἔμφασις (= *innuendo*) is a traditional figure of thought, and Hermogenes makes it a μέθοδος, but only because it instantiates the general σεμνὴ μέθοδος of speaking 'in a precise manner, as if we have knowledge'.[2] Again, the *idea* ἐπιείκεια relies heavily on μέθοδοι that lower the tone, and two special cases are ἐλάττωσις (diminution) and παράλειψις (omission), both of them traditional figures of thought.[3]

More commonly, however, figures of thought in the traditional sense have come through into *Peri Ideon* not as μέθοδοι but as σχήματα, though μέθοδοι may still govern their use. Thus, in the section on ἀλήθεια, many of the σχήματα correspond to traditional figures of thought, for example ἀποστροφή (360. 14), διαπόρησις (361. 4), ἀποσιώπησις (361. 12), and ἐπιδιόρθωσις (362. 2), and these are subsumed under a μέθοδος which has to do with how such emotional σχήματα are expressed—with or without deliberate introductory statements like: 'I am amazed', 'I am angry' (353. 16 ff., 354. 19 ff.).

However, the claim that μέθοδος continues the category figure of thought makes more sense if we look at the general statements about figures of thought that are made in ancient rhetoricians, who quite often define figuration of thought as an oblique or unnatural way of expressing

---

[1] Alexander Noumeniou, 10. 14 ff.: Quintilian, *IO* 9. 1. 17.

[2] See Rutherford (1988).

[3] παράλειψις: Alexander, 23.10 ff. Sp., Phoebammon, 51. 4 ff. Sp., Tiberius, 60. 27 ff. Sp.; also Herodian, *Peri Skhematon* 94. 14 Sp.; Quintilian does not regard it as a figure, although Roman orators use it (see Usher 1965); ἐλάττωσις at *Ad Herennium* (4. 50).

something.[4] This type of definition—analogous, of course, to the standard definition of verbal figures as deviant or unusual patterns of syntax[5]— could easily be applied to the adapting, mediating function of μέθοδος.[6] In this context special attention might be reserved for the account of figures of thought in Herodian, *Peri Skhematon* (90. 20 ff.), in which the scope of figures of thought has been narrowed down to two techniques: first, irony;[7] second, using inappropriate words deliberately to defuse grandiose subjects. The terminology of intensifying and slackening is a little misleading, since the techniques are not exact opposites. Most of what mainstream theory calls figures of thought are naturally excluded from this narrow category, and the section of verbal figures is correspondingly enlarged.

Part of the background here is that σχῆμα λόγου and ἐσχηματισμένος λόγος have another sense in rhetoric: the techniques of innuendo and oblique language.[8] The tendency has been to separate *figure-σχῆμα* and *innuendo-σχῆμα* as if they were semantically distinct.[9] But there are a number of indications that the *innuendo* sense has a place in figure-

---

[4] Alexander Noumeniou, 11. 19Sp.: σχῆμά ἐστι διανοίας μετάπλασις διανοήματος ἐκ τοῦ κατὰ φύσιν, πλάττουσα πρὸς τὸ χρησιμώτερον τὴν ἀναγκαίαν διάνοιαν (a figure of thought is a configuration of thought away from the natural, shaping the necessary thought in the direction of what is more useful); Tiberius Rhetoric, 59. 6Sp.: [text Ballaira] ἔστι τοίνυν σχῆμα τὸ μὴ κατὰ φύσιν τὸν νοῦν ἐκφέρειν μηδ' ἐπ' εὐθείας, ἀλλ' ἐκτρέπειν καὶ ἐξαλλάσσειν τὴν διάνοιαν τῇ πλάσει κόσμου τινὸς ἢ χρείας ἕνεκα (A figure is not to express the meaning in accordance with nature, nor directly, but to divert it, and change the thought for the sake of ornament or usefulness); Herodian, 90. 22Sp.: ἔστι δὲ σχῆμα διανοίας τὸ μὴ κατὰ φύσιν ἐκφέρειν τὸν νοῦν μηδὲ ἐπ' εὐθείας, ἀλλ' ἐκτρέπειν καὶ ἐξαλλάσσειν τὴν τῆς διανοίας φράσιν (Figuration is not expressing the meaning in accordance with nature or directly, but diverting and changing the thought in respect of expression for the sake of ornament or usefulness.).

[5] On which see Barwick (1957), 87 ff.

[6] The main limitation to this is that, as we have seen, Hermogenes also wants μέθοδος to cover cases where an ἔννοια is directly expressed and its quality is preserved. But the direct, quality-preserving function of μέθοδος is to be seen as an extension from a more fundamental oblique, quality-modifying function. There is an analogous situation with respect to the σχήματα: whereas earlier rhetoric defines verbal figures as deviant or unusual patterns of syntax, Hermogenes classes as σχήματα not just marked syntactic patterns of syntax, but unmarked ones as well; for example the direct sentence structure that he calls ὀρθότης, or common constructions like 'so . . . that . . .'. I would venture the generalization that, whereas earlier stylistic theory tends to single out specially marked highlights, *idea*-theory attempts to give a comprehensive account of oratorical language. There is a good discussion of this in Patillon (1988).

[7] The application of the term σχῆμα διανοίας to irony is rare; the only other case I know is *Peri Politikou Logou*, c. 43 (18. 14 ff.). On figures in Herodian, see Müller (1904).

[8] See Penndorf (1902), Russell (1981*b*), Ahl (1984).

[9] See Schenkeveld (1964), 116 ff.; the semantics of σχῆμα are discussed by Sandoz (1971), Kojic-Slapsak (1977).

theory.[10] So Herodian's account of figuration of thought seems merely to be the most conspicuous case of their overlapping.

Μεταχείρισις in *On Plainness* seems to be somewhat similar to μέθοδος (I discuss this further in Appendix C. 2).

---

[10] (1) In general discussions of the meaning of the term σχῆμα, two sources cite the rhetorician Zoilus to the effect that it means 'pretending to say one thing and really saying another' (Phoebammon, 44. 2–3Sp.; Quintilian, *IO* 9. 1. 14). (2) Quintilian, *IO* 9. 2. 65 ff., discusses ἐσχηματισμένοι λόγοι among the figures of thought. (3) Some play is made on the two senses of σχηματίζομαι ('form', 'pretend') in the introduction to Alexander (12. 7 ff. Sp.). (4) The manuals often mention 'pretence' when describing the operation of particular figures of thought (e.g. Tiberius, 44. 2Sp.). No rigid distinction, then, can be made between the two senses.

APPENDIX C

The Relation between *Peri Ideon* and *Peri Aphelous Logou*

I. WAYS OF EXPRESSING EMOTION IN *PERI APHELOUS LOGOU* AND *PERI IDEON*

Earlier on I suggested that *Peri Apheleias* might have been a source for *Peri Ideon* (p. 76). By way of filling out this hypothesis, I present below discussions of two other possible links between the two works. A pattern we meet more than once in comparing *Peri Aphelous Logou* and *Peri Ideon* is that a contrast which in *Peri Aphelous Logou* serves to distinguish ἀφέλεια from πολιτικὸς λόγος in *Peri Ideon* is redeployed so as to describe a contrast *within* the πολιτικὸς λόγος of Demosthenes (shown schematically in Table 8).

TABLE 8. *Stylistic Contrasts in* Peri Aphelous Logou *and* Peri Ideon

	styleme A	styleme B (= not A)
Peri Aphelous Logou	ἀφέλεια	πολιτικὸς λόγος
Peri Ideon	πολιτικὸς λόγος type A	πολιτικὸς λόγος type B

A brief example will show what I mean. The technique of ὑποστροφή seems to mean a 'turn' or 'twist' in the plain flow of the narrative and takes the form of a parenthetical clause, for example a postponed causal statement. According to *Peri Aphelous Logou* this effect produces πολιτικὸσ λόγος, and it is associated with the quality γοργότης,[1] while ἀφέλεια is not supposed to use it at all. In *Peri Ideon* ὑποστροφή is still associated with γοργότης, but as such it is a mark of only one desirable πολιτικός style (the

---

[1] This could well be the first attestation of the term. At Dionysius, *De Compositione Verborum* 86. 14 ff., one MS has γοργότερον, applying to a κῶλον, which Hagedorn (1964), 54 seems to believe. But there αὐτουργότερον ('crude made'—as at *Dem. Lex.* 212. 18) makes a perfectly adequate contrast to ἀκριβέστερον, and γοργότερον is probably a corruption due to a Byzantine scribe familiar with Hermogenes. For the athletic associations of the word, see Pleket (1970) and Poliakoff (1982), 108 n. 4.

Demosthenic). It is not associated with Xenophon, but its absence is characteristic of Isocratean ὑπτιότης, another form of πολιτικὸς λόγος.

A similar pattern is found if we compare *Peri Aphelous Logou* and *Peri Ideon* on the portrayal of emotion. According to *Peri Aphelous Logou* ἀφέλεια requires that expression of emotion be restrained, whereas free expression of emotion suggests πολιτικὸς λόγος. Interestingly, a very similar division is found in *Peri Ideon*, according to which restrained expression of emotion suggests ἀφέλεια, whereas unrestrained expression of emotion suggests not πολιτικὸς λόγος *per se* but rather the specific *idea ἀλήθεια*.

Let us have a close look at the account of the presentation of emotion in *Peri Aphelous Logou*. The following passages are particularly important (summarized schematically in Table 9):

1. In c. 21 (80. 1 ff.): a contrast is drawn between ἀφέλεια, represented by the first sentence of the *Memorabilia* Xenophon writes: 'I have often been surprised', and the political style, which might have repeated 'I have often wondered' several times.

2. c. 22 (90. 14 ff.): a contrast is drawn between ἀφέλεια, represented by the same passage of the *Memorabilia*, and political style, which would have said: 'deserving of reproach'. In ἀφέλεια one does not 'mark' (ἐπισημαίνεται) the points in this way. The difference between these styles is described as a difference of μεταχείρισις.

3. c. 31 (85. 16 ff.): in ἀφέλεια one avoids passing judgement and using value-laden epithets, because this would not be consistent with giving the impression that the speaker is a good man. The example given is the first line of the *Anabasis*: 'Tissaphernes slandered Kuros to his brother.' The political way of putting this would be: 'A thing most dreadful and cruel Tissaphernes cast into the mind of Kuros' brother', perhaps even adding: 'ashamed of neither gods nor justice nor of a most dreadful course of action'.

4. c. 91 (109. 3 ff.): a similar contrast: whereas Demosthenes says (19. 15): 'standing up he uttered words, ye gods, deserving the death penalty many times over', the ἀφελής man would say: 'coming forward, he said this.'

TABLE 9. *Expression of Emotion in* Peri Aphelous Logou

	ἀφελής	πολιτικός
(1)	single utterance of qualification	repetition of qualification
(2)	(context is something worthy of anger) meiosis	saying it is worthy of anger
(3–4)	omission of quality terms (no ἐπισημαίνεσθαι)	expressing quality terms (ἐπισημαίνεσθαι)

Note the key word ἐπισημαίνεσθαι, which seems to mean: 'to mark what the speaker is doing, or the significance of what he is saying, or the fact that it is deliberate'.[2]

If we compare *Peri Ideon*, we find that Hermogenes is interested in the same sort of contrasts, but has to some extent inverted the antithesis. Thus in the section on ἀλήθεια, he contrasts two types of emotional utterance: either one can begin with a statement to the effect that one is performing a certain sort of speech act ('I swear, I do not know what to do, I beseech you', etc.), or one can just perform the speech act without any introductory statement. It is the latter which produces ἀλήθεια, while the former produces ἀφέλεια. This distinction may owe something to figure-theory; Alexander Noumeniou and Caecilius of Caleacte distinguished the technical figures of rhetoric from the natural figures of everyday language.[3] However, Hermogenes' discussion seems to me more reminiscent of techniques such as (1) and (2) in *Peri Aphelous Logou*. He could well have been thinking of the first sentence of the *Memorabilia*, which contains a splendid example of τὸ προλέγειν. Notice, however, that Hermogenes reverses the thesis of *Peri Aphelous Logou*: he agrees that a single utterance of an introductory formula like 'I am surprised' can produce ἀφέλεια is part of political language; he does not mention multiple utterance; and thinks that the most effective political language is produced by omitting such statements entirely.

The technique of τὸ ἐπισημαίνεσθαι is not mentioned by Hermogenes in his discussion of τὸ προλέγειν, but he does mention it a little later on in the section on ἀλήθεια, where he talks about 'using insults without marking it' (ταῖς λοιδορίαις ἄνευ τοῦ ἐπισημαίνεσθαι, 358. 8 ff.).

For marking is not characteristic of an impassioned heart or an emotional disposition, or of a man who has lost his temper and does not know what he is saying; it is a sign rather of someone who is sober and knows it, and is going to insult his opponent deliberately and eagerly.

Here the contrast does not involve ἀφέλεια, but one could still see in this an implied criticism of *Peri Aphelous Logou* for claiming that τὸ ἐπισημαίνεσθαι is an invariable feature of πολιτικὸς λόγος.

---

[2] We find the term also at *Peri Politikou Logou*, c. 102 (40. 20 ff.), c. 120 (47. 15 ff.), c. 138 (54. 2 ff.), c. 27 (83. 1 ff.), c. 43 (91. 12 ff.), cc. 81–2 (105. 7 ff.), *Peri Ideon* 346. 5, 358. 8 ff. Ernesti (1795) fails to interpret this term accurately. He says: 'ἐπισημαίνεσθαι dicitur orator, si promittit auditoribus de aliqua re se velle imprimis verbis facere, ut ab ea re recte sibi cavere possint . . .'. He goes on to cite only *Peri Politikou Logou*, c. 102 (40. 20 ff.), but his inaccurate interpretation is based on a misunderstanding of this passage.

[3] Paradoxically, the more complex figure that was previously considered more technical is now thought to suggest ἀφέλεια.

If the author of *Peri Aphelous Logou* opposes ἀφέλεια to πολιτικὸς λόγος on the grounds that the former is more deliberate, involving τὸ ἐπισημαίνεσθαι, Hermogenes seems to argue that, on the contrary, πολιτικὸς λόγος, at least where it partakes of the quality ἀλήθεια, can exhibit greater spontaneity than ἀφέλεια. Hermogenes has inverted a hierarchical antithesis in *Peri Aphelous Logou*, he has, in other words, deconstructed his position (see Table 10). The point is confirmed by the terminology he uses for the quality. One term he uses is ἄμψυχος λόγος, a concept which is grounded in an earlier antithesis between speech and writing, the latter being 'dead' in the sense that it represents empty words, devoid of the mind of a speaker. That antithesis then gets reinterpreted as one between two styles of written language: one that sounds like spontaneous, 'live' speech, and one that sounds like 'dead' writing.[4] A similar antithesis seems to underlie the application of a second term, ἐνδιάθετος λόγος, which in philosophy denoted the internal language of thought, and formed one side of a contrasting pair with προφορικὸς λόγος, 'expressive language'. The application of a philosophical term for 'language of thought' to a style of rhetoric implies a striking paradox, and one which I imagine Hermogenes was well aware of.[5]

TABLE 10. *Expression of Emotion in* Peri Aphelous Logou *and* Peri Ideon

	more spontaneous	less spontaneous
Peri Aphelous Logou	ἀφέλεια	πολιτικὸς λόγος
Hermogenes	ἀλήθεια	ἀφέλεια
	(both part of πολιτικὸς όγος)	

---

[4] See in particular 355. 21 ff. Dionysius also used ἔμψυχος of Demosthenic style (Geigenmüller (1908), 62); also Ps. Lucian, *Dem. Enc.* 14: μόνος γέ τοι τῶν ῥητόρων ἔμψυχον, ὡς Λεωσθένης ἐτόλησεν εἰπεῖν, οὐ σφυρήλατον παρεῖχε (for only he among the orators, as Leosthenes ventured to say, produced language that was alive, not hammered out like a statue), reading οὐ . . . rather than καὶ . . . This opposition between 'live' and 'dead' language goes back to Plato, *Phaidros* 276a.

[5] Both terms are from philosophy; see Pohlenz (1933), appendix; Mühl (1962). The philosophical term may have passed into general usage; see Pohlenz (1933), 85–6, citing a papyrus letter from the 4th century AD, *Pap. Amherst* II. 145. 12: τὸ σὸν εἰν ἡμᾶς ἐνδιάθετον. That Hermogenes' use of the term reflects the philosophical usage seems to me to be suggested by the fact that it is λόγος that he calls ἐνδιάθετος (as in philosophy) and by the fact that the association with ἀληθής is found several times in Philo, where, as Pohlenz (1933), 85–6, notes, it is obviously borrowed from a Stoic source.

2. *METAKHEIRISIS* IN *PERI APHELOUS LOGOU* AND *METHODOS* IN *PERI IDEON*

In the last section I mentioned à *propos* of c. 22 the term μεταχείρισις. I want in this section to look at it in greater depth, comparing it with the parallel concept of μέθοδος in *Peri Ideon*.

The term μεταχείρισις is introduced in *Peri Aphelous Logou* c. 4 (71. 16 ff.) as the second of five axes distinguishing πολιτικὸς λόγος and ἀφελὴς λόγος. The other four are the strata (ἐπινόημα, σχῆμα, ἀπαγγελία, ῥυθμός).[6] In πολιτικὸς λόγος the μεταχείρισις is obvious, so that the audience can easily follow the argument, but in ἀφέλεια the argument is hidden, and does not resemble a strategic approach (ἐπιβολή).[7] This text presents some parallels with the methodology of *Peri Ideon*, which often contrasts manifest and hidden effects (though he usually calls the 'hidden' element 'real' rather than 'hidden'). The closest parallel in *Peri Ideon* is in the account of δεινότης, where the second type (376. 5 ff.), ἡ οὖσα δεινότης, particularly useful in private speeches, is defined as a matter of pretending to be simple (the word ἀφελής is among those used), while in fact working toward one's rhetorical aims by covert strategy.[8]

Now let us consider the general function of μεταχείρισις in *Peri Aphelous Logou*. There are two main ones. The first has to do with the way the argument proceeds. This is illustrated by c. 13 (76. 3 ff.), where the author of *Peri Aphelous Logou* discusses the opening of the *Kuropaidia*, which begins in an offhand and desultory manner (*Kuropaidia* 1. 1. 1: 'The thought once occurred to us'), then finally, after reflections on why it is difficult to rule men, reaches the point (*Kuropaidia* 1. 1. 8: 'Kuros, however, ruled an immense number of men. Kuros, then, must have been a man of immense worth'). The same passage is discussed again in cc. 84 ff., where the author observes that οἱ πολιτικοί take their beginnings from the subject itself, whereas Xenophon does not (citing the same example).[9]

---

[6] For the strata see c. 2 (71. 8 ff.). The omission of μεταχείρισις from this list is predictable in so far as it is not, like the other strata, a formal feature of language but a way of treating it.

[7] In *Peri Ideon* this seems to mean *initial approach* or *impact* (227, 330. 9); a similar meaning is found in Ulpian on Demosthenes 14 (διὰ ἐπιβολὴν προοιμίου); and at Menander Rhetor, περὶ ἐπιδεικτικῶν 419. 16Sp. (132. 19 Russell and Wilson) ἐπιβολὴν θρήνων means 'beginning of the dirges', but that may not be a technical usage. In the *Peri Aphelous Logou*, on the other hand, it seems to mean 'strategy', 'strategic approach' (here and at c. 28, 84. 1 ff.). Other meanings are ἐπαναφορά, e.g. at Rutilius Lupus 1. 9 (6. 66 ff. H.) and Phoebammon, *Peri Skhematon* 55. 105Sp.; and 'rhetorical ornament' at Dio Chrysostomus, 18. 14; cf. ἐπιβεβλημένη at Philostratus, *Vit. Soph.* 1. 20. 2 (see glossary to Philostratus, *Lives of Sophists*, ed. Wright).

[8] For δεινότης, pp. 31 ff.

[9] There are various parallels in *Peri Ideon*: Hermogenes discusses μέθοδοι that involve putting a proof before saying what point it supports or the λύσις to an

The second function of μεταχείρισις has to do with the level of expression. Things are simpler in *Peri Aphelous Logou* than in *Peri Ideon* because *Peri Aphelous Logou* is mainly concerned with only two styles. The author argues that the two can coincide in respect of one or more of the strata, in any particular passage there will always be one stratum that makes a difference. In c. 22 (80. 14 ff.), μεταχείρισις is described as playing up or playing down the emotional level of the utterance. In the same category belong the application of μεταχείρισις in c. 92 (109. 12 ff.), where Xenophon is said to have 'chopped up' (κόψας) his subject matter; this points forward to certain techniques described in the γοργότης section of *Peri Ideon* which have to do with dividing language into κόμματα or short clauses.[10]

The two major functions of μεταχείρισις—the organization and ordering of thoughts and their stylistic presentation and adaptation—both have parallels in the account of μέθοδος in *Peri Ideon*, which is partly a matter of the presentation of an individual ἔννοια, and partly one of sequences of ἔννοιαι.

The parallel between μέθοδος and the traditional category 'figure of thought' is therefore quite strong, at least as regards the paradigmatic or transforming μέθοδοι, while it does not provide a very good parallel for the syntagmatic μέθοδοι. Perhaps Hermogenes derived μέθοδος from figure-theory, and then the author of *Peri Aphelous Logou* modelled μεταχείρισις on that. On the other hand, it is also possible that *Peri Aphelous Logou* precedes *Peri Ideon*, that Hermogenes was familiar both with μεταχείρισις and with the traditional concept of σχῆμα διανοίας, and that he combined them into a new concept, applying to it the new term 'μέθοδος'.[11]

ἀντίθεσις before the ἀντίθεσις itself (283. 17 ff.; 238. 6 ff.); in his analysis of οὖσα δεινότης and elsewhere he describes how to conceal the purpose of one's speech; finally, one of the ἔννοιαι of ἀφέλεια consists of giving the impression that one's discourse is unmotivated and that no one has asked for it (322. 15 ff.).

[10] I am thinking of τμητικὸς λόγος.

[11] The parallels I have in mind are not verbal ones; hence, perhaps, Schmid (1917), 138, who was interested mainly in verbal parallels, failed to notice them.

Translation of *Peri Aphelous Logou*

Different Properties of Political and Plain Language

(1) Since we have shown you the qualities of political language and its virtues, you must also hear about the qualities of plain language. For nothing needs to be considered as much as the qualities of plain and simple language, and the differences between it and language that is political and contentious. This is no easy task, since all language belongs to the same *genus* and has the same nature. However, there are certain differences and distinguishing qualities. (2) Obviously, all language consists of thoughts, and expression, which is comprised of diction, figure, and rhythm. We must consider what are factors which constitute differences between political and plain language. For the thoughts of plain language and political language are not the same; for, if the thought is the same, the diction will not be the same; or if the diction is the same, the rhythm will not be the same; or if the rhythm is the same, there will be a difference in respect of figure. (3) The first thing to realize (to summarize greatly) is that the primary distinctions between plain and political language are derived from sentiments. Political thoughts are rougher and more important, derived from important sentiments, and more pungent from their greater rarity and importance, while plain thoughts are simple, common, and unimportant, being derived from unimportant sentiments. So much by way of a few select remarks about thoughts. (4) The next distinction concerns handling, since this exists in

Note. *Peri Aphelous Logou* is of great importance for understanding the taste for Xenophon in the early empire. The text is often difficult, and certainly harder than *Peri Politikou Logou*, *Peri Ideon*, or *Peri Heureseos*. I have generally followed Schmid's text; occasional emendations are marked in the notes. A special problem is that the author's citations from Xenophon and other texts are often inaccurate: in some such cases the transmission of *Peri Aphelous Logou* may be to blame, but in other cases he may have misremembered the texts, or he may be using a different text from ours. Consequently it is uncertain to what extent we should try to bring his text into line with our texts of Xenophon. I print his citations in italics when there is at least a rough correspondence with the actual text. In some cases, it seemed helpful to supply more of a passage that the author cites, and I have used parentheses to mark the parts of citations that I have supplied.

The text is full of technical terms, and ideally, I would have glossed all but the most familiar technical terms. However, for reasons of space I have elected to gloss only the more obscure, using footnotes.

plain language, just as in political language. The difference between the two sorts of handling is this: in political discourse it must be apparent; for speech proceeds in a political manner if the audience can follow the points at issue. In plain discourse, this is not the case. Rather, the points at issue are sometimes hidden and no one even knows what the speaker's purport is, because the discourse does not bear any resemblance to a strategic approach. (5) The figures in political language are rough, vehement, refuting, and violent, whereas in plain language they are relaxed, simple, implying no refutation or examination, but more ordinary and humble. The former make language tense and political, whereas the plain ones make it personal and conversational.(6) Nor are they the same in respect of diction either, there is a difference here also, for in political language, whether a thought is completed, or whether it needs the interruption of another thought, the speech must progress with complete sureness and intensity. Conversely, in plain language the diction seems to proceed at random, suggesting that it is neither planned nor deliberate. (7) Again, in political language whatever one wants to express must be the only meaning implied by the diction, whereas in plain language the same diction can convey one or two or three things on occasion. (Also placement of words next to each other produces beauty of diction, such as the horse-trainer of horses, the swineherd of swine.)[1] (8) In respect of rhythm also I would say that there is a difference between political language and plain language, and the ground of the difference between the two is this: it is a mark of plainness for speech to proceed simply and for the ear always to follow smoothly and that there should never be any obstruction in the language or acoustic impediment; whereas ὑποστροφή as the sentence proceeds and the resulting acoustic impediment makes the figure contentious and the rhythm political. Such things divert the hearer, and do not allow him just to follow along, in the way that plainness does. Consider this example from Xenophon's *Sumposion* (2. 3) (I will now cite examples of these techniques for you, so that the principles of plainness become clearer for you): *But women, especially if they happen to be wives like those of this Niceratus and Critoboulos, do not need more perfume*; and the ὑποστροφή: *For this is what they smell of.* What would have been expected is: 'they do not need more perfume from a man, for they have it already, being wives.' It is worth noticing the figure of ὑποστροφή. The progression was plain as far as: *They do not need more perfume*; but the explanation added by the figure of ὑποστροφή (*For this is what they smell of*) made the language extremely agile, and the rhythm has perhaps become political. (9) So much for expression.

---

[1] The citations here seem to allude to Xenophon, *Sump.* 1. 1. 2.

Low Thoughts

Again, there are thoughts which fall under plainness, such as the use, if
appropriate, of even quite unimportant thoughts. For example, Xenophon wanted to argue that Kuros was a remarkable man (*Kur.* 1. 1).
Consider how he arranges this. The premiss is political and the demonstration that Kuros was remarkable is political in the extreme, but the
thoughts vary between political and plain. The sentiment that Kuros was
a remarkable man, that he easily achieved the most difficult thing of all—
ruling men—is political. If you adapted it in a political manner, you
would express it like this: 'Kuros was a remarkable man. What was most
difficult he achieved—ruling men. Why? Because men are not readily
ruled; many empires have fallen and many tyrannies as the result of men
who do not want to be ruled.' Thus far, then, the thoughts are political.
(10) But when you come to establish the difference between men and
animals, and you say: 'it is easier to rule oxen and sheep and any herd of
animals than to rule men', then I say that you lead the argument into
plainer thoughts, since they are connected with character and behaviour,
which maintain the plainness of the speech. The political man sets out
first the main point and appends the supporting considerations, in this
way adding more and more political thoughts. For example, a statement
which involves unpolitical actions, such as: *shepherds however are rulers*,
or again: *we have never seen herds collecting* . . . would never be uttered by
a political man, but Xenophon has provided appropriate variety in respect
of arguments. (11) When the thoughts are the same, the diction and figure
are different. Thus, in the passage which starts with *The thought once
occurred to me* (*Kur.* 1. 1): *. . . of those who undertook to be tyrants some were
soon completely destroyed*, he avoids saying: *paid the penalty*; and in: *even if
they continued in power any length of time*, he chose not to say: 'those who
took cities by force and very firmly consolidated their control'. (12) I have
shown you that some thoughts are specially selected, while others are
indiscriminate, and that some of them are derived from important things,
others from small and inconspicuous things. Thus, plain men use
indiscriminate thoughts, they are not satisfied with ones derived from
the subject matter, but sometimes use ones which another man would
scorn and steer clear of because they are extraneous or unimportant. But
plain men do not abstain from these. (13) This is one example of the use
of handling of thoughts.

Apparent Lack of Order[2]

Another is for the points that support the point at issue not to be spoken
as if leading up to it, but for the speech to proceed as if its purpose was
unclear. For example, not having stated in advance that he wants to show

---

[2] Cf. c. 81. below.

that Kuros is a remarkable man, he adds: *The thought once occurred to me,* and after setting out first (?) all the supporting points—that it is hard to rule men, harder than this or that—only then he adds (1. 1. 3): *But Kuros ruled the greatest number of men, so Kuros was a remarkable man.* And this is the handling appropriate to plain language, when it is not obvious that what is said is the point at issue.

Need for Variety (Sumposion *1. 1*)

(14) In many cases thoughts should not all be strong, like those of political language, but one should arrange some in a restrained manner—those that seem less impressive—while others could appear humorous, if possible, such as at the start of *Sumposion,* where he says: *But to me it seems that it is not only the serious deeds of gentlemen that deserve to be related, but also what they do in jest.* The thought that one should accept what gentlemen do at play involves character. It is a principle of plain language, then, that one should not consistently pursue thoughts that are distinguished and great, but also those that seem low and that invite disdain. (15) On the level of style neither thought—neither: *The thought once occurred to me . . .* nor: *But to me it seems . . .*—is expressed roughly. Since the point in the *Sumposion* about relating what men do in play seems unimportant, and no political man would do it since it is unimportant, he has introduced it with the apology: *But to me it seems . . .* If the sentence had begun with a declarative statement, i.e.: *It seems to me,* it would have been rougher and more in the manner of someone like Critias. (16) On the level of figure, one should use a relaxed form of figuration. One would not create a plain effect by stretching it out, as a political man did (cf. Dem. 3. 1): *My opinion about good men is not the one held by most men; for most men think that the only memorable things about them are those that they do with serious intent, whereas I am different. The things that men do in jest seem to me no less worthy of record than the things they do in earnest.* Instead of proceeding in this way, Xenophon employed a relaxed form of figuration and variety: *But to me it seems . . .*, followed by words that are also full of character, in accordance with the properties of this style: *fair and good gentlemen.* Another example is (*Sump.* 1. 2): *As the horse-race finished.* The figure seems relaxed and laid back. The political man would choose a more intense manner of expression: 'After the horse-race finished', or something of this sort. (17) To provide variety, plain and political men of the classical period used the same figures. Those figures that make the style pungent in political language make the other style plain.

Rhythm, with Special Reference to Agesilaos *1. 5*

The rhythm of the diction should as it were move forward and advance without urgency, not like political language where authors add value-judgements: 'most terrible of all', or: 'at which you will all be upset', or: 'this as outrageous'. Political men indicate the quality before stating the thing that they are referring to, or rather sometimes they can state the quality beforehand, and sometimes they can add it afterwards. (18) Another example of good rhythm is (*Ag.* 1. 5): *And yet, except for the fact that he was judged worthy of the highest honour by the best men in the strongest city, what further proofs of his virtue before he began his reign are required?* This seems to me also to produce good rhythm in the language, in so far as the use of *peribole* and completing the thought is what brought it to a standstill, so that what is said after it ((1. 6) *But when he came to control men . . .*) is not linked to it and seems to begin a second thought. Xenophon does not often use this figure,[3] since it is rougher and more forensic, and we usually add this when the facts are demonstrated and we are either forcing our way or giving the impression of speaking violently. (19) Another remarkable aspect of his good deployment of rhythm here is the use of a series of divisions in one continuous sentence (*And yet then . . . in the strongest city . . . judged by the best men . . . to be thought worthy of the greatest honour*), and the exposition of many thoughts set out independently in a single sentence also creates power and rhythm.

Tropes

(20) With respect to diction, plain writers also delight in transference from one thing to another, as in the *Agesilaos* (1. 19) where Xenophon says: *he made many men lovers of his friendship.* The normal sense of 'lover' is different. Another example is: *themselves seeing the followers of the Greeks* (1. 30), where again he uses a word of less significance than the subject, since the word 'followers' is more usually said of slaves, but Xenophon has not hesitated to call the rearguard of the army 'followers'. Again, in the *Memorabilia* he says (1. 1. 20): *I am amazed at how they were persuaded that Socrates was not of sound disposition on the subject of the gods.* In this case he has transferred the phrase ('of sound disposition') since it is appropriate to the genre.

Subdued Expression, variation, argumentation, with reference to
Memorabilia *1. 1. 2*

(21) Notice furthermore how even though he uses words that are subdued for the sake of *plainness*, he still expresses the seriousness of the subject in the appropriate way. So at the start (of the *Memorabilia*): *I have often wondered at the arguments by which the accusers of Socrates persuaded the Athenians that he deserved the death-penalty from the city. The indictment against him was this, that Socrates commits injustice not respecting the gods*

---

[3] I take it the 'figure' here is the one in *Agesilaos* 1. 5.

whom the city observes, and in other respects also corrupting the young men.
For 'I have wondered' and 'often' contain a suggestion of things that are
not insignificant, and what follows makes it clear. A political man would
have repeated both meanings several times; but Xenophon was satisfied
by a statement of the simple meaning. (22) Now, sometimes the *thoughts*
coincide, and it is the handling that makes the difference. You can see
plainness of words here too (*Mem.* 1. 1. 1), for although the subject matter
deserves anger and reproach (such being the quality of the proposition,
namely that a man as valuable as Socrates has been condemned),
Xenophon speaks like a plain man: *I have often wondered* and not: . . .
which would provoke one to anger or . . . *which deserves reproach.* For in
plain language, there is neither force nor spirit nor vehemence, nor is the
disposition of the subject matter like this,[4] nor is it such as to mark the
points as they are introduced. And this is particularly characteristic of
plain language. (23) It is good also to speak about things one knows as if
one is querying something, for example: . . . *at the arguments by which* (he
did not say 'accusations' or 'denunciations', which would have suited
political language, but: . . . *at the arguments by which they persuaded the
Athenians*), and it is good also to refer to the genus, i.e. not (the species)
'Anytus and Meletus', but (the genus): 'those who indicted Socrates'.

Something else that is appropriate to plain language is variation: *He
commits injustice on the one hand not respecting the gods whom the city
observes . . . he commits injustice on the other hand corrupting the young
men as well.*[5]

(24) Then in what follows, the proofs are extremely political. He shows
aggression against the points that belong to the argument (*Mem.* 1. 2. 1):
*This too seems to me surprising that some were persuaded that Socrates
corrupted the young men. First then . . .* With *first then*, he does not assert a
proposition, and then add points that support it, but simply develops the
subjects first. Notice the handling of the supporting points: a political
man would have taken them by genus, saying: 'he was so temperate, so
restrained, and so enduring of all kinds of labour.' Xenophon, however,
takes them by species, saying: 'he was restrained in respect of stomach
and sexual desire, and held out against winter and summer.' Furthermore, he mixes more serious points with less serious ones: *How then
would he be making them impious or lawless or gluttonous?*

---

[4] 'Disposition' = διάθεσις, a difficult term, occurs in a similar sense in cc. 31, 41,
135.

[5] This is based on *Mem.* 1. 2. 1, cited also in c. 21 (some words are omitted in c.
21; I underline them): ἀδικεῖ Σωκράτης οὓς μὲν ἡ πόλις νομίζει θεοὺς οὐ νομίζων, ἕτερα
δέ καινὰ δαιμόνια εἰσφέρων, ἀδικεῖ δὲ καὶ τοὺς νεοὺς διαφθείρων. There may be a
corruption; 'variation' would be a better description of: οὓς μεν . . . ἕτερα δέ . . .

Extraneous Thoughts

(25) Plain men often make use of thoughts extraneous to the subject, for example (*Kur.* 1. 1. 2): *We have never seen herds collecting round the shepherd*, and thoughts of this sort which are not suited to a political man. For even if political men use extraneous thoughts, such as if someone were to argue from examples or from history or from something of this sort, they should use ones related to the subject, which is why they are accustomed to modify them either by an explanation of causes or by an introduction. For example (to cite one from many) (Demosthenes, *Or.* 20. 11): *. . . therefore, so that you recognize that it is inconsistent also with the customs of our city to pass such a law*, and then: *The Thirty Tyrants are said to have borrowed money . . .* In plain language, on the other hand, extraneous thoughts are introduced from almost all areas of life. When the name or place is prestigious the things added from outside produce magnitude in language.

(26) In every case one must take care that rhythms, figures and names are appropriate to plain language, and one must be aware of thoughts that involve the same rhythmical pattern, such as (*Mem.* 1. 1. 19): *. . . being said, being done, being deliberated*, and all figures that suit them. In all cases one should take note of the plain quality that resides in them.

The Beginning of the Sumposion[6]

(27) Many principles are shared by the plain and political styles, for example making marking statements about things you are about to say, considering their nature and the objection that can be made that you are speaking about small and worthless things. An example of plainness is this scene (*Sump.* 1. 11 ff.): Philip the comedian came in and was weeping, those reclining at the *sumposion* kept laughing and the Syracusan provided wonderful entertainment (*Sump.* 2. 1). All this subject matter is common to either political or plain language, but the handling of the items is Xenophon's own. Similarly, the promise at the start of the *Sumposion* (1. 1) is common: *I wish to relate events which I have knowledge of, having been present at them*, but what follows is uncommon and novel,[7] since, instead of following up his promise straight away, he goes on to one of the things about Socrates. The events he was present at are those which happened in the home of Callias, but these are not related at once, but he takes it right from the beginning preceding these events. It is more like a narration.

Character: Introductory Comments

(28) One should be versatile in this form of language,[8] and one should produce in some places solemnity, in others *peribole*, in others dignity,

---

[6] Cf. the discussion in c. 14.
[7] 'Common' here seems to mean both 'shared by both styles' and also 'ordinary'.
[8] Translating Schmid's suggestion in his apparatus.

and achieve elsewhere character and grace, still elsewhere comedy, if possible, as in the passage mentioned earlier (*Sump.* 1. 11): *Philip the comedian, striking the door* . . . Character is extremely graceful, which is appropriate to plain language. Removing strategic approaches, using the words themselves, following the nature of the subjects, and not fearing their insignificance or vulgarity is a mark of a simple and noble soul. This is why rhetorical handbooks were invented, since from them even things lacking innate magnitude in themselves can acquire it; sometimes the qualities suggested can be of the same sort, sometimes they suggest some falsehood. An example of the latter is (*Sump.* 1. 5); *You are always making fun of us. You gave Protagoras a great deal of money in return for wisdom.* This remark suggests a quick touch of grace, but at the same time it contains malice. (29) In some sentiments no additional overtones are heard, but others have character.

Character is not simple but varies: there is graceful character and virtuous character; character can suggest sweetness, goodness, and there is a form that instantiates solemnity, as, for example (*Sump.* 1. 8): *So Autolycus sat down by his father.* Making the son sit down by his father is also very solemn in respect of thought, for such thoughts are solemn, but he particularly protected the effect of character by not employing the development that would naturally follow: Autolycus sat down by his father, as was right for a son with his father. That is political, and has lost the impression of character and solemnity. (30) Some of these passages, as I said, have a covert[9] and deliberate character, such as the foregoing example (*Sump.* 1. 5): *You are always making fun of us*; others are simple and suggest no malice, as, for example (*Sump.* 1. 7): *some scraping themselves, others washing themselves.* This expresses nothing more than the bare event. Where there are malicious innuendos which obstruct the style, you must not correct the offending utterance you have introduced absolutely, but rather do so with qualifications you add, such as (*Sump.* 1. 8): *As soon as he realized what was happening, he would have thought that beauty was something regal by nature*, with Xenophon's qualification: . . . *especially if like Autolycus one possessed it with a sense of restraint and modesty.* Since the subject under discussion was beauty, no one could resist interpreting this *in malam partem*.

Character and Moral Excellence

(31) First, the *ethos* of plain language must be one that suggests goodness. Goodness is excellence of judgement, moral choice made with intention and judgement and fairness of habits. This *ethos* shuld not be shown in itself, but it should be left behind in the minds of the hearers, so that it

---

[9] Translation 'covert' (for ὑποκαθημένον) suggested by Dr D. C. Innes.

seems innocent of intrigue. Consequently, one should not *mark* dangerous things as dangerous or terrifying things as terrifying, but it is sufficient just to say, for example (*Anab.* 1. 1. 3): *Tissaphernes slandered Kuros to his brother*. It was enough to convey from the genus what sort of thing it is to slander one brother to another. The value-judgement and attitude, in so far as it has any, he leaves you to consider. If you were to express it in a contentious manner, you might say: *Most dreadful and cruel was the slander which Tissaphernes put into the mind of Kuros' brother*. If you wanted to heighten it and supply considerations that should have prevented such slander, you might add: . . . *ashamed of neither gods nor justice nor of a most dreadful course of action*.

(32) The techniques one might expect to produce character in political writers might also be effective in plainness, but less so, since their manner and effect is different in the two genres. In political oratory one can produce character by hinting at something or suggesting something different, or even the very opposite of one's literal meaning, but in the other style this is not as effective, since it would be (?) an example of plainness and simplicity of thought. (33) To take an example from both styles: what does Demosthenes say when he wants to convey *ethos*? (passage unknown): *it would be highly appropriate for you to place the highest value on such a man and rightly regard him as a benefactor*. An example of character in Xenophon is (*Kur.* 7. 3. 8): *And the hand followed him*. By examining the arrangement in each case we could discover character in each.[10]

(34) Xenophon produces character first by looking at the idiosyncracies of the individuals whom he happens to be writing about, and second by observing the particular occasions and, in addition, the circumstances and the factors that accompany them. Reasoning from these he discovers how to produce character in his writing and indeed the effect of emotion also.

(35) To begin from the works themselves, the *Sumposion* contains every virtue, including the style and simplicity of thought that one would call 'character'. In fact it is pretty well pervasive in the work. How did he achieve it? By observing the nature of the occasion, the subject, and the attendant circumstances, by observing, for example, what sort of thing a *sumposion* is, and what sort of things are spoken of and take place in it. Looking to factors of this sort, he produced character[11] right at the start of the work: *But to me it seems that it is not only the serious deeds of gentlemen that deserve to be related, but also what they do in jest*. The thought that what great and good men do in jest should be welcomed also involves character; and indeed it is a principle of plainness that one should not seek important and high material unconditionally but also things that seem low and easy to condemn.

---

[10] The theme of character in Demosthenes is never returned to.
[11] Emending from λόγον.

(36) Again, in the *Memorabilia* in framing the style he looks to what he has learned of Socrates' moral choice. Although the subject deserves anger and reproach, that a man of such worth as Socrates should have been condemned,[12] he nevertheless here too shows the character of a plain man, and says: *I have often wondered . . .*, and not: 'at which one would be angry', or: 'which deserves reproach'. Notice particularly that although the words are restrained for the sake of plainness, they express equally well the magnitude of the event in the appropriate way, since 'I wondered' and 'often' suggest things that are not insignificant.

(37) Again, in the *Kuropaidia* notice the handling in the words: *The thought once occurred to me*. The thought is, how Kuros was brought up as a child, what form of education he had, what deeds he did, and that he was the most fortunate of men. But the significance of this to Xenophon is different. His choice was not to praise Kuros, nor was he concerned with how Kuros was educated or brought up, but, since his style involves character, the real line of thought his pen traces is, what should a good man be like, what upbringing and education should he have, what should he be like as a child and as an adolescent, and what actions and activities are suited to a gentleman.

(38) His method of handling such writing is similar in the *Memorabilia*, in which he deals with a more varied range of subjects—how one should behave with regard to one's country, one's friends, and one's family. But he does not state it as a direct recommendation as if it were a thesis: one should behave in this way toward one's friends, or: one should behave in this way toward one's brothers, or: there must be a demonstration of government before a man becomes wise and competent. Instead, he teaches you how to do such things by impersonating other characters. For example, he describes Chaerephon quarrelling with his brother (2. 3. 1): 'tell me, ' he says, 'do you alone not recognize that one must behave in this way toward one's brother', but he impersonates another person.[13] So when you are composing with character, do not introduce a subject as if it were a thesis (one should do this or that . . .), but impersonating another person, say that he was that sort of person, and that he did the things that you want that someone to do.

Other Forms of Character (i.e. not involving virtue)

(39) Simplicity of thought is not the only source which seems to produce character in speech. There is also a form which is exactly the reverse of the other one which consists in using a harsher, rough style, when the subject is of this sort, or when it is someone in love, supplying an appropriate style that is angled toward pathos in all respects, as in the

[12] Cf. c. 22.
[13] i.e. Xenophon speaks in the person of Socrates.

Kuropaidia (6. 1. 31–7. 20) Xenophon produced pathos from the circumstances in his account of Abradates and his wife. The entire excellence of this passage consists in maintaining the true properties of each. Thus he represented Cyanaxares as consistently irascible, and others as consistently possessing some other mental quality. This produces great character in the language. You would maintain it, if you follow the earlier thought and purpose of the discourse, looking for its significance and observing the peculiar nature of your subject.

Tacit Delineation of Character

(40) Depictions of character in plain style acquire force and dignity if someone communicates his own opinion and leaves an impression of character on the basis of thought alone. For example, if you said by way of marking the quality: the gods gave gifts to Cheiron and honoured him, as was right, since he was just and had performed the deeds of a good man, admiring him, or, that he was just and pursued the rest of virtue. In such passages you communicate your own opinion of such men. But Xenophon was content to break off in silence, and to rely on the thought alone: (*Cyneg.* 1. 1) *(they gave to) Cheiron because of his justice*, and so on. (41) Another habit of Xenophon and of all plain men is to make their characters as good as possible, without marking this for what it is. From this point of view consider the following aspect of plain characterization, whether you do not think that a good man who is going to die would want both his sons to be present. Darius was good and loyal to his own family to such a degree that he wanted both his sons to be present (*Anab.* 1. 1. 1): *When Darius was ill and suspected the end of his life, he wanted both his sons to be present*. This is the behaviour of a good character. He displays the disposition of father, and it is a virtuous judgement and a goodness of character appropriate to a plain man. He portrays good character also in the *Sumposion* saying of the woman who performs amazing feats (2. 11): . . . *so that the audience were frightened* . . . A good character shows here also—the fact that the audience were scared at the unexpected sight. (42) A different sort of character again is invisible and hidden, as is appropriate in plain language (*Anab.* 1. 1. 2): *Kuros goes inland taking Tissaphernes, as if he was a friend*. What need was there to say: 'taking Tissaphernes, the man who particularly plotted against him, as if he was a friend? Hiding this point and passing it over contained character.

(43) Pay particular attention to this point: the only exception to the generalization that plain men do not mark meanings, and let them show themselves, is if a suitable occasion should ever appear, as in the *Kunegetikos* (1. 18): *I advise young men not to despise hunting*. The use of the form of recommendation: *I advise*, said in his own person, after

such digressions, is appropriate and involves remarkable character. (44) When you intend the opposite of the literal meaning and you relax the intensity,[14] you produce character. For you are not saying: 'to be involved with hunting and be keen on hunting', but rather: 'not to despise hunting nor the rest of education'.

The effect of vulgarity is prevented also by setting something important in parallel with something that does not seem so: *not to despise hunting nor the rest of education.* To bind together greater with smaller, and genus with species suggests a man of understanding, e.g. (*Mem.* 1. 2. 7): *From this they become good in respect of war and in respect of other things also.*[15] The explanation is common to both political language and plain language, but the figuration is different—not binding it together and saying: not only for the war, but also for other purposes.[16]

Miscellaneous Techniques Related to Character

(45) Again, Xenophon produces character combined with sweetness in *Memorabilia* (1. 2. 7): *Indeed he is thought to have the greatest advantage, possessing a good friend.* He produces sweet character by the use of understatement. Instead of saying that the property of friends all becomes his, or that he derives help in life from friends, he uses a single word, which suggests both sweetness and character: *possessing a good friend.*

(46) The use of criticism by denying the opposite produces character. For example, after saying: *he himself did not neglect*, what would naturally have followed was: 'he blamed those who neglected', but what he says is *Mem.* 1. 2. 4): *Yet he himself did not neglect his body, and he did not praise those who neglected theirs.* (47) Another source of good character and one which is Socratic is to avoid strict consistency, for example in (*Mem.* 1. 1. 16): *he himself discoursed on human subjects, considering what was pious and what impious,* then moving from neuter adjectives to nouns, *what temperance was, what madness, what bravery, what cowardice, what a*

---

[14] Reading ἐπίτασις; other MSS have ἐπίστασις.

[15] Text adds: τόδε οὖν χρὴ ποιεῖν διὰ τόδε ('This should be done for this reason'), which Dr D. C. Innes suggests might be a gloss on the following αἰτιολογία ('explanation').

[16] This theme is reprised in c. 53, which may have been misplaced from here: 'There is character and solemnity in implying piety toward the gods and good deeds toward friends, and one must pay particular attention to these. You see, a very large number of the most important rhetorical principles have to do with thoughts, and thoughts are derived from within the author. The expression of thoughts about piety and obedience strongly suggests the moral choice of plain men. As I said, they do not much like to use didactic statements, unless they are forced to, for example: "one must be pious", "one must obey the gods who rule us", but they adumbrate thoughts about what one must do, not asserting that one must do these things in a didactic manner, but making general statements, such as: "when men do things like this, these things are accustomed to happen".'

city, what a man of the city. In the same passage he produced beauty by employing asyndeton in each case.

(48) Instances of irony also produce character. For example, all the passages in which he represented Socrates as discoursing and teaching young men as if he himself did not know, but rather inquired.

(49) Some words produce character in speech independently of their subject matter. For example (*Sump.* 1. 3): *I have met you at an opportune time.* Here character is generated purely by the words: *I have met you at an opportune time.*[17]

(50) While figures of comparison are very plain, and suggest historical writing instead, they also furnish character. For example (*Sump.* 1. 4): . . . *more with men such as you than with generals, officers of the cavalry, and campaigners for office* . . . But if you linked this with its opposite and said, e.g. 'whoever choose such men as they see superior to others in respect of offices or honours or similar powers, I think that they do wrongly', this would instead suggest the style of Critias or that of ancient sophists.

(51) I say that the plain man uses unemphatic diction, figure, and rhythm, for example (*Anab.* 1. 1. 1):[18] *When Darius was ill and suspected the end of his life, he wanted both his sons to be present.* The rhythm here is not tightly knit and tying the thoughts together, like that of political language, but relaxed, disconnected, and with the thoughts expressed directly,[19] as it were. (52) Expressing the thoughts in a direct manner instead of an indirect one generates pungency. Indirect expression would have been: Darius being ill . . . The plainness would probably have approached vulgarity because of the unemphatic use of most of the words as in the example the use of the unadorned word *was ill.* Thus he has used synonyms to avoid vulgarity: *When Darius was ill and suspected the end of his life* . . .[20]

Solemnity

(54) Solemnity comes about in many ways in plain language, particularly when you transfer from persons to things. Putting a proposition in terms of a person, e.g. 'beautiful people are kings by nature' (this is childish) is different from expressing it in the abstract (*Sump.* 1. 8): *beauty is regal by nature.* Solemnity is also the cause of the thought added after this: *especially if one possesses it like Autolycus along with a sense of restraint and modesty.* (55) Solemnity is also produced by interweaving, e.g. (*Sump.*

---

[17] Cf. the discussion of the same passage at c. 122.

[18] The same example appears in c. 41.

[19] The MSS here have πλάγια, which would mean 'oblique, subordinated, usually by use of genitive absolute', associated with the terms πλαγιάζω and πλαγιασμός. I follow the suggestion of Dr D. C. Innes that we really expect οὐ πλάγια.

[20] For c. 53 see under c. 44 above.

2. 1): *a boy very pretty and playing the cithara and dancing very beautifully.*
Weaving together different points removes the subdivisions of the genus.
(56) You make the language solemn when you introduce things that are
about to happen or are happening at the present as if they have already
happened, e.g. (*Sump.* 2. 2): *When the flute-girl had played for them, and
the boy had finished playing the cithara.* (57) When you interrupt with
solemn words, you produce force along with solemnity and beauty, e.g.
(*Kuneg.* 1. 4): *Zeus and Cheiron were brothers, sons of the same father, but
the mother of one was Rhea, the other a Naiad nymph.* Making them share
something in common (*sons of the same father*), but also stating the
difference (*the mother of one was Rhea, of the other* . . .) produces solemnity
along with plainness. (58) Stating something by genus is more solemn
than saying it by species, for example (*Sump.* 2. 11): *lest she suffer
something* (there is a difference between the expression of the specific:
lest she be pierced through, lest she be butchered, and gathering all the
species together and expressing them with a single phrase: *lest she suffer
something*).

Peribole

(59) *Peribole* comes about in plain language when one subordinates[21] a
thought and inserts another one when the first is not yet finished, and
completion has not yet been achieved, so that there seems to be a single
thought, e.g. (*Ag.* 1. 7): *When the Lacedaimonians were considering the
matter, Agesilaos declared* . . .; then the verb that completes it: *that he
would cross*, not employing subordination any more. '. . . that having
crossed he would do *x* and *y* . . .' would have been over-long, so he says: . . .
that he would cross.[22] (60) All *peribole* produces force in language. We must
consider how force in plain language differs from political language. So
consider (Demosthenes, *Or.* 1. 23): *For success that is undeserved is a source
for contempt from foolish people.* I would claim that a demonstrative
figure[23] is of no profit in plain language, since although it adds dignity
and force, it is not simple or ordinarily human, so that one just states the
subject in that way, but it is exalted and inflated. The same is true of the
subordinating particle (?) (*Or.* 1. 23): *For success* . . . Such particles force a
sentence to enclose thoughts within itself and become rounded, harsh and
twisted together. Hence one should not add subordinating particles when
one wants to introduce a sign of force, but instead begin with simple

---

[21] πλαγιάσας usually means 'use the genitive absolute' (see on c. 51 above), but
here it is used more generally of subordination by use of participle.

[22] The point here is that the sentence goes on: 'that he would cross and that he
would . . .'. Xenophon might have expressed 'cross' as a participle also, but he held
back from such a high degree of subordination.

[23] ἀποφαντικόν, i.e. a construction which sets out a subject, rather than ques-
tioning, ordering or something similar.

verbs.[24] (61) Another feature that contributes to *peribole* and makes the language significant and important is when one does not introduce subjects just by themselves or describe them on the basis of the specific subjects (e.g. Callias appeared a worthy sight because he was overcome with love for Autolycus), but adds some general addition extraneous to the specific theme in question, for example (*Sump.* 1. 10): *All those possessed by other gods appear to be a worthy sight* . . . If you wanted to pass quickly to the subject matter and not to elevate the style to a great extent, you would just have said: particularly those possessed by love. As it is, it has been elevated much more because different matters have been inserted in the interval before the subject is added: *Some appear more vigorous to look upon and to speak more effectively and to be more forceful* . . .[25] (63) Another case of *peribole* is in the *Sumposion* (2. 9): *Socrates said: by many other facts and most clearly by the feats of this girl* . . . where Xenophon creates *peribole*. What creates the *peribole* here? The introduction of something general and the transition to something specific: in many other cases, and clearly among them that of the girl. It is a Socratic and old-fashioned technique to draw some advantageous example from anything, since the original subject of the speeches was excellence (?), and their greatest tenet is that the virtue of men and women is the same.

Sweetness

(64) Sweetness of diction, we have stated,[26] is derived from comedy and Plato and Xenophon. Plain men also use poetic words, when they want to add grandeur to style through rhetorical principles. It is a feature of comic style to begin with particles of partition (i.e. the μὲν . . . δὲ . . . construction) and from particles of addition, such as 'and yet', 'however', 'but', 'accordingly', 'but indeed'. Such words add plainness to the style. (65) When you want to produce sweetness, use a particular type of metaphor, transferring words that naturally apply to one thing to another. It is also produced when you do not keep to words used in a strictly literal sense, for example the literal sense is 'they gave', and the transferred expression applied to it is (*Kuneg.* 1. 1): *and they honoured Cheiron because*

---

[24] This refers to Demosthenes, *Or.* 1. 23, a clear case of periodic συστροφή. The author is saying: do not start with e.g. an articular infinitive, since this makes the sentence over complex, but start with simple verbs.

[25] c. 62 seems to be out of place. (Much more suggestive of historical writing is direct use of figures, whereas indirect use suggests political language, since it involves dignity and *peribole*. If you were to use an indirect construction, you would say: 'with the horse-race having ceased', whereas the direct construction is (*Sump.* 1. 2): *As the horse-race ceased*. This seems relaxed and laid back. The political man would not do this but compose in a tenser manner: 'After the horse-race ceased.' Just as political language is twisted together and combines thoughts, so plain language is relaxed and stretched out.)

[26] Not in our MSS.

of his justice, instead of 'they gave'. (66) Sweetness is also produced by saying important things in an unimportant way and *vice versa*, and this truly remarkable trope which adds sweetness to speech expressing unimportant things in an important way is exemplified by speaking of a war between a dog and a wild beast (*Kuneg.* 10. 1): *First, the dogs of each species must not be just any dogs, so that they are ready to fight the wild beast.* (67) He produces remarkable sweetness in the *Agesilaos* also when he says (6. 7): *But whenever he travelled, he led the army arranged in the most advantageous way possible to provide support*, then he supplies an example, in the manner of a plain man conveying sweetness along with solemnity: *Quietly,[27] just as a girl of the greatest modesty would walk.* An impression of relaxation is produced by the diminishing effect of the example and the fact that the comparison is not appropriate in every way; for in what respect is a girl like an army? Nevertheless saying 'the modest girl' would sound vulgar, but reversing it, and placing the attribute before the person would have produced solemnity along with sweetness: just as the most modest girl.[28] (68) As for sweetness, I have stated already in an earlier passage its effects in political language and in plain language. It is probably more a virtue of plain language.

Beauty

(69) Plain language acquires beauty from details, if they are available, or from other circumstantial factors, such as when he calls a city (*Anab.* 1. 2. 7) *great and fortunate*, and in the case of a river when he specifies its source or its breadth, since all of this adds beauty to the language. Going through all the properties of a river, a city, or a plain dissipates the plainness, but to do so by genus (e.g. *great and fortunate*) preserves the beauty and the simplicity. (70) Juxtapositions of similar things make the style beautiful and pungent, as in the *Anabasis* he says of Kuros (*Ag.* 1. 25):[29] *he proposed prizes for the formations of horse, to be awarded to whoever should ride his horse best.* (71) The elaboration and the figuration in plain writers is invisible. This is something which makes ancient writers valuable. Notice how Xenophon fashions figures in: . . . *for the formations of horse, to be awarded to whoever should ride his horse best.* This is different from saying 'for the horsemen', for this would probably make the style quick moving and contentious. The figuration moves from a plurality to a singular, and it is expressed directly. It is next to a similar construction: . . . *for the formations of horse, to be awarded to whoever should ride his horse best, and*

---

[27] ἡσυχῶς is not in extant MSS of Xenophon.

[28] The distinction seems to hinge on the difference between 'sweetness and solemnity' (generated when the superlative follows), and 'solemnity with sweetness' (when it precedes). Alternatively, the text may have originally said (as Schmid believed): 'but reversing it . . . would not produce . . .'.

[29] A rare case of a misattribution.

for the formations of hoplites, whoever should be in the best physical condition.

Truth[30]

(72) The most important thing in plain language is for the style to seem as truthful as possible and for what is said to be the sort of thing that one would think would be easy for anyone to think up. This happens most when the author derives a thought from the very subject which is being introduced, for example, in the *Agesilaos* (1. 8): *to plan to fight spending his money rather than that of the Greeks.* He derives the thought from something done by Agesilaos (he was about to speak of his crossing into Asia), introducing a thought by which he could show that Agesilaos was a sensible man, and in this way he particularly gives the impression of saying the truth about him. (73) Truth is also produced by introducing something which seems to go against you, and admitting it and letting it go without refuting it, for example (cf. *Kur.* 6. 2. 20; Demosthenes, *Or.* 2. 22; 11. 15): *if one of you seeing the enemy supposed them to be terrifying, his view seems to me to be right.* To create the impression that the other things that Kuros says to the soldiers are truthfully spoken, he has him not only fail to refute this point—although it seems to be against him—but actually corroborate it. (74) The impression of truth is also created by introducing points in the form of a narrative, even if they are fabricated or insignificant. The reason is that in saying them in this way one presupposes that they actually happened. (75) A truthful effect is also produced by saying something briefly and putting many points side by side. For example (*Kur.* 5. 1. 2): . . . *summoning* (next, who?) *Araspes* (then, where was he from?) *the Mede* (then the reason for his knowing him) *who had been his friend since childhood* (then another point) *to whom he had given the robe* . . . (76) These techniques seem to be sufficient for expression with a truthful effect (? literally 'with an effect also'). But it comes about particularly when you do not accept something true said about you, and this is characteristic of the plain man. For example, Socrates says (*Sump.* 1. 5): *you are always making fun of us.* Character has been created by the restrained quality of the thought, and by the fact that he is not inflated by his praise, but treats it as a joke. What the other one said in earnest, he reacts to as if he is being made fun of.

Arrangement

(77) Arrangement of a speech is appropriate order, the expectation of what is said, thoughts being connected sequentially, and also arguments

---

[30] Schmid (1926) calls ἀλήθεια "ἀξιοπιστία" (see his heading on p. 101), which creates the impression that *Peri Apheleias* is more like *Peri Politikou Logou* than it really is. In fact, the words ἀξιοπιστία and ἀξιόπιστος do not occur in the text of *Peri Aphelous Logou*.

related to the subject matter, as well as all the other principles that belong to plain arrangement. What I mean is that if there is a single heading, one should state without anticipation the necessary strong points on behalf of oneself, then lay down anticipation of the good points that can be made against the opponent, and then consider if they themselves make some point on our behalf. If, on the other hand, the points that come from the opponent are several, one must consider the subject. The method is the same: the basic point is that we must show the weakness of our enemies' points and the strength of the points in our favour. Anyone can see how it could happen and that it would always be the same.

Diction

(78) On the subject of diction, I would say that one should only use nouns and verbs that one finds in classical literature, and to put it simply one could say that one should not use all words in all types of language, but treat differently each element of plainness, pathos, character, and anger. The elements of Demosthenes' speeches contribute much to the quality of diction, but Xenophon alone consistently produces plainness in his diction. Anger, pathos, wrath, or sharpness and other emotions belong to dignity or roughness, and to the change and encitement of emotions, the type of thought typical of Demosthenes.

Examples

(79) The use of examples is Socratic, and it does not suit political language very well. Sometimes Xenophon introduces what he wants to say by examples even before stating the subject itself, and for the most part his arguments involve examples. He does this in all his works, but it is particularly clear from the *Memorabilia*. In that work one can discover by examination that his representation of Socrates discoursing and proving things follows this pattern. (80) Examples that are introduced, through which you make a display, must be similar to the subject and have something in common with it in respect of genus, or strength, or time, or consequences, or properties, or some other similarity, and this is successful in this form of language and produces simplicity most effectively. This is an extremely rich source, and the wheeling in of additional features makes the language appear plain because what is being said not only gains in solemnity but also, from the new elements, in vividness— which appears to be more the task of conversation.[31]

Arguments

(81) As for arguments, Demosthenes and those who compose forensic speeches make selections and divisions, and they mark the qualities

---

[31] λαλιαί are mentioned only here and in 82. See Mras (1949).

individually, reasonably so, since their style is contentious, so that the
audience can at once learn the strength of each and consider each of them
carefully. (82) But I do not think this fits plain language, since the style
should appear as much as possible uncontrived, simple, and pure.
Xenophon arranges each thought so that it is free of marking, as in the
Agesilaos. As a result, one might think that these thoughts had been
thrown in at random.[32] However, far from being thrown in at random,
they are expressed with care, but lack any detailed examination of
arguments, addition, transference, change in quality, and all alterations
of this sort. Hence there are many breaks—they are continuous—and
beginnings of thoughts which are not integrated into the context but
asyndetic. Further, the argument seems to vary a great deal, and the
composition is not a single web, but expressed clause by clause, in the
manner of a conversation. (83) The same effect is produced by the
appearance these words give of being a narrative of the actions of a
good man. However, this does not fit in all cases into plain language, and
one must understand this more than any other idiom of Xenophon's, and
this more than anything, in my view, makes his style plain.

Beginnings

(84) Let us learn about the beginning of a work and Xenophon's practice
in this area. In all cases one must manage in advance what in the subject is
useful and either refute possible objections or make them support one's
own point of view. In this respect it is the same as political language, but
plain language is unique in its manner of handling and style. (85) Political
men derive their beginnings from the subject itself, or use beginnings that
lead into the subject. Xenophon does not use beginnings that lead into the
subject in all cases, and he does not usually derive them from the subject.
So in the *Kuropaidia* he says: *The thought once occurred to me . . .* He does
not begin from the deeds of Kuros, but develops his theme from outside
by a long argument. Hence proceeding subtly from outside he creates
amplification. (86) But he did derive the beginning from the subject in the
Memorabilia, so that it would seem completely forensic at the start of
presentation of the subject,[33] if the thought were not brought to a
conclusion: *Often*, he says, *I have wondered at the arguments with which
they persuaded the Athenians . . .* (87) A principle in all Xenophon's
beginnings is not to divide off the first thought and speak as if introducing
a second within it, but to suggest further points that depend directly on
the first, and to develop them at length. A peculiar quality of plainness is
to express a thought in general terms first without changing the quality of
the thought (a political man would have done the same, but he would have

---

[32] Cf. *Kunegetikos* 13. 6, mentioned above on p. 68.
[33] ὑποβολή; some MSS gave ἐπιβολή.

elevated the language with dignity), for example (*Kur.* 1. 1. 1): *The thought once occurred to me* (the same technique is also found in the passage concerning the nature of the beautiful *(Sump.* 1. 8)), then the specific point . . . *all the democracies and all the tyrannies.* Another peculiar quality of plainness is to avoid the use of a declarative figure, such as (*Sump.* 1. 8): *nothing is harder to persuade than human nature*; instead he uses a question, in a particular human manner: *The thought once occurred to me*, and diction that is not relaxed but tightly coiled: *The thought once occurred to me . . .* (88) The final section of a phrase or any other unit should come to rest on a long element. The *kola* should be independent, and the speech should be plain, with clean divisions in respect of *kola*, and suggesting an effect in style or quality of crowdedness, and a novel and plain interweaving. This effect is produced by a single word, e.g.: *The thought once occurred to me*, instead of: 'We once considered . . .'.[34]

(89) In general the beginnings should be derived from the beginning of the events described, for example (*Anab.* 1. 1. 1): *Darius and Parysatis had two sons . . .* In that case even if the theme is great, its origin is in simple matters.

Plain Language and Political Language[35]

(90) In the two types of prose the greatest difference is subject matter. Political writers show confidence when dealing with important and well-known affairs and characters, whereas the historical writer endows even important subject matter with plainness by expressing doubts and reservations. (91) Most important of all in plainness is that the expression of the subjects should be pure and lacking in elaboration, without marking the individual qualities. For marking is characteristic of the political man, when you state not just the subjects but add the quality— that it is great, if it is great, that it is dangerous, if it is dangerous. Plainness must be free of this. For example, the plain man would say '. . . coming forward he said this . . .', while Demosthenes says (*Or.* 19. 15): *. . . standing up he uttered words, ye gods, deserving the death penalty many times over . . .*

(92) Xenophon often uses Demosthenic frequency of force in respect of thought, and differs from him only in the handling of it. Take the passage from the *Anabasis* (2. 5. 16 ff.), in which he expresses certain argumentation in the case of Tissaphernes, namely that he was not plotting against the Greeks. Since Tissaphernes' character was one that might well be suspected of wanting to hatch plots and since he could not prove his point

---

[34] This paragraph ends with a probably corrupt sentence: . . . acute brevity creates plainness, so that when the principle is removed, instead of plainness roughness or dignity results, but mild dignity instead results from '. . . once occurred . . .'.

[35] Cf. the discussion at cc. 11 ff.

on grounds of judgement, he shifts his ground to a proof from capacity: *If we are capable of harming you but in fact do not do so, it is clear that we do not want to.* What has made thoughts as forceful as these *plain* is the manner of *handling* them: he arranges the thoughts in pairs of positive and negative,[36] and cuts them up, putting it like this: *Is it that you are in your homeland and we in a foreign country? Is it that you are in a good condition and we in a bad one?* There is nothing else to relax the thought except the manner of expression. (93) In the *Agesilaos* he does the same thing, making the handling plain, since the thought of the passage was rough (*Ag.* 1. 1):[37] *(it would not be good) if he did not win even moderate praise because he was exceedingly virtuous.* What I mean is that if the thought is of this type, ⟨he handles it in such a way as to become plain⟩.[38] He avoided an indignant outburst like that of Demosthenes (Ps. Demosthenes 7. 1): *it would be a terrible thing if the letters sent from Philip . . .* Some usages are peculiar to plain language, and you could not in any way transfer them to become political, as here: *. . . he was exceedingly good.*

(94) In general, wherever Xenophon makes many disconnected points in a short space and makes the thought independent, his style has a good rhythm, as in (*Kur.* 5. 1. 5): *When she stood up, all those with her stood up as well.* One must not combine many things in plain language, as Demosthenes does (*Or.* 1. 8): *If when we came after helping the Euboeans . . .*, but express things in brief units, so that one's language becomes easy to follow.

Diction

(95) The use of words without emphasis produces vulgarity. Hence there is a risk that plain language becomes vulgar, since it approaches it closely as a result of the use of such words. Avoidance and removal of vulgarity can come from the juxtaposition of synonyms, such as: *When Darius was ill and suspected the end of his life . . .*

(96) The metaphorical use of words is characteristic of plain writers, for example (*Ag.* 1. 19): *he made many men lovers of his friendship*, and again (*Ag.* 1. 30): *the followers of the Greeks* (he does not hesitate to call the rearguard 'followers').[39] Again, the repeated use of the same word (Demosthenes, *Or.* 19. 93): *they persuaded . . . we were persuaded*, and those that cut up the thought into separate units: *we sent ambassadors.* For a sequence of independent units makes the style plain and suggests

---

[36] ἐξ ὑπάρξεως καὶ στερήσεως is found only here; it can be compared to the σχῆμα of 'denial and assertion' (τὸ κατ' ἄρσιν καὶ θέσιν) described by Hermogenes at 293. 16 ff.

[37] The word 'exceedingly' may come from *Ag.* 1. 1. 36.

[38] The text literally says: 'he makes the handling rough', which must be wrong, perhaps a negative has been omitted.

[39] The same example is used in c. 20.

character, as if someone is relating actual events quickly. (96) Words for places and locations that suit plain language should be selected, and against those that have less force and are less approved of, such as 'gymnasium', 'hippodrome'. And if you actually combine them, adding one to the other,[40] e.g. (*Ag.* 1. 25): *gynasia of men exercising, hippodromes of horsemen training*, the effect is one of plainness.

(98) In plain language words should not only be used in one meaning but to signal two or three things. For example, 'depart' has several aspects, and all must be examined; it includes 'near' and 'far', 'by land' and 'by sea', 'having trouble' and 'causing trouble', and countless other significations also. (99) Words of the kind that refer to barley, wheat, or olive oil seem to produce plainness, since that style involves less important things. A political man would hesitate to approach such words, and if he does, he must be well aware that they will be introduced for the sake of vividness, or to produce character.

Rhythm can be different without affecting the subject matter, so that the difference from political language comes down to matters of style, not thought. Language that is perfect and fully political should be so in respect of both thought and style.

(100) Sometimes the thought is plain but the style political, as in the *Against Callicles* of Demosthenes (*Or.* 55. 24): *(She said that) of the barley not even three medimnoi were wet and she saw them being dried, and that of wheat a half a medimnos; a container of oil, she said, was knocked on its side, but it suffered no harm.* This involves solemnity, since direct expression would have produced vulgarity, if one had said, for example: *. . . it was not spilt . . .* Demosthenes, however, instead of using the proper term and naming the species, puts it more generally: *. . . but it suffered no harm.*

Interweaving (τὸ ἐπιπλέξαι) in Demosthenes

(101) Interweaving by the use of the same words seems to be plain,[41] and it slackens the force of political language, as in *On the False Embassy* Demosthenes says (19. 83): *Who does not know that it is by the military prowess of the Phocians, and by the fact that the Phocians are masters of Thermopylae (that we have security against the Thebans and assurance that neither Philip nor the Thebans will invade the Peloponnese or Euboea or Attica).* But he adds (19. 84): *This security of place and circumstance . . .,* and this gives force, as if he is summing up.

---

[40] Or perhaps ἐπιπλεκόμενος in the sense of 'interweaving' (cf. cc. 101, 109, 110) instead of ἐπιλεγόμενος, which might be repeated from earlier on.

[41] 'Interweaving' is ἐπιπλέκω, as in 109–10 (also c. 97?). Here it seems to involve repetition of the same word (*Phocians . . . Phocians*; *Thebans . . . Thebans*). I take it that the author thinks that 19. 84 represents a change of style.

Miscellaneous Techniques

(102) To assume an opinion is plain, for example: knowing well, and thinking, and supposing. It is also good to insinuate thoughts as if derived from other people's opinion. Xenophon uses this particularly in the *Kuropaidia*, repeatedly saying, for example, *if any of you thinks this*.[42]

(103) It is also plain not to be upset by things that one might be upset by, and not to be amazed at things that warrant amazement, but simply to relate the events on one's own authority without marking them.[43]

(104) Beginning with the nominative case makes the style plain, as does breaking up the thoughts into brief clauses.

Plain men often use extraneous additional thoughts, such as (*Kur.* 1. 1. 2): *We have never seen herds collecting round the shepherd.* Political men also use extraneous thoughts, such as histories or examples, but they adapt them by the use of introductions and explanations.

(105) Appropriate to plain language are variations, such as: 'he thinks, not thinking', and beginning from the same points (?)

Plain too is not using rough words, but restrained ones.

Rough is: 'this in private, that in public', whereas the plain man says (*Mem.* 1. 1. 2): *at home and on the altars.*

Additions such as: (ibid.): *for so too it was rumoured*, are also plain.[44]

The Optative

(106) Optatives seem to be more a feature of plainness, for example 'may he be worthy', and 'if they were pious', and 'as Socrates would say', and in the *Anabasis* (1. 1. 5): *So that they would be capable of fighting . . .*, and (following it, in the same figure), *. . . and would have good will toward him.* Optatives make the style pure.

Three Techniques from Agesilaos *1. 3–8*

(107) Plain also is not speeding up the tension of the style, but slowing down, and proceeding at leisure, e.g. (*Ag.* 1. 3): *But one could not even hold this against them (the fact that though kings the state they rule is quite ordinary).*

As for digressions, political men usually examine untoward happenings, which is a source for roughness, whereas plain men examine good events, e.g. (*Ag.* 1. 4): *While no other government (. . . can claim an unbroken existence, this kingdom alone stands fast).*[45]

(108) Another plain technique is not to overextend oneself either in

---

[42] There is no precise parallel for this in the *Kuropaidia*; the example seems intended to give a type of statement, not an exact quotation.

[43] Cf. c. 22, c. 91 above.

[44] Cf. c. 125.

[45] Xenophon uses history to show the excellence of the Spartan system; political orators are presumably more interested in crisis and disaster.

respect of action or thought, and the use of transitions such as 'however' and 'but in this way', and it is very plain not to give one's own judgement when something is worthy of praise but a commonly held judgement, e.g. (*Ag.* 1. 8): *At once the majority were amazed* . . . And here there is another principle—not to exaggerate and say 'all were amazed', but to be more restrained and say: . . . *the majority were amazed.*

More Miscellaneous Techniques

Another characteristically plain technique is to omit supporting arguments and to use points that are less supportive, for example:[46] *to have hopes for safety in awareness of no impiety on their part concerning the gods nor any act of injustice concerning men.*

(109) Another plain technique is to place words in parallel and bound together with no elaboration, e.g.: 'also Ionians and Aeolians and Hellespontians'.

Also, not refraining from words that have less force and less prestige, e.g. saying 'market' and 'in the market', and specific terms, e.g. 'iron-workers' and 'cobblers'. This too gives plainness.

Two Points in Agesilaos *1. 35–6*[47]

(110) Often when the difference is great (?), you interweave clauses in this way (*Ag.* 1. 35): . . . *Now however there are some who actually revolted*, and sometimes you can state it free of any elaboration, sometimes you add the cause, e.g. . . . *striving for freedom.* Using figures of inquiry instead of figures of demonstration is plain; an example of the figure of demonstration having vividness (1. 36) is: *that man ruling many cities in the mainland, and also ruling islands.* Vividness also comes about in political language,[48] for example (Demosthenes, *Or.* 18. 319): *Philammon did not leave Olympia without a crown because he was defeated by Glaucus the Carystian* . . .

Still More Miscellaneous Techniques

(111) Also plain is not to argue by way of a proposition that something is good, but by way of a comparison to argue that it is better than some other good.

Plain and elegant is using a denying hyperbole instead of a straightforward denial, e.g. (*Ag.* 5. 5): *Not even if I were to (become the fairest and strongest and swiftest man on earth)*, and instead of what would follow to

---

[46] The source for this is unknown; Schmid (1926) suggests it might be from *Kur.* 8. 8. 7.

[47] Cf. cc. 133 ff. below.

[48] The MSS here have 'vividness is also found in plainness', but this cannot be right; I would propose some suitable emendation here.

deny the opposite, e.g. (*Mem.* 1. 2. 4): *he did not neglect*, instead of: 'he cared for' (which would naturally follow).[49]

(112) Asyndeton is plain, since it breaks up the rhythm. It is opposite to political language, and suits plainness, e.g. (*Ag.* 2. 6): *Athenians, Thebans, Argives, Corinthians.*

Plain also is not speaking of things universally. An example of speaking universally is 'the Persians'; an example of speaking partially is 'the possessions of the Persians'.

(113)[50] Again, often using the same word in different cases and reversing it is plain.

(114) Another feature in the same style is without hiding either the thing or its name to say it obliquely, e.g. (*Anab.* 1. 2. 12): *it was said that (Epyaxa gave) to Kuros . . .*

(115) It is historical to introduce in addition to specific names also an indefinite element (if complete speech is needed (?)), e.g. (*Sump.* 1. 5): *Gorgias, Prodicus, and many others.*

(116) When a thought is completed by one word which finishes it off, and depends on a single word at the end, as in this case (*Sump.* 1. 7): *since he was obviously worried that they would not follow, they went along*, the effect is historical and suggests character.

(117) The naming of individual things, for example (*Ag.* 2. 7): *all the bronze and all the red dye*, is plain, whereas the naming of things *en masse* suggests *peribole* and dignity.

Interweaving (συμπλοκή)

(118) Interweaving is more appropriate to contentious language, but it may sometimes have a role in plain language also, when the beginning of a sentence is coiled together with interweaving, but what follows is disconnected, e.g. *he was both burning and sacking.* Pungency is produced when interweaving is combined with anaphora, e.g. (*Ag.* 1. 33): *simultaneously he was both burning [and sacking the area of the town], simultaneously he was revealing through an announcement (?)*, not 'was announcing', or 'was ordering to announce'.

Philip at the Door: Sumposion *1. 11*

(119) In plain language it is sufficient to mention not only what happened but how it happened, e.g. (*Sump.* 1. 11): *Philip the comedian beating on the door.* The words 'beating on the door' are chosen carefully, because he is described not only as knocking on it but actually beating on it.[51] Some

---

[49] For the latter point, cf. c. 46.

[50] Here I omit a sentence which seems to be corrupt and to duplicate c. 120 below.

[51] Cf. Schmid (1887–97), i. 106.

disagree, but that it is good Greek is not in question. If you wanted to amplify this in a political manner, you could add qualities: 'Philip was a comedian, who suddenly appears, and when he found no one nearby, his first thought was to leap at the door, but he decided to signal to someone else, and so came up and knocked on the door.'

And Yet More Miscellaneous Techniques

(120) To say some things relying on the opinions of others is plain, e.g. (Thucydides, 1. 24. 4): *(having been in a state of stasis with each other for many years), as is said.* The political man, on the other hand, introduces most points on his own authority, for example, to take the plain statement of Thucydides just mentioned, if he had said, *'after (ἐπειδή) they had been in a state of stasis . . .'*, he would have made the style rough.

(121) Some things are fine for plain men but low in political discourse, e.g. 'living the life of gulls'.[52] This was said for the purpose of abuse, and it has its place. But there is a difference in speech between plainness and vulgarity. When you want to abuse, divide it into individual elements, as Demosthenes does (*Or.* 18. 260): *chief-dancer, leader, ivy-carrier.*

In elegant style and in dialogues it is appropriate for plainness to be mixed in with the first principles[53] of dignity.

Ending on the same element (in a manner stretched out, however, so as not to destroy the style) creates plainness.

Sentence Structure at Anabasis 1. 2. 13 (Midas)

(122) In plain language it is very fine to use an indirect construction (i.e. direct speech?), and it has remarkable vividness, for example if you wanted to say, using the indirect construction[54] 'he himself came and said that he had met them at a good time', then follow Xenophon (*Sump.* 1. 3): *I have met you at an opportune time.* To cut short the construction, and make a new beginning, is plain.

(123) In such passages when you vary the construction, and make many beginnings, articulating the structure into independent units, it suggests a more novel and a more delicate style, e.g. (*Anab.* 1. 2. 13): *By the road was a fountain called after Midas the king of Phrygia*; then a new beginning: *here Midas hunted down the satyr*; then another beginning, supplying the manner of the hunting: *he mixed wine with it.* Such beginnings and the continual use of the direct construction show that the style is finer. (124) But it is a mark of the older style to stretch out the sentence with a single

---

[52] Of unknown origin; the phrase 'life of a gull' is used proverbially for the life of a wandering sailor at Aelian, *Ep.* 18; alluded to perhaps at Aristophanes, *Clouds* 591; Dio of Prusa, 33. 24.

[53] As Schmid says in his apparatus, the sense of ἀρχαί here is obscure.

[54] πλάζω seems to mean 'vary the construction' (I owe this suggestion to Dr D. C. Innes).

unbroken complex: *By the road was a fountain called after Midas the king of Phrygia, where Midas is said to have hunted the satyr,* (then the manner) *mixing wine in with it.* The sentence has been produced in one complete unit, and this is typical of Xenophon.[55]

Further Techniques

(125) On the subject of obscure things, I have often said that one must attribute them to hearsay, which suits plain language, e.g. (*Anab.* 1. 2. 12): *and it was said that Epyaxa gave much money to Kuros.*[56]

On the subject of mythological events, one should say not that they happened, but that they are said to have happened.

Kainoprepeia/*Novelty*

(126) We said that novelty suits plainness. It is sensible to use an example here also, the passage in the *Anabasis* (1. 2. 10) where Xenophon says: *he sacrificed the Lycaea.* This is very novel, and the syntax is peculiar, since he uses the name of the festival as if it were the offering itself, applying the place in which it happened and the reason it happened to the action. The normal mode of expression would have been: *at the Lycaea,* but *to sacrifice the Lycaea* was novel, as if you were to say 'he sacrificed the Panathenaea' or 'he sacrificed the Olympia'.[57]

Apollo and Marsyas

(127) It is characteristic of elaborate style to combine factors that relate to place—where, near what, under what,[58] as in the *Anabasis* (1. 2. 8): *The great king has a palace in Celaenae, strong, at the fountain of the Marsyas river, under the acropolis,* then the same epanalepsis (?), so as to create a new beginning: *it flows through the city and gives out into the river Maeandros.* Another example of distinction is: *there it is said that Apollo flayed Marsyas, quarrelling with him about wisdom.* (128) Of mythological subjects, as we said before, one should know that one should say not that they happened, but that they are said to have happened. Again, one should also know that the old-fashioned manner, when the subject is an important one, does not employ the same elaboration, but it is enough to state the things and how they happened without any elaboration. Elaborating and dwelling on them because they are important detracts from the

[55] Unusually here the author suggests that the ideal style, with many beginnings, is not the one illustrated by Xenophon.

[56] Κῦρον in Schmid's text implies that the author misquotes the *Anabasis* here; I read Κύρῳ, with Spengel. The same example is cited in c. 114 (Schmid has Κύρῳ there!).

[57] Here Schmid rightly brackets the comment: *it is normal to say that he sacrificed sacrifices. This is just normal speech.*

[58] Reading ὑπὸ τῷ, following some MSS, suggested to me by Dr D. C. Innes.

old-fashioned quality of the style. So in: *there it is said*, he does not say: 'there is the flute-player Marsyas, a Phrygian by birth, who learnt a great lesson.' (129) Note also that he changed the order. Naturally first was to say that he quarrelled, then that he was defeated, and then what he suffered. When you reverse the natural order in this way, and put the last item first, and then successively the points leading up to it, it will add speed and beauty, as when after saying that Marsyas suffered Xenophon explains why: *quarrelling with him about wisdom*. Old-fashioned also is not to specify the species and say: 'quarrelling about flute-playing and music', but to say: *about wisdom*. (130) As for Marsyas' hide, another writer might have said *hanged* (using the middle voice), but Xenophon uses a novel form of expression (*Anab.* 1. 2. 9, using the active): *hanged the hide in the cave, from where the fountains* . . . Notice also how basic and unelaborate it is: *for this is why the river is called Marsyas*. Notice also the restraint of the ancients, since he did not mention the misfortune which is why he gave his name to the Marsyas river, or refer to the fate of the flute-player. Xenophon does none of this, and is content to say: *this is why the river is called Marsyas*. (131) Then another beginning from something important (*Anab.* 1. 2. 9): *There Xerxes, when he was defeated in battle and left Greece* . . . Notice again the restraint: there is no reference to Salamis here, no expedition, no numerous foot-army, no massive numbers of infantry or triremes, nor how he was defeated, how he withdrew, nor any of the many things that happened to Xerxes, just the bare fact: *when* . . . *he left Greece*. You have learnt now how the ancients proceed and how much restraint they have.

Ordering of Points and Anabasis *1. 1. 9*

(132) In the area of thoughts take particular care that points that sum up should have been deployed and placed last, so that the style also has an element of solemnity. Notice also that in plain language, even if some things are greater and more important than others, they always tend to put the less important first, for example in this case: it is a major and prestigious thing for Kuros to give so much money to Clearchus, but Xenophon did not start with this, but first described his reasoning (*Anab.* 1. 1. 9): *he admired him and gave him ten thousand darics*. As for the opening: *Clearchus was a Spartan exile. Kuros got together with him . . .*, there is remarkable effect of character in not saying: 'Kuros after making trial of him', or, seeing him to be worth a great deal and an excellent commander, but simply: *Kuros got together with him*. What follows on immediately is designed to produce the maximum amount of character: *he admired him and gave him ten thousand darics*.

Comparison, with Special Attention to Agesilaos *1. 35*

(133) I have often stated that comparison is plain, for example (*Anab.* 1. 1. 4): *he loved Kuros more than he loved Artaxerxes who was king*, and (*Anab.* 1. 1. 5): *so as to be friendlier to him than to the king.* Plain also is using less forceful words, and applying less distinguished words to greater things. Thus in the *Anabasis* (1. 1. 5): *he cared for the barbarians with him*, insignificant language is applied to a significant thing. 'Caring' applies properly only to things of moderate importance, as one might say: he cared for his home, but to use such a term of an army is less appropriate. Again in the *Agesilaos* (2. 5 = *Hell.* 4. 3. 9): *he remained there again pleased by the deed*, the use of less forceful words—not saying: exulting, or, exalted by the victory, but: *pleased by the deed*—is plain. (134) Change of tenses is plain, for example what scholars define as historic present, as in (*Anab.* 1. 1. 2): *he sends for Kuros from his command*, instead of: 'sent for'. The change of tense created plainness. We should sometimes treat what has happened as happening, e.g.: he calls him into his house and talks to him, as if what happened long ago is happening now. There is novelty in this.[59] (135) If you use comparison to detract from magnitude, elegance results, as in the *Agesilaos* (1. 35): *the king of the Persians thinking that of all these things Tissaphernes was the cause, sent Tithraustes, and had his head cut off. Had his head cut off* is plain, and the word *thinking* implies the attitude toward the subject, since he did not say: 'since the affairs of the barbarians were in a bad way, and there was so much riot and trouble, and they had lost so many battles, and finally they were shut up and under siege', but simply: *thinking*, and he did not say: 'on the one hand angered by what had happened, on the other hand thinking . . .'; he has none of this, but simply: *thinking*. Then comes the comparison: *After this the affairs of the barbarians became more hopeless.* He did not say: 'were in great hopelessness', but simply *more hopeless. Plain* also is the use of a partitive expression: *the affairs of the barbarians*, and not just: 'the barbarians' [(?) e.g. (*Ag.* 1. 36): *who ruling many cities in the mainland and also ruling islands. (?)*]

Points about Semantics

(136) Some words signify strongly, some less. For example: 'he passed through, drove through', signify strongly, while: 'he journeyed' signifies weakly. So in the *Agesilaos* (2. 5): *On the next day crossing the Achaean mountains of Phthia he journeyed the rest of the way through friendship to the borders of Boeotia.* The element of novelty here also contains plainness, since he applied something that has to do with a person to a place, and instead of saying 'through the land of friends', he says: *through friendship*, and instead of 'through the land of allies', he says: *through alliance.*

[59] Xenophon is an example of the historic present in *Peri Hupsous* 25.

(137) Plain men also make subtle use of 'there'. It signifies both place and time. 'He caught him there' is of place. The asyndeton is plain, setting the thought apart from what precedes. Sometimes he uses a complete deictic pronoun 'over there', sometimes an incomplete one 'there'.

(138) On the subject of tropes in historical writers, one should realize this much, that they should not be derived from important or solemn things, but from what is lower and common, as in the *Sumposion* (1. 4): *to these men cleansed in respect of their souls.* The trope *cleansed*, which is derived from furniture or vessels, transferred from the common to the solemn, to men and their souls, is not a pure trope, but is guarded and historical. Such tropes are more normal for plainness, e.g. (*Ag.* 1. 20): *inhabited on the one hand, sown on the other, it would produce eternal food.*[60] Such a figure belongs wholly to the encomiastic form of language. (139) The order of points should be such as seems to suit the genre: in histories the bare events produce the order of the narration, whereas in didactic and informal writing one can use whatever order one likes.

Conclusion

(140) After exact study and training in these principles, you will be able to produce elegance where there was dignity and dignity where there was elegance, and in all cases there will be the sort of plainness that has the strength of these principles. This is a sufficient and detailed demonstration of what I set out to show—word-by-word principles about character, the beginning of the work, handling of thoughts, sweet diction, plain diction, narratives, mythological sections, and beauty in writing, and all of these I have analysed separately.

---

[60] I restore the optative in place of the indicative, following the MSS of Xenophon.

Bibliography

1. *Principal Editions of Rhetorical Texts Consulted*

For many Greek rhetorical texts the best or only edition is in the nine-volume *Rhetores Graeci* of Christian Walz (Stuttgart, 1832–6), abbreviated 'W.') or the three-volume *Rhetores Graeci* of Leonard Spengel (Leipzig, 1853–6, abbreviated 'Sp.'), of which the first volume was re-edited by C. Hammer (1894, abbreviated 'Sp.-H.'). For some minor Latin texts, the best edition is Karl Halm's *Rhetores Latini Minores* (Leipzig, 1863, abbreviated 'H.').

Alexander Noumeniou, Περὶ σχημάτων, Sp. iii. 9–40.

Anonymous, Περὶ σχημάτων λόγου (sc. in the works of Hermogenes), Sp. iii. 110–60.

Anonymous Seguerianus, Τέχνη ῥητορική, Sp.-H. 352–9.

Apsines, Τέχνη ῥητορική, Sp.-H. 217–329.

Apsines, Περί τῶν ἐσχηματισμένων προβλημάτων, Sp.-H. 352–98.

Caecilius of Caleacte, *Fragmenta*, ed. E. Ofenloch (Leipzig, 1907).

Demetrius, Περὶ ἑρμηνείας, ed. W. Rhys Roberts (Cambridge, 1902).

Dionysius of Halicarnassus, *Opera*, ed. H. Usener and L. Radermacher, 2 vols. (Leipzig, 1899, 1929).

Herodian, Περὶ σχημάτων, Sp. iii. 85–104.

Hermogenes of Tarsus, *Opera*, ed. H. Rabe (Leipzig, 1913).

John the Sicilian, Ἐξήγησις εἰς τὰς ἰδέας τοῦ Ἑρμογένους, W. vi. 56–504.

Julius Rufianus, *De Figuris Sententiarum et Elocutionis*, H. 38–62.

Menander Rhetor, Περὶ ἐπιδεικτικῶν, ed. D. A. F. Russell and N. G. Wilson (Oxford, 1981).

Philodemus, Περὶ ῥητορικῆς, ed. S. Sudhaus, 2 vols. (Leipzig, 1892–6).

Philostratus, *Lives of the Sophists*, ed. W. C. Wright (Harvard, 1922).

Phoebammon Sophistes, Περὶ σχημάτων ῥητορικῶν, Sp. iii. 43–56.

Phrynichus Arabius, *Die Ekloge des Phrynichos*, ed. von Eitel Fischer (Berlin: de Gruyter, 1974).

Ps. Aristides Α΄, Περὶ τοῦ πολιτικοῦ λόγου and Β΄, Περὶ τοῦ ἀφελοῦς λόγου, ed. W. Schmid (Leipzig, 1926).

Ps. Dionysius, Τέχνη ῥητορική, the Usener-Radermacher edition of Dionysius, 2. 253–387.

Ps. Hermogenes, Περὶ εὑρέσεως, in Rabe's edition of Hermogenes, 93–212.

Ps. Hermogenes, Περὶ μεθόδου δεινότητος, ibid. 414–56.

Ps. Longinus, Περὶ ὕψους, ed. D. A. F. Russell (Oxford, 1964).

Quintilian, *Institutio Oratoria*, ed. M. Winterbottom (Oxford, 1970).

Rutilius Lupus, *Schemata Dianoeas et Lexeos*, ed. G. Barabino (Genoa, 1967).

Syrianus, *Scholia to the Works of Hermogenes*, ed. H. Rabe, 2 vols. (Leipzig, 1892–3).

Tiberius Rhetor, Περὶ σχημάτων, (i) Sp. iii. 59–82, (ii) ed. G. Ballaira (Rome, 1968).

Trypho, Περὶ τρόπων, Sp. iii. 191–206.

2. Books and Articles

AHL, F. (1984), 'The Art of Safe Criticism in Greece and Rome', *AJP* 105: 174–208.

ALBINI, U. (1968), Περὶ πολιτείας *di Erode Attico* (Florence).

ALPERS, F. (1910), *De Luciani Samosateni quae fertur Demosthenis laudatio* (Leipzig).

ANASTASSIOU, A. A. (1966), *Zur antiken Wertschätzung der Beredsamkeit des Demosthenes* (Diss. Kiel).

ANDERSON, G. (1986), *Philostratus: Biography and Belles Lettres in the Third Century A.D.* (London).

ARRIGHETTI, G. (1960), *Epicuro, Opere* (Turin).

AUSTIN, T. R. (1984), *Language Crafted: A Linguistic Theory of Poetic Syntax* (Indiana).

AVEZZÙ-TENUTA, E. (1974), "πλεονασμός, πλεονάζειν nelle testimonianze di retori greci", *BIFG* 1: 5–29.

AX, W. (1997), 'Quadripertita Ratio. Bemerkungen zur Geschichte eines aktuellen Kategoriensystems (Adiectio—Detractio—Transmutatio—Immutatio', in D. J. Taylor, ed., *The History of Linguistics in the Classical Period* (Amsterdam and Philadelphia), 191–214.

BAKHTIN, M. (1984), *Problems of Dostoevsky's Poetics*, ed. C. Emerson (Minnesota).

BALLAIRA, G. (1968), 'La Dottrina delle figure retoriche in Apollodoro di Pergamo', *QUCC* 5: 37–91.

BARCHIESI, A. (1966), 'Poetry, Praise and Patronage: Simonides in Book 4 of Horace's Odes', *CA* 15: 5–47.

BARWICK, K. (1957), *Probleme der stoischen Sprachlehre und Rhetorik* (Berlin).

BAUER, A. (1914), *Lukians Δημοσθένους Ἐγκώμιον* [= *Rhetorische Studien*, 3] (Paderborn).

BAUMGART, H. (1874), *Aelius Aristides als Repräsentant der sophistischen Rhetorik des zweiten Jahrhunderts der Kaiserzeit* (Leipzig).

BAUMGARTEN, D. (1932), 'Quid Xenophonti debeat Heliodorus Emesensus', *Studia Leopolitana* 4: 1–36.

BECKER, H. (1896), *Hermogenis Tarsensis de rhythmo oratorio doctrina* (Münster).

BEHR, C. A. (1981), *P. Aelius Aristides: The Complete Works*, translated into English (Leiden).

BOCOTTI, G. (1975), 'L'asindeto e il τρίκωλον nella retorica classica', *BIFG* 2: 34–59.

BOLAFFI, E. (1958), *La critica filosofica e letteraria in Quintiliano* (Collection Latomus 30) (Brussels).

BOMPAIRE, J. (1989), 'Le Sacré dans les Discours d'Aelius Aristide', *REG* 102: 28–39.

BONNER, S. F. (1935), *The Literary Treatises of Dionysius of Halicarnassus: A Study in the Development of his Literary Method* (Cambridge).

BOULANGER, A. (1923), *Aelius Aristide et la sophistique dans la province d'Asie au IIe siècle de nôtre ère* (Paris, republished 1968).

BOWERSOCK, G. (1969), *Greek Sophists in the Roman Empire* (Oxford).

BOWIE, E. L. (1970), 'Greeks and their Past in the Second Sophistic', *Past and Present* 46: 3–41 (= M. I. Finley, ed., *Studies in Ancient Society* (London, 1974), 166–209).

——(1985), 'The Greek Novel', in Easterling and Knox (1985), 683–99.

——(1989), 'Greek Sophists and Greek Poetry in the Second Sophistic', *ANRW* II. 33. 1, 209–58.

——(1990), 'Greek Poetry in the Antonine Age', in Russell (1990*a*), 53–90.

BRANCACCI, A. (1985), *Rhetorike philosophousa: Dione Crisostomo nella cultura antica e bizantina* (Elenchos 11) (Rome).

BRANDSTÄTTER, C. (1894), *De Notionum Πολιτικός et Σοφιστής Usu Rhetorico* (Leipziger Studien 15).

BÜRGI, E. (1930), 'Ist die dem Hermogenes zugeschriebene Schrift περὶ μεθόδου δεινότητος echt?', *WS* 48: 187–97.

CICHOCKA, H. (1990), 'Hermogenes' Treatise on Types of Style and its Reputation in the Renaissance (Selected Points)', *Eos* 79: 225–36 (in Polish).

CLAUSSEN, J. D. D. (1873), *Quaestiones Quintilianae*, Jahrbuch Suppl. 6: 2, 317–94.

COUSIN, J. (1936), *Études sur Quintilien, Tome I: contribution à la recherche des sources de l'Institution Oratoire* (Paris).

DAMON, C. (1991), 'Aesthetic Response and Technical Analysis in the Rhetorical Works of Dionysius of Halicarnassus', *MH* 48: 33–58.

DE LACY, P. (72), 'Galen's Platonism', *AJP* 93: 27–39.

DENNISTON, J. D. (1954), *The Greek Particles* (Oxford).

DESIDERI, P. (1978), *Dione di Prusa: un intellettuale greco nell'impero romano* (Florence).

DIELS, H., and KRANZ, W. (1954), *Die Fragmente der Vorsokratiker*, 7th edn. (Berlin).

DÖRRIE, H. (1955), *'Ὑπόστασις: Wort- und Bedeutungsgeschichte* (Göttingen).

DOUGLAS, A. E. (1956), 'Cicero, Quintilian and the Canon of Ten Attic Orators', *Mnemosyne* 9: 30–40.

DRERUP, E. (1923), *Demosthenes im Urteile des Altertums von Theopomp bis Tzetzes: Geschichte, Roman, Legende* (Würzburg).

EASTERLING, P. E., and KNOX, B. M. W. (eds.) (1985), *The Cambridge History of Classical Literature*, i. *Greek Literature* (Cambridge).

ERNESTI, J. C. T. (1795), *Lexicon Technologicae Graecorum Rhetoricae* (Leipzig).

FANTHAM, E. (1973), 'Ciceronian *Conciliare* and Aristotelian *Ethos*', *Phoenix* 27: 262–75.

FEHLING, D. (1969), *Die Wiederholungsfiguren und ihr Gebrauch bei den Griechen vor Gorgias* (Berlin).

FORSSMAN, B. (1982), *"ἀφελής"*, *Serta Indogermanica. Festschrift G. Neumann* (Innsbrucker Beiträge zur Sprachwissenschaft 40) (Innsbruck): 65–9.

GEIGENMÜLLER, P. (1908), *Quaestiones Dionysiacae de Vocabulis Artis Criticae* (Leipzig).

GEMOLL, H. (1933), "Caecilius' Stellung zu den *Σχήματα Διανοίας*", *RM* 82: 59–66.

GIGANTE, M. (*Nomos Basileus* (Naples).

——(1969), *Saggio critico su Demostene e Aristide* (Testi e documenti per lo studio dell'antichità 27; Milan).

GILL, C. (1984), 'The Ethos/Pathos Distinction in Rhetorical and Literary Criticism', *CQ* 78: 149–66.

GOLDSTEIN, J. A. (1968), *The Letters of Demosthenes* (New York).

GRANT, M. (1924), *Ancient Rhetorical Theories of the Laughable in the Greek Rhetoricians* (Madison).

GRUBE, G. M. A. (1952), 'Thrasymachus, Theophrastus and Dionysius', *AJP* 73: 251–67.

——(1961), *A Greek Critic: Demetrius on Style* (Phoenix Suppl. 4; Toronto).

——(1965), *The Greek and Roman Critics* (London).

GUTHRIE, W. (1969), *A History of Greek Philosophy*, iii (Cambridge).

HWR = *Historisches Wörterbuch der Rhetorik*, ed. G. Ueding, G. Kalivoda, F.-H. Robling (Tübingen, 1992–).

HAGEDORN, D. (1964), *Zur Ideenlehre des Hermogenes* (Hypomnemata 8) (Göttingen).

HAGEN, H. M. (1966), *'Ηθοποιΐα. Zur Geschichte eines rhetorischen Begriffs* (Erlangen).

HARRY, J. E. (1894), 'On the Authorship of the Leptinean Orationes Ascribed to Aristides', *AJP* 15: 66–73.

HEATH, M. (1989), 'Dionysius of Halicarnassus "On Imitation"', *Hermes* 117: 370–3.

HEGNAUER, S. (1981), *Systrophe: The Background to Herbert's Sonnet 'Prayer'* (Berne, Frankfurt, and Las Vegas).

——(1982), 'The Rhetorical Figure of Systrophe', in *Rhetoric Revalued*, ed. B. Vickers (Binghamton, NY), 179 ff.

HINCK, H. (1873), *Polemonis Declamationes Quae Extant Duae* (Leipzig).

HIRZEL, R. (1895), *Der Dialog* (Leipzig).

HÖFLER, A. (1935), 'Der Sarapishymnus des Ailios Aristeides', *Tübinger Beiträge zur Altertumswissenschaft* 27 (Tubingen).

HOLLINGSWORTH, J. E. (1915), *Antithesis in the Attic Orators from Antiphon to Isaeus* (Mensha, Wis.).

HOLTZ, M. L. (1979), 'Grammairiens et rhéteurs romains en concurrence pour l'enseignement des figures de rhétorique', in R. Chevallier, ed., *Colloque sur la rhétorique [Calliope I]* (Paris), 207–20.

HUBBELL, H. M. (1920), *The Rhetorica of Philodemus* (Transactions of the Connecticut Academy of Arts and Sciences 23) (New Haven, Conn.).

INNES, D. C. (1979), 'Gigantomachy and Natural Philosophy', *CQ* 29: 165–71.

——(1985), 'Theophrastus and the Theory of Style', in W. W. Foitenbaugh, P. M. Huby, and A. A. Long (eds.), *Theophrastus of Eresus: On his Life and Work. Rutgers University Studies in the Classical Humanities*, ii (New Jersey), 251–67.

——and WINTERBOTTOM, M. (1988), *Sopatros the rhetor: Studies in the Text of the Διαίρεσις Σητημάτων* (BICS Suppl. 48) (London).

JOCELYN, H. D. (1979), 'Virgil Cacozelus (Donatus, *Vita Vergilii* 44)', *Papers of the Liverpool Latin Seminar* 2: 67–142.

JONES, C. P. (1978), *The Roman World of Dio Chrysostom* (Cambridge).

KAHN, C. H. (1969), 'Stoic Language and Stoic Λόγος', *AGPh* 51: 158–72.

KENNEDY, G. A. (1963), *The Art of Persuasion in Greece* (Princeton).

——(1972), *The Art of Rhetoric in the Roman World* (Princeton).

——(1983), *Greek Rhetoric Under the Christian Emperors* (Princeton).

KERFERD, G. B. (1981), *The Sophistic Movement* (Cambridge).

KITTAY, J., and GODZICH, W. (1987), *The Emergence of Prose: An Essay in Prosaics* (Minneapolis).

KÖRTE, A. (1936), 'Homer und Menander', *Hermes* 71: 221–2.

KOHL, R. (1915), *De Scholasticarum Declamationum Argumentis ex Historia Petitis* [= *Rhetorische Studien*, 4] (Paderborn).

KOJIC-SLAPSAK, S. (1977), 'La Transformation sémantique du mot σχῆμα et ses derivés et composés et ses traductions', *ZAnt* 27: 347–98 (in Serbo-Croatian).

KOLLER, H. (1958), 'Die Anfänge der griechischen Grammatik', *Glotta* 37: 5–40.

KROEHNERT, O. (1897), *Canonesne Poetarum Scriptorum Artificum per Antiquitatem fuerint?* (Königsberg).

KROLL, W. (1918), " '*Ev "Hθει*", *Philologus* 75: 68–76 (= Stark (1968), 464–72).

——(1936), *Das Ἐπιχείρημα* (Vienna).

KUSTAS, G. L. (1973), *Studies in Byzantine Rhetoric* (Thessalonika).

LIMC = Lexicon Iconographicum Mythologiae Classicae, ed. L. Kahil (Münich, 1981–).

LANG, K. (1925), *Das Σχῆμα Κατ' Ἄρσιν Καὶ Θέσιν bei Demosthenes* (Erlangen).

LAUREYS, M. (1991), 'Quintilian's Judgement of Seneca and the Scope and Purpose of *Inst.* 10, 1', *AA* 37: 100–25.

LIERS, H. (1885), 'Zur Geschichte der rhetorischen Ideenlehre', *Jahrbuch für Klassische Philologie* 132: 577–89.

LINDBERG, G. (1977), *Studies in Hermogenes and Eustathius* (Lund).

LLOYD, A. C. (1971), 'Grammar and Metaphysics in the Stoa', in A. A. Long (ed.), *Problems in Stoicism* (London), 58–74.

LONG, A. A. (1971), 'Language and Thought in Stoicism', in *Problems in Stoicism* (London), 75–113.

LOSSAU, M. J. (1964), *Untersuchungen zur antiken Demosthenesexegese* (Palingenesia 2; Bad Homburg).

MORPURGO-TAGLIABUE, G. (1979), 'Il χαρακτὴρ δεινὸς di Demetrio e la sua datazione', *RAAN* 54: 281–318.

MORRISON, J. S. (1961), 'Antiphon', *PCPS* 187: 49–58.

MORSON, G. S., and EMERSON, C. (1990), *Mikhail Bakhtin. Creation of a Prosaics* (Stanford).

MRAS, K. (1949), 'Die προλαλιά bei den griechischen Schriftstellern', *WS* 64: 71–81.

MÜHL, M. (1962), 'Der Λόγος Ἐνδιάθετος und Προφορικός von der älteren Stoa bis zur Synode von Sirmium 351', *Archiv für Begriffsgeschichte* 7: 7-56.

MÜLLER, R. (1904), 'Zu ΗΠΩΔΙΑΝΟΥ ΠΕΡΙ ΣΧΗΜΑΤΩΝ', *H'rmes* 39: 444–60.

MÜNSCHER, K. (1920), 'Xenophon in der griechisch-römischen Literatur', *Philologus Supplementbände* 13. 2 (Leipzig).

NICOLAI, R. (1992), *La storiografia nell'educazione antica* (Biblioteca di materiali e discussioni per l'analisi dei testi classici 10; Pisa).

NORDEN , E. (1898), *Die antike Kunstprosa* (Leipzig).

NORTH, H. (1952), 'The Use of Poetry in the Training of the Ancient Orator', *Traditio* 8: 1–33.

OFENLOCH, E. (1888), *Caecilius Calactinus Fragmenta* (Leipzig).

PANOFSKY, E. (1968), *Idea: A Concept in Art Theory*, tr. J. J. S. Peale (New York).

PATILLON, M. (1988), *La Théorie du discours chez Hermogène la rhéteur:*

essai sur les structures linguistiques de la rhétorique ancienne (Collection
d'Études Anciennes 117; Paris).

PATTERSON, A. M. (1970), *Hermogenes and the Renaissance, Seven Ideas of
Style* (Princeton).

PENNDORF, J. (1902), 'De Sermone Figurato Quaestiones Rhetoricae',
Leipziger Studien 20: 169–94.

PERNOT, L. (1981), *Les Discours siciliens d'Aelius Aristides (Or. 5–6):
Étude littéraire et paléographique: édition et traduction* (New York).

PERRY, B. E. (1930), 'Chariton and his Romance from a Literary-
Historical Point of View', *AJP* 51: 93–134.

PETERSON, W. (1891), *M. Fabi. Quintiliani Institutionis Oratoriae Liber
Decimus* (Oxford).

PLEKET, N. W. (1970), '*ΓΟΡΓΟΣ*: A Note on Epictetus III. 12. 10',
Mnemosyne 23: 304–6.

POHLENZ, M. (1913), 'Eine byzantinische Recension plutarchischer
Schriften', *NGG* 338–62.

——(1924), 'Anonymus περὶ νόμων', *NGG* 19–37 (= id. (1965), ii. 314 ff.).

——(1933), '*Tò Πρέπον*: Ein Beitrag zur Geschichte des griechischen
Geistes', *NGG* 53–92 (= id. (1965), i. 100 ff.).

——(1939), 'Die Begründung der abendländischen Sprachlehre durch
die Stoa', *NGG* 151–98 (= id. (1965), i. 39 ff.).

——(1965), *Kleine Schriften*, ed. M. Dörrie (Hildesheim).

POLIAKOFF, M. (1982), *Studies in the Terminology of Greek Combat Sports*
(Beiträge zur Klassischen Philologie 146) (Königstein/Ts.)

POWELL, J. U. (1925), *Collectanea Alexandrina* (Oxford).

PRITCHETT, W. K. (1975), *Dionysius of Halicarnassus: On Thucydides*
(Berkeley).

PROVOT, E. M. (1910), *De Hermogenis Tarsensis Dicendi Genere* (Strasbourg).

——'Pindaric Encomium and Isokrates', *ETagoras*', *TAPhA* 117: 131–
55.

RACE, W. H. (1987), 'Pindaric Encomium and Isokrates' *Evagoras*',
TAPhA 117: 131–55.

RADERMACHER, L. (1897), 'Studien zur Geschichte der griechischen
Rhetorik, II: Plutarch's Schrift de se ipso citra invidiam laudando',
RM 52: 419–24.

——(1912), 'Hermogenes, Rhetor aus Tarsus', *RE* 15: 865–77.

REARDON, B. P. (1971), *Courants littéraires grecs des IIe et IIIe siècles après
J.-C.* (Paris).

ROBERTSON, N. (1986), 'A Point of Plataea. The Dispute between
Athens and Sparta over Leading the Procession', *Hesperia* 55: 88–
106.

ROHDE, E. (1900), *Der griechische Roman und seine Vorlaüfer*, 2nd edn.
(Leipzig).

RUSSELL, D. A. (1979), 'De Imitatione', in D. West and T. Woodman (eds.), *Creative Imitation and Latin Literature* (Cambridge), 1–16.

—— (1981a), 'Longinus Revisited', *Mnemosyne* 34: 72–86.

—— (1981b), *Criticism in Antiquity* (London).

—— (1983), *Greek Declamation* (Cambridge).

—— (1990a), *Antonine Literature* (Oxford).

—— (1990b), 'Aristides and the Prose Hymn', in Russell (1990a), 199–219.

—— (1992), *Dio of Prusa. Orationes VII, XII and XXXVI* (Cambridge).

RUSSELL, D. A. F. and WINTERBOTTOM, M. (eds.) (1972), *Ancient Literary Criticism: The Principal Texts in New Translations* (Oxford).

—— and WLSON, N. G. (1981), *Menander Rhetor. Edited with an Introduction and Notes* (Oxford).

RUTHERFORD, I. C. (1988), " Ἔμφασις in Tractatus Coislinianus c. 7", *Maia* 40: 125–9.

—— (1990), review of Patillon (1988), *CR*, 40: 252–3.

—— (1992), 'Inverting the Canon: Hermogenes on Literature', *HSCP* 94: 355-78.

—— (1994a), 'Decorum', *HWR* 2: 467–72.

—— (1994b), 'Denotes', *HWR* 2: 423–34.

—— (1994c), review of Nicolai, *CR* 45 (1995), 49–50.

—— (1995), 'The Poetics of the *Paraphthegma*: Aristides and the *Decorum* of Self-Praise', in D. Innes, H. Hine, and C. Pelling (eds.), *Ethics and Rhetoric* (Oxford), 193–204.

>—— (forthcoming), 'Καταλογάδην Catalogued: Articulations of a Prose-Culture', in volume of papers on genre, ed. D. Obbink and M. Depew.

SACKS, K. S. (1983), 'Historiography in the Rhetorical Works of Dionysius of Halicarnassus', *Athenaeum* 60: 65 ff.

SANDOZ, C. (1971), *Les Noms grecs de la forme* (Neuchâtel).

SCHENKEVELD, D. M. (1964), *Studies in Demetrius On Style* (Amsterdam).

SCHMID, W. (1894), 'Zur antiken Stillehre aus Anlass von Proklos' Chrestomathie', *RM* 49: 133–61.

—— (1887–97), *Der Attizismus in seinen Hauptvertretern von Dionysius von Halikarnass bis auf den zweiten Philostratus* (Stuttgart).

—— (1917), 'Die sogenannte Aristidesrhetorik', *RM* 72: 113–69, 238–57.

—— (1926), (ed.), *Ps. Aristides A′, περὶ τοῦ πολιτικοῦ λόγου* and B′, *περὶ τοῦ ἀφελοῦς λόγου* (Leipzig).

SCHMID, W., and STAHLIN, F. (1924), *Geschichte der griechischen Literatur*, 2 vols. (Munich).

SCHNEIDER, B. (1983), 'Die Stellung des zehnten Buches im Gesamtplan der Institutio oratoria des Quintilian', *WS* NS 16: 109–25.

SCHWAB, T. (1916), *Alexander Numeniou περὶ σχημάτων in seinem Verhältnis zu Kaikilios, Tiberios und seinen späteren Benutzern* (Paderborn).

SMEREKA, J. (1927), 'De Dinosi', *Eos* 30: 227–56.

—— (1928), 'De Dinosi', *Eos* 31: 87–114.

SMITH, B. H. (1968), *Poetic Closure* (Chicago).

SMYTH, H. W. (1894), *The Sounds and Inflections of the Greek Dialects*, i. *Ionic* (Oxford).

SOHLBERG, D. (1972), 'Aelius Aristides und Dionysius von Babylon', *MH* 29: 256–77.

SOLMSEN, F. (1938), 'Aristotle and Cicero on the Orator's Playing upon the Feelings', *CP* 33: 390–404.

SPEYER, W. (1971), *Die literarische Fälschung im heidnischen und christlichen Altertum* (Munich).

STADTER, P. A. (1967), 'Flavius Arrianus, the New Xenophon', *GRBS* 8: 155–61.

——(1976), 'Xenophon in Arrian's *Cynegeticus*', *GRBS* 17: 157–67.

——(1980), *Arrian of Nicomedia* (Chapel Hill).

STANFORD, W. B. (1936), *Greek Metaphor* (Oxford).

STARK, R. (1968) (ed.), *Rhetorika* (Hildesheim).

STEGEMANN, W. (1936), *RE* 33: 551 ff., s.v. *Nicostratus*.

STEINMETZ, P. (1964), 'Gattungen und Epochen der griechischen Literatur in der Sicht Quintilians', *Hermes* 92: 454–66 (= Stark (1968), 451–63).

STEPHENS, S. (1983), 'The Arginousai Theme in Greek Rhetorical Theory and Practice', *BASP* 20: 171–80.

STURM, J. (1571), *Hermogenis Opera* (Strasbourg).

SÜSS, W. (1910), *Ἦθος: Studien zur älteren griechischen Rhetorik* (Leipzig).

SYKUTRIS, J. (1936), review of F. Walsdorff, *Die antiken Urteile über Platons Stil*, *Gnomon* 6: 527–39 (= Stark (1968), 438–50).

TAVERNINI, N. (1953), *Dal libro decimo dell'Instituto Oratoria alle fonti tecnico-metodologiche di Quintiliano* (Università di Torino, Pubblicazioni della facolta di lettere e filosofia 5.4) (Turin).

THOMPSON, W. E. (1968), 'Γοργότης nell'orazione "De Pace" di Andocide', *Maia* 20: 271–5.

TRAPP, M. B. (1990), 'Plato's *Phaedrus* in the Second Century', in Russell (1990a), 141–73.

TURASIEWICZ, R. (1978), 'Zakres semantyczny ἦθος w scholiach do tragików (Quid ἤθους notio in scholiis in tragicos significaverit)', *Eos* 66: 17–30.

USENER, H. (1889), *Dionysii Halicarnassensis Librorum De Imitatione Reliquiae Epistulaeque Criticae Duae* (Bonn).

USHER, S. (1965), 'Occultatio in Cicero's Speeches', *AJP* 86: 175–92.

——(1974), *Dionysius of Halicarnassus: The Critical Works in Two Volumes*, i (Cambridge, Mass.).

VALGIMIGLI, V. (1912), *La critica letteraria di Dione Crisostomo* (Bologna).

VINCE, J. H. (ed.) (1930), *Demosthenes 1*, Loeb (Cambridge).

VOIT, L. (1934), *Δεινότης, Ein Antiker Stilbegriff* (Leipzig).

WADE-GERY, H. T. (1945), 'Kritias and Herodes', *CQ* 39: 19–33 (= *Essays in Greek History* (Oxford, 1958), 271–92).

WALLACH, B. P. (1980), 'Epimone and Diatribe: Dwelling on the Point in Ps. Hermogenes', *RM* 123: 272–322.

——(1981), 'Ps. Hermogenes and the Characterising Oath', *GRBS* 22: 257–67.

WEGEHAUPT, J. (1896), *De Dione Chrystostomo Xenophontis Sectatore* (Diss. Gotha).

WILAMOWITZ-MOELLENDORF, U. VON (1900), 'Asianismus und Atticismus', *Hermes* 35: 1–52 (= *Kleine Schriften*, iv (Berlin, 1969), 223 ff.).

WILSON, N. G. (1983), *Scholars of Byzantium* (London).

WOOTEN, C. W. (1983), *Cicero's Philippics and their Demosthenic Model: The Rhetoric of Persuasion* (Chapel Hill).

——(1987), *Hermogenes' On Types of Style* (Chapel Hill and London).

——(1989), 'Dionysius of Halicarnassus and the Style of Demosthenes', *AJP* 110: 576–88.

ZETZEL, J. (1984), 'Recreating the Canon: Augustan Poetry and the Alexandrian Past', *Critical Inquiry* 10: 83 ff. (= Robert von Hallberg (ed.), *Canons* (Chicago, 1984), 107–29).

ZUCKER, F. (1953), "Ἀνηθοποίητος. Eine semasiologische Untersuchung aus der antiken Rhetorik und Ethik" (SBAB 4), reprinted in id., *Semantica, Rhetorica, Ethica* (Berlin, 1963), 33–47.

Index of Passages Cited

General Index